Making Sense of Motherhood

Making Sense of Motherhood

Biblical and Theological Perspectives

Edited by
Beth M. Stovell

Foreword by
Lynn H. Cohick

WIPF & STOCK · Eugene, Oregon

MAKING SENSE OF MOTHERHOOD
Biblical and Theological Perspectives

Copyright © 2016 Wipf and Stock Publishers. All rights reserved. Except for brief quotations in critical publications or reviews, no part of this book may be reproduced in any manner without prior written permission from the publisher. Write: Permissions, Wipf and Stock Publishers, 199 W. 8th Ave., Suite 3, Eugene, OR 97401.

Wipf & Stock
An Imprint of Wipf and Stock Publishers
199 W. 8th Ave., Suite 3
Eugene, OR 97401

www.wipfandstock.com

PAPERBACK ISBN 13: 978-1-62564-675-0
HARDCOVER ISBN 13: 978-1-4982-8824-8

Manufactured in the U.S.A.   02/01/2016

Scripture quotations marked with NRSV are taken from the New Revised Standard Version Bible, copyright 1989, Division of Christian Education of the National Council of the Churches of Christ in the United States of America. Used by permission. All rights reserved.

Scripture quotations marked with NAB in this work are taken from the New American Bible, revised edition © 2010, 1991, 1986, 1970 Confraternity of Christian Doctrine, Washington, D.C. and are used by permission of the copyright owner. All rights reserved.

Beth M. Stovell's "The Birthing Spirit, the Childbearing God: Metaphors of Motherhood and Their Place in Christian Discipleship" first appeared as an article by the same title in *Priscilla Papers* 26 (2012) 16–21, http://www.cbeinternational.org/sites/default/files/Birthing_Stovell.pdf.

A longer version of Cristina Lledo Gomez's "Matrescence and the Paschal Mystery: A Rahnerian Reflection on the Death and Rebirth Experiences of Mothering Infants" (including a table outlining some of the possible crosses, deaths, and resurrection experienced in motherhood) first appeared as "Early Motherhood and the Paschal Mystery: A Rahnerian Reflection on the Death and Rebirth Experiences of New Mothers," in *Australasian Catholic Record* 88 (2011) 131–50.

To my mother, Mary Louise Moskowitz,
my children, Elena and Atticus,
and to all mothers.

Contents

Contributors | ix

Foreword | xiii
  —Lynn H. Cohick

Acknowledgments | xvii

Can We Really Make Sense of Motherhood? An Explorative Introduction | xix
  —Beth M. Stovell

Part I: The Hebrew Bible and Motherhood

1 Lot's Daughters and Tamar: Mothers Positively Reimagined in Genesis Rabbah | 3
  —Shayna Sheinfeld

2 Moses: Mother of Israel? | 16
  —Anthony Rees

3 The Birthing Spirit, the Childbearing God: Metaphors of Motherhood and Their Place in Christian Discipleship | 27
  —Beth M. Stovell

Part II: The New Testament and Motherhood

4 She Forgets Her Suffering in Her Joy: The Parable of the Laboring Woman (John 16:20–22) | 45
  —Ruth Sheridan

5 The Inward Groaning of Adoption (Rom 8:12–25): Recovering the Pauline Adoption Metaphor for Mothers in the Adoption Triad | 65
  —Erin M. Heim

6 *Pater Nutrix:* Milk Metaphors and Character Formation
  in Hebrews and 1 Peter | 81
   —Alicia D. Myers

7 "As Long as It's Healthy": Responses to Infanticide
  and Exposure in Early Christianity | 100
   —Louise A. Gosbell

Part III: Christian Theology and Spirituality and Motherhood

8 Matrescence and the Paschal Mystery: A Rahnerian Reflection on the
  Death and Rebirth Experiences of Mothering Infants | 121
   —Cristina Lledo Gomez

9 Reverend Mother: Conversations in Motherhood and Ministry | 136
   —Rebecca Lindsay

10 Motherhood as a Metaphor for Contemporary Latina Theology
   and Spirituality: Pregnant Mary (Maria) on a Pilgrimage | 154
    —Claudia H. Herrera

11 Matrescence and Spiritual Transformation: Finding God
   in the Disorientation of New Motherhood | 166
    —Sarah Foley Massa

12 The Loss That Does Not Diminish: Transition Parenting
   as a Response to God's Covenant | 190
    —Patricia A. Smith

13 Conclusion: Motherhood Made Complex | 205
    —Beth M. Stovell

Modern Authors and Subjects Index | 213
Ancient Documents Index | 221

Contributors

Lynn H. Cohick holds a PhD in New Testament and Christian Origins from the University of Pennsylvania and serves as a professor of New Testament in the Department of Biblical and Theological Studies at Wheaton College and Graduate School. She is an associate editor for Story of God Bible Commentary series and has written several books, including *Melito of Sardis: Setting, Purpose, and Sources* (Brown Judaic Studies, 2000), *Women in the World of the Earliest Christians: Illuminating Ancient Ways of Life* (Baker Academic, 2008), commentaries on Philippians (Story of God Bible Commentary Series, Zondervan, 2013) and Ephesians (New Covenant Commentary, Cascade Books, 2010), and several articles on women in early Judaism and early Christianity. She and her husband reside in Wheaton, Illinois.

Cristina Lledo Gomez is a visiting international research fellow at Boston College's School of Theology and Ministry. She holds a PhD in Theology from Charles Sturt University and a Master of Theology from the Sydney College of Divinity. Her doctoral dissertation explored the use of "Mother Church" as metaphor in key early patristic writing and the Vatican II documents. Cristina is also a postgraduate researcher for Charles Sturt University's Public and Contextual Theology Strategic Research Centre and has presented conference papers at the Australian Catholic Theological Association, Motherhood Initiative for Research and Community Development, and for the Ecclesiological Investigations International Research Network in Australia, Italy, the UK, and the US. She has published in the areas of ecclesiology, motherhood, Karl Rahner, and early patristics.

Louise Gosbell is a PhD candidate in the Ancient History department of Macquarie University. Her doctoral thesis explores the use of disability-related language as a means of social categorization in the gospels of the New Testament. Louise serves as an adjunct lecturer at both Mary Andrews and Excelsia Colleges in Sydney teaching in various New Testament subjects as well as a course on disability and the Bible. Louise is also the Regional Coordinator for CBM's Australia's Luke 14 program, which aims at assisting churches to become more welcoming of people with disabilities.

Claudia H. Herrera is a PhD candidate in Practical Theology and the first lay Director of Campus Ministry at St. Thomas University in Miami, Florida. Her dissertation title is "Understanding Contemporary Latino/a Theology through the Lenses of Latinas in Their 20s: A new Marianismo?" She explores the religious identity and lived experiences of first- and second-generation college-aged Latinas through participatory action research. She is an associate member of the Academy of Catholic Hispanic Theologians of the United States. She recently published "Christian Education in Colombia" in *Encyclopedia of Christian Education* (Scarecrow, 2015).

Erin Heim is an assistant professor of New Testament at Denver Seminary. She earned a PhD from the University of Otago, an MA from Denver Seminary, and a BMus from the University of Minnesota. Her thesis on the Pauline adoption metaphors was named an exceptional thesis in the division of the humanities at the University of Otago.

Rebecca Lindsay is a part of the ministry team at Hope Uniting Church in Maroubra, Sydney. She has received an MTh from Charles Sturt University, as well as honors degrees in theology and linguistics. Rebecca has taught Old Testament and Hebrew as a sessional lecturer at United Theological College campus of Charles Sturt University. She is interested in the ways theological and biblical reflection enliven congregational life.

Sarah Massa is the mother of three children and works part-time as a physiotherapist in the field of lymphoedema. She completed her MA in Theology at University of Newcastle in Callaghan, Australia. Sarah and her family are active in ministry in their local church. She is passionate about knowing God in "ordinary" day-to-day life and seeks to integrate desert spirituality into family life via the practice of meditation and mindful living. She hopes to participate further in future study in meditation and healing.

Alicia D. Myers is an assistant professor of New Testament and Greek at Campbell University Divinity School in Buies Creek, North Carolina. Prior to teaching at Campbell, she taught at United Theological Seminary. She earned her PhD in Biblical Studies with an emphasis on the New Testament from Baylor University and is the author of *Characterizing Jesus: A*

Rhetorical Analysis on the Fourth Gospel's Use of Scripture in its Presentation of Jesus (T&T Clark, 2012) and co-editor with Bruce G. Schuchard of *Abiding Words: The Use of Scripture in the Gospel of John* (SBL, 2015).

Anthony Rees is a lecturer in Old Testament/Hebrew Bible at Charles Sturt University. He has taught in a number of Australian colleges and at Pacific Theological College in Suva, Fiji. He spent 2014 as a research fellow of the Centre for Public and Contextual Theology at Charles Sturt University. He is the author of two books: *[Re]Reading Again: A Mosaic Reading of Numbers 25* (Bloomsbury, 2015) and *Voices of the Wilderness: An Ecological Reading of the Book of Numbers* (Sheffield, 2015).

Shayna Sheinfeld is a visiting assistant professor at Centre College in Danville, Kentucky, and was awarded her PhD from McGill University in 2015. She is the author of numerous articles on Second Temple Judaism, early Christianity, and rabbinic Judaism, including "A Note on the Context of the Phrase 'Women are Temperamentally Lightheaded' in BT Kiddushin 80b" in *Women in Judaism*. She has also written (with Ann W. Duncan) the article "Recognizing the Whole Student: Balancing Family and Academia." When not writing and teaching courses on Bible, Judaism, and Apocalypticism, she remains attached to reality through the machinations of her four children and her husband.

Ruth Sheridan is a post-doctoral research fellow at United Theological College, Australia. She was awarded her PhD in 2011 from the Australian Catholic University and is the author of *Retelling Scripture: The Jews and the Scriptural Citations in John 1:19–12:15* (Brill, 2012), which won the 2013 Manfred Lautenschlaeger Award for Theological Promise (formerly the John Templeton Prize).

Patricia Smith is the mother of five adult children and holds a B.Ed (Hons) from the University of Sydney, a BA and M.Litt. from University of New England in New South Wales, and a MA in Theological Studies from the Broken Bay Institute in New South Wales. She is currently working as a pastoral musician in Kuringgai Chase Catholic parish in the diocese of Broken Bay, Australia.

Beth M. Stovell is an assistant professor of Old Testament at Ambrose Seminary of Ambrose University in Calgary, Canada. Prior to teaching at Ambrose, she taught at St. Thomas University in Miami Gardens, Florida. She earned her PhD in 2012 in Christian Theology with a concentration in Biblical Studies at McMaster Divinity College. She has authored *Mapping Metaphorical Discourse in the Fourth Gospel: John's Eternal King* (Brill, 2012), co-edited *Biblical Hermeneutics: Five Views* (InterVarsity, 2012) with Stanley E. Porter, and has contributed to several edited volumes. Beth is currently co-writing a book on interpreting biblical language with Stanley E. Porter for InterVarsity Press and is writing commentaries on the Minor Prophets for the Story of God Bible Commentary series from Zondervan.

Foreword

Lynn H. Cohick

"*Jambo Mama C.J. Habari yako?*" My Kenyan friends would greet me with these words and a smile. During our three years in Kenya, I was not identified as "Lynn" but as the mother of my son, C. J., or my daughter, Sarah. Such greetings seem uncomplicated on the surface, for they praise the good fortune of the woman who has birthed children. But underneath these apparent still waters run deep currents of one's self-worth, identity, and place in society.

I was delighted when my friend Beth Stovell invited me to offer the foreword to this volume. Over the years, Beth and I have met several times at conferences. I recall one time when we sat on the floor in a deserted hallway, resting our feet and talking about work and family. So I was not surprised when Beth told me about this book project, because it has been a topic of longstanding interest to her and to me. That is why I am grateful that she gathered this group of solid and reflective scholars to explore the reality of motherhood—in the flesh and in metaphor, in society and within the deepest hollows of the heart. The contributors to *Making Sense of Motherhood* do not shrink from navigating murky and forbidding waters. In so doing, they sketch a map for the reader of these somewhat unchartered territories and offer companionship for the journey. With its fearlessness in addressing deep anxieties about labor, delivery, and possible failure at mothering, *Making Sense of Motherhood* stands as a word of vulnerable hope to mothers and society today. The authors embrace ambiguity and messiness amidst the tedium and joy of mothering, paradoxically drawing strength in not having the final word on the subject. Instead, they invite the reader to participate in the meaning-making process.

Since my graduate school days in the 1980s at the University of Pennsylvania, I have been intrigued by the metaphor of "mother" within theological reflection and the reality of motherhood within the biblical text. In an ironic twist, I studied Julian of Norwich's *Showings* during the year my first child was born. This mystic describes her revelation about God and sin and in one section portrays Jesus Christ as mother. Julian stands in a long line of Christian reflection on images and metaphors of God and/or Jesus Christ as mother.[1] Alongside theological reflection on the concepts of mother and motherhood, I continue to reflect on women's lives as noted in the New Testament and early Jewish and Christian writings. In my book *Women in the World of the Earliest Christians*, I explore the historical setting of Jewish and Gentile mothers, their experiences in birthing and raising their children, and their relationships to their adult children.

In a more recent study, I explore the early third-century female Christian martyrs Perpetua and Felicitas as they reflect theologically on their experience of childbirth and nursing.[2] Perpetua's diary makes up the bulk of this martyrdom account. Distraught at being unable to nurse her young son in prison, Perpetua rejoices when she is released to a different section of the prison to nurse him. Later she despairs when her father refuses to return her son, and she marvels that God miraculously dries up her milk upon this sudden weaning. The themes of nursing and milk continue in Perpetua's first vision, which features a good Shepherd nursing sheep. He gives her some of the milky cheese to eat, and the sweet taste remains in her mouth as her vision ends. In this, Perpetua reflects the church's discussion of Eucharist as milk from the Savior, but also her own complicated and conflicted identities as a mother and a martyr. Felicity, the young slave woman, gives birth prematurely a few days before she is to face the beasts in the arena. Watching her painful labor, a male guard mocks her suffering as only the beginning of her agonies. She retorts that when she faces the beasts, there will be another in her that will suffer with her, for she is suffering for Jesus. Later the narrator links the blood shed in birthing with the blood of her second baptism, the martyrdom she so willingly embraces. The words invite the reader to consider the daughter inside Felicitas brought safely to life (to be raised by a fellow believer) with Felicitas's own second birth and safe "delivery" to her heavenly reward.

Felicitas, like Julian of Norwich one thousand years later, understood the power of the metaphor of motherhood. *Making Sense of Motherhood*

---

1. Bynum, *Jesus as Mother*.

2. Cohick and Amy Brown Hughes, tentatively titled, *Christian Women in the Patristic World*, forthcoming.

continues in this rich vein. For example, Ruth Sheridan held me spellbound as she wove together her traumatic, near-death birth experience with the words of Jesus in John 16 about a woman's pain in labor and her joy at her child's safe delivery. Sheridan challenges a facile reading that assumes once labor is finished, the woman no longer remembers her pain or emotional turmoil. She notes the fear that gripped her because of her ill-defined and later ignored sense that something was wrong in her labor. And (spoiler alert) with the delivery of a healthy baby, she feels a surge of guilt that she had not done enough to prevent the trauma. Sheridan's poignant story, set down with such piercing power, provided space for me to reflect on my own children's traumatic births. Sheridan argues convincingly and compellingly that it is precisely at the point of remembering that mothers, and all disciples, can link the past and current suffering with hope and new life.

Beth Stovell addresses God as birthing mother and mighty warrior, drawing on Isa 42 and the concept of rebirth in the Spirit (see John 3 and 16), biblical themes that prove so rich in the martyrs' tradition. Stovell highlights how the biblical texts reinforce the reality of struggle, pain, and sorrow as a natural part of the Christian journey. She reminds us of the images of God as a mother birthing her child—a metaphor that echoes from martyr Felicitas to mystic Julian and on to mothers today. Again, Perpetua's vision connects the rite of Eucharist with her experiences of nursing in complicated ways. Alicia Myers explores the ways in which ancient conversations about moral formation use language of milk and lactation. She identifies gender constructions related to the male and female body that underlie various discussions within the Greco-Roman world and specifically in Hebrews and 1 Peter in the New Testament.

How I wish I had had this book to read when my children were young! These authors push back against the culture's rosy, simplistic attitudes towards pregnancy, birthing, and motherhood. They write with bold vulnerability and appropriate candor. They make space for the reader to walk alongside their experiences and allow readers to think about their own experiences in fresh ways.

Making Sense of Motherhood is not just for mothers, or even just for women. A hidden strength of this work is its unflinching focus on the reality of the embodied life. These contributors wrestle with how their faith, the biblical text, and their cultural codes shape their experiences. In this, mothers are but a particular example of the human condition, as body and mind together imagine the future and process the past while walking in the present. Questions about identity and personhood, about self-worth and self-denial, are especially poignant for mothers but not unique. Thus Erin Heim's chapter on adoption could be equally engaging for an adopted son as for an adopted daughter. Heim bestows voice to the figure that is so often silenced: the birth mother who gives up her daughter. One could explore this further by looking at fathers and grandparents whose stories and identities link with the adopted child. Rebecca Lindsay provokes necessary engagement with our patterns of ministry today that touch pastor/fathers as much as pastor/mothers. She challenges the naïve notion that fatherhood and pastoral ministry are easily linked in uncomplicated ways, offering the ideas generated by women in ministry to help men and women better represent the self-giving Christ.

The reader will not want to hurry through these chapters, but to savor them. I found myself pausing after finishing a chapter and sitting quietly, letting the observations and ideas soak in. After a bit, I wanted to share my reactions with my friends, including the mamas in Kenya. This is a book that is to be enjoyed not just by the reader alone, but also with others—a lot like mothering.

Bibliography

Cohick, Lynn H. *Women in the World of the Earliest Christians: Illuminating Ancient Ways of Life*. Grand Rapids: Baker Academic, 2009.

Cohick, Lynn H., and Amy Brown Hughes, tentatively titled, *Christian Women in the Patristic World: Influence, Authority, Legacy*. Grand Rapids: Baker Academic, forthcoming.

Walker Bynum, Caroline. *Jesus as Mother: Studies in the Spirituality of the High Middle Ages*. Berkeley: University of California Press, 1982.

Acknowledgments

This book has been a labor of love for many, and they deserve my express gratitude. I would like to extend my thanks to all of the contributors for sharing their time and insight on this project. I deeply appreciate how you shared not only your scholarship, but also other aspects of your lives in this unique volume. I am proud of our collaborative community. Your patience, passion, and wisdom have birthed this volume. I would particularly like to thank Cristina Lledo Gomez and Ruth Sheridan. Cristina provided the initial vision for this project, and Ruth worked with me on extending that vision. Both supported this volume to its completion. Without you, this volume would not exist.

I also wish to thank Matthew Wimer and the editorial team at Wipf and Stock for their work on this project. I am thankful that Wipf and Stock saw the value of such a diverse work.

I would like to thank my husband, Jon, for his encouragement over the long process of envisioning and coordinating this volume. He has empowered me to be the mother-scholar that I am. Additionally, my colleagues at Ambrose University and my longtime friends and fellow alums from Regent College and McMaster Divinity College deserve thanks for their insights and support. And thanks to Miriam Neufeld for her help indexing.

I further wish to thank the mothers (biological, legal, and spiritual) who have encouraged me to see the deep value of mothering through the ways they have mothered me. To Mary Louise Moskowitz, Deb Lightbown, Ovelina Stovell, Cindy Westfall, and Maxine Hancock, you have inspired this book!

Finally, I wish to thank our readers of this volume. I hope and pray that this volume will provide new insights into the theological depths of motherhood.

Can We Really Make Sense of Motherhood?

An Explorative Introduction

BETH M. STOVELL

Motherhood and Birthing a Book

In 2006, I became a mother for the first time with the birth of our daughter, Elena, and my life was irrevocably changed in both large, obvious and small, nearly imperceptible ways. Despite the many books I had read about the medical and health dimensions of motherhood, I was shocked by the experiences of loss and pain alongside joy that came not only from birthing, but also from becoming a mother. I felt at a loss to understand myself and my changing view of God in relation to this new life. As a biblical theologian in training at the time, I desperately wanted to make sense of motherhood in its biblical and theological dimensions alongside its practical ones. How could I understand the self-emptying of motherhood in relation to Christ's kenosis and passion? How could I see in new ways God's self-depiction as a mother and see my own imperfect mothering as strangely echoing the *Imago Dei*? In 2009, I began exploring these questions in earnest while pregnant with our second child, our son Atticus. During this pregnancy, I wrote what would become my chapter in this volume, in which I explore the picture of God as mother in Isa 42 and John 3. I remember standing, nine months pregnant, as I presented this paper at the Evangelical Theological Society, functioning like a living *ikon* for this deeply mysterious divine metaphor.[3]

---

3. This experience caused me to think deeply about notions of the *Imago Dei* and mothers' bodies. This pursuit is present in my chapter in this volume, but such themes can also be found in works exploring the picture of Jesus as mother in the work of Julian of Norwich. See Baker, *Julian of Norwich's Showings*, esp. chapter 5, "Reimagining the Imago Dei: The Motherhood of Jesus and the Ideology of Self," 107–34; Nuth, *Wisdom's*

My continued longing to "make sense of motherhood" ultimately led to the birthing of this book.

In some ways, motherhood makes perfect sense. Babies are born every day, transforming the women who give birth to them into mothers. We understand the basic life events that make a woman into a mother. We can study the anatomy and physiology of motherhood, the practices of motherhood, the struggles of motherhood, and yet in a sense we cannot therefore state that we have "made sense of motherhood." This is particularly true as we approach how motherhood shapes our thinking about Scripture and theology. Scripture abounds with stories of mothers, with metaphors related to mothering, and with mothers who hold theological significance. In Christianity and Judaism alike, motherhood has impacted notions of personhood and theology. How do we make sense of this complex diversity in the portrait of motherhood in Scripture, theology, and spirituality? This question is particularly true if we agree with Ruth Sheridan, who states elsewhere in this volume that "motherhood can never be fully understood or reduced conveniently to a formula that would give it meaning or 'make sense' of its entirely and for all persons; it is ever elusive and ever changing as it is lived."[4]

Studying Motherhood in Biblical and Theological Ways

Motherhood has been the topic of many studies in a variety of fields associated with biblical studies, theology, and Christian spirituality. In the area of biblical studies, many recent books have focused on depictions of God's motherhood in Scripture or depictions of mothers in Scripture.[5] Within systematic and practical theology, many books have focused on the concept of motherhood in relation to gender. For example, several works discuss motherhood as part of a broader feminist theology.[6] Some feminist theologies begin with motherhood as one of the chief feminist depictions of God, whether seeing the Holy Spirit as mother or the entire Godhead as mother.[7] The metaphor of motherhood has also frequently played a chief role in

---

Daughter, 65–68, 95–97; Pelphrey, *Christ Our Mother*; Palliser, *Christ, Our Mother of Mercy*.

4. Sheridan, "She Forgets Her Suffering In Her Joy," 49.

5. Maier, *Daughter Zion, Mother Zion*; Dille, *Mixed Metaphors*, 398; Bronner, *Stories of Biblical Mothers*.

6. Hogan, *From Woman's Experience to Feminist Theology*; Carr and Fiorenza, *Motherhood*; Kirk-Duggan and Pippen, *Mother Goose, Mother Jones, Mommie Dearest*.

7. Ruether, *Gaia & God*; McFague, *Models of God*.

ecclesiological discussions.[8] Others discuss motherhood as part of a theology of marriage and family.[9] Some studies have focused on motherhood and theology in specific historical contexts or in connection to a particular theological theme.[10] In the areas of Christian spirituality and ministry, studies of motherhood have often focused on Mary's role as the mother of God for broader Christian understanding.[11] Other related books have focused on the spirituality of motherhood within Christian spiritual traditions.[12]

The unique value of this volume is its ability to provide a single resource that demonstrates the diversity of these approaches to motherhood across these disciplines, while forging ahead with new scholarly material and touching upon frequently overlooked areas of motherhood. While this volume is similar to Carr and Schüssler Fiorenza's *Motherhood* as an edited volume that crosses different areas of theology with a diversity of scholars, this volume is contrastingly not focused on feminist theology as its primary foundation for interpretation (although feminist theology certainly comes into play in several chapters). Connecting international scholars from across North America, Oceania, and the Third World representing Jewish and ecumenical Christian perspectives, this edited volume works across the disciplines of biblical studies, systematic theology, practical theology, and Christian spirituality. In this way, this volume provides an approach to the diversity of maternal understanding that will also contribute to the broader understanding of women in the history of Christianity. This volume also incorporates types of motherhood often overlooked in other works on motherhood and theology, including contextual and practical theological approaches to motherhood, alongside otherwise marginalized views of motherhood (e.g., motherhood in Latina culture, adoptive mothers, and grief and motherhood).

The diversity of contributions in this volume reflects the deep tension in motherhood between the pain, crisis, and association with death that accompanies motherhood and the joy, transformation, and life that also accompanies motherhood. There are few metaphors in Scripture (or in life) that stand so firmly between life and death, love and loss, and joy and deep pain. After all, motherhood's meaning arises again and again at these crucial crossroads. While including negative aspects of the experience of

---

8. Braaten, *Mother Church*; Cuneen, *Mother Church*.

9. Rubio, *A Christian Theology of Marriage and Family*; Browning, *Equality and the Family*; Miller-McLemore, *Also a Mother*.

10. Grenholm, *Motherhood and Love*.

11. Braaten and Jenson (eds), *Mary, the Mother of God*; Flusser, Lang, and Pelican (eds), *Mary*; Gaventa, *Mary*.

12. Sanna, *Motherhood*; Palliser, *Christ, Our Mother of Mercy*.

motherhood, this vision is not a pessimistic one, but it reveals something powerful about what motherhood actually means. Many people (including theologians) focus on the positives of motherhood without realizing that part of the essence of mothering is this side of struggle and pain. Scripture and theology, however, again and again focus on this very complexity of mothering. This book captures this reality in the world and this truth revealed within Scripture and theology.

The approach to this volume is both academic and personal. At times, it captures the humor of motherhood, the pain of motherhood, the loss of motherhood, and the joy of motherhood through intimate interweavings of the academic and the experiential. For the majority of the authors of this book, motherhood is more than simply a concept or a theoretical notion; it is a lived experience that shapes how they "make sense of motherhood" in their own lives and in the lives of those around them. The scholars in this volume show a side of motherhood rarely seen in academic circles and take off the masks of distance and objectivity academics wear, revealing the inner spaces of mothering. Several of these scholars expressed to me how writing their contributions for this volume became a unique experience for them, one that involved self-revelation in surprising ways at times. This experience of self-revelation becomes an opportunity for readers to peek into the depths of motherhood in new ways.

Laying Out the Book

This book includes three major parts: motherhood in the Hebrew Bible, the New Testament, and in Christian theology and spirituality. Part I charts the images of motherhood in the Hebrew Bible. In chapter 1, Shayna Sheinfeld presents a picture of "subversive mothers," examining the stories of Lot's daughters and Tamar in Genesis and midrash. Her chapter demonstrates how the rabbinic scholars valued the motherhood of these women because of their ultimate role in leading to the messiah. In chapter 2, Anthony Rees explores the complicated relationship between Yhwh and Moses as co-parents of Israel. This somewhat humorous exchange between Yhwh and Moses provides a window into questions about Israel's parentage and into metaphors of mothering and children in the Hebrew Bible. Chapter 3 functions as a hinge between Part I and Part II as I describe the continuity in the picture of God as mother. My chapter compares the use of God as mother and God as warrior in Isa 42 and the depiction of spiritual rebirth in John 3, suggesting that these images of motherhood hint at a more complicated picture of God as mother and rebirth by the Spirit than has been previously considered, a picture that includes the pain and uncertainty of birth alongside its joy and new life.

Part II explores New Testament depictions of motherhood and issues related to motherhood in the early church. In chapter 4, Ruth Sheridan continues the exploration of the Fourth Gospel. Through her examination of John 16, Sheridan plunges her reader into the pain, fear, and loss of birthing alongside its joy and shows how this is an apt metaphor for Jesus' death and resurrection. Erin Heim provides a personal exploration of adoption by way of a theological reflection on the intersection between contemporary adoption narratives and the adoption metaphor in the Pauline narrative of Rom 8 in chapter 5. This personal and academic engagement provides deeper insight into adoptive mothering, into the too often overlooked experiences of biological mothers, and the complexity of the experiences of adoptees as children with two mothers. In chapter 6, Alicia Myers explores milk metaphors in the New Testament with a focus on their ancient milieu to demonstrate how nursing and milk provide windows into notions of gender and mothering in the ancient world. Myers demonstrates how these masculinized motherhood metaphors provide new insight into the complexities of representations of Jesus' gender and of gender assumptions around Christian discipleship. In chapter 7, Louise Gosbell also rethinks our notions related to mothering in the ancient world. Gosbell explores conceptions of exposure and infanticide in the early church and its surrounding context with an awareness of how this makes us question our own assumptions about infanticide today.

Part III turns to the impact of motherhood on Christian theology and spirituality. In chapter 8, Cristina Gomez demonstrates the links between motherhood and the paschal mystery, illuminating how Christ's death and resurrection become mirrored in the lives of new mothers and thereby become a means of salvation. Rebecca Lindsay explores questions of motherhood and ministry in chapter 9 by listening closely to the voices of four feminist theologians. Lindsay suggests new ways that motherhood provides reflection on being a minister of the Word and on a more expansive view of spirituality for women and men alike. Chapter 10 moves to the value of reflection on Mary's motherhood for Latina spirituality. Claudia Herrera uses the lens of practical theology, specifically Latina/o theology, to illumine Mary's journey of motherhood as a metaphor for Latina spirituality. She explores Mary's motherhood as showing the value of *lo cotidiano* ("everyday experiences" or "daily life") in her journey to Judea and examines Mary's role as representative of all people, particularly the poor and oppressed. Herrera suggests that Mary's motherhood, in its pathway to Bethlehem and its pathway to Calvary, provides two routes through which Latinas can join in Mary's journey. Chapters 11 and 12 continue in the direction of practical and spiritual theology as they create dialogue with Hebrew Bible scholar, Walter Brueggemann. These chapters span the movement of motherhood from the earliest stages of mothering to the transitional space of releasing children on to adulthood. In Chapter 11, Sarah Massa dialogues with Brueggemann's notion of disorientation in the Psalms as a means of exploring the experience of disorientation of early motherhood, arguing for a new view of motherhood as insightful for spiritual transformation. In chapter 12, Patricia Smith dialogues with Brueggemann's three critical dimensions of his covenantal theology to explore the transitional space of mourning the loss of children as they move from adolescence to adulthood.

Chapter 13 provides a conclusion to the volume that explores the implications for future research and reflection based on the contributions in this volume. This chapter explores in what way this volume has "made sense of motherhood" and points to further pathways for "sense-making" in the future.

Bibliography

Baker, Denise Nowakowski. *Julian of Norwich's Showings: From Vision to Book*. Princeton University Press, 1994.
Braaten, Carl. *Mother Church: Ecclesiology and Ecumenism*. Minneapolis: Fortress, 1998.
Braaten, Carl E., and Robert W. Jenson, eds. *Mary, the Mother of God*. Grand Rapids: Eerdmans, 2004.
Bronner, Leila Leah. *Stories of Biblical Mothers: Maternal Power in the Hebrew Bible*. Lanham, MD: University Press of America, 2004.
Browning, Don. *Equality and the Family: A Fundamental, Practical Theology of Children, Mothers, and Fathers in Modern Society*. Grand Rapids: Eerdmans, 2007.
Carr, Ann, and Elizabeth Schüssler Fiorenza, eds. *Motherhood: Experience, Institution, Theology*. Edinburgh: T&T Clark, 1989.
Cuneen, Sally. *Mother Church: What the Experience of Women Is Teaching Her*. Mahwah, NJ: Paulist, 1991.
Dille, Sarah. *Mixed Metaphors: Mixing Metaphors: God as Mother and Father in Deutero-Isaiah*. Journal for the Study of the Old Testament Supplement Series 398. London: T&T Clark, 2004.
Flusser, David, Justin Lang, and Jaroslav Pelican, eds. *Mary: Images of the Mother of Jesus in Jewish and Christian Perspective*. Philadelphia: Fortress, 1986.
Gaventa, Beverly Roberts. *Mary: Glimpses of the Mother of Jesus*. Philadelphia: Fortress, 1999.
Grenholm, Cristina. *Motherhood and Love: Beyond the Gendered Stereotypes of Theology*. Grand Rapids: Eerdmans, 2011.
Hogan, Linda. *From Woman's Experience to Feminist Theology*. Sheffield: Sheffield Academic, 1995.

Kirk-Duggan, Cheryl A., and Tina Pippen, eds. *Mother Goose, Mother Jones, Mommie Dearest: Biblical Mothers and Their Children*. Semeia Studies 61. Leiden: Brill, 2010.

Maier, Christl M. *Daughter Zion, Mother Zion: Gender, Space, and the Sacred in Ancient Israel*. Minneapolis: Fortress, 2008.

McFague, Sally. *Models of God: Theology for an Ecological, Nuclear Age*. Philadelphia: Fortress, 1987.

Miller-McLemore, Bonnie. *Also a Mother: Work and Family as Theological Dilemma*. Nashville: Abingdon, 1994.

Nuth, Joan M. *Wisdom's Daughter: The Theology of Julian of Norwich*. New York: Crossroad, 1991.

Palliser, Margaret Ann. *Christ, Our Mother of Mercy: Divine Mercy and Compassion in the Theology of the Shewings of Julian of Norwich*. Berlin: DeGruyter, 1992.

Pelphrey, Brant. *Christ Our Mother: Julian of Norwich*. London: Darton, Longman, & Todd, 1989.

Rubio, Julie Hanlon. *A Christian Theology of Marriage and Family*. Mahwah, NJ: Paulist, 2003.

Ruether, Rosemary Radford. *Gaia & God: An Ecofeminist Theology of Earth Healing*. San Francisco: HarperSanFrancisco, 1992.

Sanna, Ellyn. *Motherhood: A Spiritual Journey*. Mahwah, NJ: Paulist, 1997.

Part I

The Hebrew Bible and Motherhood

1

Lot's Daughters and Tamar

Mothers Positively Reimagined in Genesis Rabbah

SHAYNA SHEINFELD

Introduction

In Genesis, stories of deception by women are a fairly common trope: three separate times the wives of the patriarchs lie about their relationships with their husbands while sojourning in a foreign land in order to keep their husbands safe (Gen 12:10–20, 20:1–18, 26:1–17); Lot's daughters use alcohol to impede Lot's senses in order to gain offspring by him (Gen 19); Rebekah tricks Isaac into giving her favorite (younger) son, Jacob, the blessing intended for the firstborn Esau (Gen 27); Rachel steals her father's *teraphim*, hiding them in her saddlebags and sitting upon them while feigning menstruation (Gen 31); and Tamar deceives Judah into having sex with her after he denies her his last son through a levirate marriage (Gen 38). Two of these instances—the Gen 19 account of Lot's daughters and the Gen 28 story of Tamar—focus on the use of deceptive tactics to become pregnant and achieve motherhood. While the narratives as told in Genesis are neutral in terms of casting judgment upon these characters seeking motherhood, they are reimagined in midrashic interpretation with a decidedly positive spin.

This chapter examines the characterization of Lot's daughters in Gen 19:30–37 and of Tamar in Gen 38, both of whom use deceptive means in order to become mothers. These women are re-characterized in the early midrashic collection known as *Genesis Rabbah*,[1] where they are portrayed as righteous despite their wiles. This rabbinic corpus is sympathetic to the plights of these mothers-to-be, providing justification for their subversive actions because the end result is considered God's will—the male offspring produced by both Lot's oldest daughter and by Tamar eventually lead to the Davidic dynasty and therefore will also one day lead to the messiah.[2] These narratives from Genesis and their reception in the midrash show how—even though these mothers' choices are incongruent with what one might expect from women in the Torah—according to the midrash, the end result justifies the deceptive means by which each mother acts. *Genesis Rabbah* makes sense of the subversive way Lot's daughters and Tamar reach motherhood by turning potentially negative stories of women into stories of motherhood that will ultimately lead to the messianic redemption of the Jewish people.

Lot's Daughters (Gen 19:30–37)

Lot, the nephew of the patriarch Abraham, lived with his family in a city called Sodom. Along with Gomorrah, Sodom was to be destroyed by God on account of its wickedness (Gen 18:16–33). Lot is saved because he invites strangers into his home; these strangers are identified as the angels (*malak*) sent to destroy the city (19:1–11).[3] At the angels' urging, Lot and his family escape with the caveat that the family is not to look back toward the city (19:12–17). Once Lot and his family have left, God destroys Sodom and Gomorrah with sulfur and fire (19:24–25). Lot's wife is turned into a pillar

---

1. *Genesis Rabbah* is one of the oldest collections of exegetical midrashim, providing (sometimes loosely connected) commentary on words, phrases, and ideas found in Genesis. *Genesis Rabbah* was written in Roman Palestine and likely redacted by the fifth century CE. I will refer to the redactors as rabbis and sometimes, for variety, as sages. For an introduction to the midrash, see Strack and Stemberger, *Introduction to the Talmud and Midrash*, 276–81.

2. The messiah, according to biblical tradition, will derive from the house of David. See Isa 11:1 and 1 Chron 22:8–10.

3. In exchange for the two strangers who are attacked by the men of the city, Lot offers his two virgin daughters. It is not clear in the text whether Lot actually gives his daughters over to the men of the city or just makes the offer. There is some discussion as to whether the two daughters who leave the city with Lot are the same two daughters who were offered to the men of the Sodom. See Bronner, *From Eve to Esther*, 116. Bronner draws this idea from the ninth-century CE midrash *Tanhuma*, which contends that "normally a father would sacrifice himself to protect his wife and daughters, whereas Lot was willing to hand them over," as in Gen 19:8 (ibid., 115). Thus, according to Bronner, the daughters at the beginning of the narrative may very well be the same as those at the end of the narrative; this leads Bronner to the interpretation that the incestuous unions could have been planned out of revenge.

of salt after she looks back toward the destruction (19:26). Left with only his two daughters and frightened by the experience, Lot removes himself and his daughters to live in a cave in the hills, far away from any civilization. Lot's daughters are concerned about their solitude and the possibility of preserving humanity, so they decide to get their father drunk and have intercourse with him with the goal of getting pregnant:

> And the firstborn said to the younger, "Our father is old, and there is not a man on earth to come in to us after the manner of all the world. Come, let us make our father drink wine, and we will lie with him, so that we may preserve offspring through our father." So they made their father drink wine that night; and the firstborn went in, and lay with[4] her father; he did not know when she lay down or when she rose. On the next day, the firstborn said to the younger, "Look, I lay last night with my father; let us make him drink wine tonight also; then you go in and lie with him, so that we may preserve offspring through our father." So they made their father drink wine that night also; and the younger rose, and lay with him; and he did not know when she lay down or when she rose. Thus both the daughters of Lot became pregnant by their father (19:31–36).

The firstborn names her son Moab, a boy who is said to have become the ancestor of the Moabites (19:37), while the younger daughter bore a son named Ben-Ammi who is said to have become the ancestor to the Ammonites (19:38).

In later analyses of the women in this narrative, the daughters of Lot are given short shrift, since the emphasis is on their mother, who is turned into salt in Gen 19:26.[5] However, it is with this particular portion of the story that our analysis begins. At issue in this discussion is the latter half of the narrative in which Lot removes himself and his daughters from society. The concerns of the elder daughter, who is the only one of the two daughters to speak, are twofold. First, she is concerned that their father is old and therefore that he may die soon. Second, she worries there are no other available men besides him, and thus with his death there will be no men at all with whom the daughters could possibly conceive.[6] Tammi Schneider notes that although it is not initially clear whether the daughters think they are indeed the last three humans or whether they simply do not have access

---

4. See below for a potential textual variant of the preposition "with" used here.

5. There is myriad secondary literature on Lot's wife. For a brief overview and an analysis, see Schneider, *Mothers of Promise*, 183–85.

6. Ibid., 189.

to other men, the use of the verb for giving the father wine also means to irrigate the ground. Thus, the daughters do not simply intend to pour their dad a glass of wine but to fully "saturate" him—that is, get him very drunk.[7] While the narrative in Genesis does not lay specific blame on any party for this incestuous encounter, the description of the daughters inebriating their father in order to carry out their plan suggests that Lot plays a passive role in the events that transpire; the general sense of the narrative implies the same conclusion. However, the daughters seem to make the choice to get their father drunk not only to commit incest but specifically in order to propagate the human race. "The young women were concerned with the future of the race, and they were resolute enough to adopt the only desperate measure that appeared to be available."[8] Thus, their goal does not seem to be simply sex or revenge.[9]

Until Gen 19:31, both daughters are treated as a unit. It is only here, when the eldest daughter speaks up, that the daughters are differentiated—not by name[10] but by birth order. The eldest daughter plays an active role both in developing and implementing the plan both sisters carry out. Schneider argues that it is only after the destruction of the primary female character of Lot's wife—a mother in her own right—that the daughters become more than just minor characters in the story: "only when their world has been destroyed, their mother turned into a pillar of salt, and they are living in a cave does the narrator separate them. Even then, there are still references to them as a unit."[11] The eldest daughter not only takes over the primary female role, she also shifts from a supporting character to become the protagonist.

In Gen 19:33 the eldest has sex with her father in order to procreate. The word used in the Hebrew, *shakab*, is a word usually reserved for what men do with women, including but not limited to potentially non-consensual encounters, such as that between Shechem and Dinah (Gen 34:2) or Reuben and Bilhah (Gen 35:22).[12] Rather than using the verb *shakab* here with the preposition *'im* (meaning "with") followed by the reference to Lot, which would indicate Lot's active participation in the act, the verb is used with the direct object marker *'et*, indicating that Lot is the object upon which

---

7. Ibid., 189.

8. Speiser, *Genesis*, 145.

9. Thus Bronner's interpretation, while appealing, is unlikely; see Bronner, *From Eve to Esther*, 115–16.

10. For more on named and unnamed characters in the Hebrew Bible, see Reinhartz, "Why Ask My Name?"

11. Schneider, *Mothers of Promise*, 187.

12. Ibid., 189.

the action is taking place. In other words, Genesis should not be understood as "the older one had (mutual) sex *with* her father" but that the sexual action is happening *to* Lot, caused by the eldest daughter. Lot's participation in the incestuous union thus seems to be excused.[13] The same situation takes place on the second night with the younger daughter, although only with the urging of her older sister: "Look, I lay last night with my father; let us make him drink wine tonight also; then you go in and lie with him, so that we may preserve offspring through our father" (Gen 19:34).

Both daughters conceive and bear sons from these illicit unions. The eldest daughter names her son Moab, which means "from my father." This descriptive name also points to the union as incestuous. The younger names her son Ben-Ammi, which means "son of my people," a more veiled reference to the incestuous situation. While the names of the sons are descriptive of their conception, they are also clearly meant to serve a negative etiological function for Israel's neighbors (and periodic enemies) the Moabites and the Ammonites. This etiology does not overtly reflect on how the narrative portrays the two daughters or Lot, but it does serve to demean them indirectly.

Unlike the narrative in Genesis, *Genesis Rabbah* intentionally portrays the daughters in a positive light. This is particularly true of the eldest daughter, who took the initiative to get herself and her sister pregnant. This positive depiction comes in spite of the fact that the daughters actively engaged in non-consensual incest with their father. *Genesis Rabbah* 51:8 states that, like in the generation of the flood (Gen 6–9), the daughters thought the world's population had been destroyed and thus their actions were justified—they were seeking to continue the human race. This reading is a near-literal interpretation of Gen 19:31: "Our father is old, and there is not a man on earth to come in to us after the manner of all the world." The main justification for the daughters' actions according to the midrash, however, is that the king-messiah will come through the line of Lot via Moab. This intertextuality draws upon the book of Ruth, in which Ruth the Moabite marries the Israelite Boaz.[14] Together they conceive Obed, who becomes the grandfather to King David.[15] This interpretation also derives from Gen 19:31: "R. Tanhuma in the name of Samuel: 'What is written is not, "So that we may keep a child alive from our father," but rather, "so we may preserve offspring through our father." That is to say, the king-messiah, who will

---

13. Ibid., 190.

14. Boaz himself was a descendent of Perez, one of Tamar and Judah's twin sons. See Ruth 4:18–22.

15. See Ruth 4:17.

come from another source'" (*Genesis Rabbah* 51:8).[16] Here it is not the child of the daughter who is important, but rather that this child continues Lot's lineage, since Lot is considered to be the forefather of the Davidic line.

However, according to *Genesis Rabbah*, Lot is not without fault in the situation, even though Gen 19:33 seems to remove any blame that might be placed on Lot based on his drunkenness. Genesis is clear that Lot had no knowledge of the plan: "So they made their father drink wine that night; and the firstborn went in, and lay with her father; he did not know when she lay down or when she rose." However, *Genesis Rabbah* 51:8 states that although Lot was drunk when his daughter lay down with him ("he did not know when she lay down"), he was sober enough to know when she got up. This is based on a peculiarity in the Hebrew text. According to the midrash, "there are dots written over the word 'when she arose,' meaning that while he did not know when she lay down, he did know when she got up." This peculiarity of the word suggested to the interpreter that while Lot did not know what was going to happen when he drank the wine, he was aware of the fact that he had sex with his daughter by the time she had left his bed. This would also suggest that Lot's willingness to drink the wine on the second night means he was complicit in the sexual relations he had with his younger daughter on that night.

Similarly, *Genesis Rabbah* 51:9 states that Lot actually desired his daughters:

> Said R. Nahman bar Hanan, "Whoever lusts after fornication in the end will be fed with his own flesh [committing incest]." R. Yudan of Galliah and R. Samuel bar Nahman, both in the name of R. Elijah Ene: "We do not know whether Lot lusted for his daughters, or his daughters lusted for him. On the basis of what is said in the following verse: 'He who separates himself seeks desire' (Prov. 18:1), it is clear that Lot lusted after his daughter."

Thus, while the narrative in Genesis puts agency into the hands of the daughters in order to produce offspring—and Lot is absolved of any choice in the situation—*Genesis Rabbah* clearly places the fault in Lot's hands. The sages use the verse from Prov 18:1, "He who separates himself seeks desire," as an interpretation of Lot's (poor) choice to live in the cave rather than to leave Sodom for a small town nearby. They argue that he made this choice so he could copulate with his daughters. This interpretation goes almost directly against the plain sense meaning of the passage in Genesis, thus redeeming Lot's daughters and placing blame into Lot's hands.

---

16. Translations of *Genesis Rabbah* are taken from Neusner, *Genesis Rabbah*.

Genesis Rabbah clearly transfers the blame from Lot's daughters to Lot, yet all the while also removing any negativity from the activity. As Bronner states:

> The rationale for the sages' tolerance was that often from evil comes good; for though the action itself was evil, they accept that the motivation had been to continue the race, a good and justified end. So worthy was this motivation, according to the sages, that Ruth, a descendent of the Moabite line, has the honor of being ancestress to the Messiah. The merit discerned by the rabbis in the other daughter, who named her son Ben-Ammi, was that she displayed modesty; thus, the pious Naamah, a wife of Solomon, sprang from her.[17]

Thus, even while placing Lot at fault for the situation, *Genesis Rabbah* does not condemn what happened, nor does the midrash blame either the daughters or the children who ultimately arise from the incestuous union. In fact, the incest is in this case justified because of the lineage it gives rise to—leading to Ruth and, through her, to King David and the messiah.

Tamar and Judah (Gen 38)

Genesis 38 breaks away from the Joseph narrative to tell the story of Tamar.[18] Judah, one of Joseph's brothers, marries a Canaanite woman and has three sons: Er, Onan, and Shelah. Er marries Tamar, but since Er was "wicked in the sight of the Lord," the Lord kills him before Tamar can conceive (38:7). Judah commands Onan to enter into a levirate marriage[19] with Tamar. Instead of performing the duty of impregnating Tamar on behalf of his deceased brother, Onan spills his semen on the ground so that Tamar would not get pregnant.[20] This too upsets God, who kills Onan as well (38:10).

---

17. Bronner, *From Eve to Esther*, 117–18. The tradition that Naamah, wife of King Solomon, came from the line of Ben-Ammi, son of Lot and his younger daughter, can be found at multiple places in the Babylonian Talmud: *b. B. Qam* 38b; *b. Yebam.* 63a and 77a.

18. The placement of the story of Tamar in the middle of the Joseph cycle has been the subject of much scholarly discussion. For overviews, see Blachman, *Transformation of Tamar*, 27–31, and Menn, *Judah and Tamar*, 73–82. See also *Genesis Rabbah* 38:9 and 38:11, both of which also make connections between the Joseph cycle and the story of Tamar.

19. See Deut 25:5–10.

20. It is not clear in the biblical narrative if this infers masturbation or *coitus interruptus*. However, *Genesis Rabbah* interprets the act as *coitus interruptus* (85:5). Similarly, the problem with Er, according to the midrash, is that he practiced anal sex (*Genesis*

Judah is now concerned that if he gives Tamar his youngest son, Shelah, he will also die, so Judah sends Tamar to wait as a widow in her father's household until Shelah is old enough to marry (38:11). However, Tamar soon realizes that Judah has no intention of giving Shelah to her. Tamar changes her clothes, discarding her widow's garments and donning a veil, and waits at the entrance to Enaim, which is on the route to Timnah. Judah, on his way to Timnah to shear sheep, approaches her because he thinks she is a prostitute. He propositions her, and she then has sex with him (38:14–16). Instead of a payment, Judah gives her as surety his signet, cord, and staff with the understanding that she will return the items when he sends a kid from his flock as payment. Judah later sends the kid, but she is no longer at the entrance to Enaim (38:17–23). Three months later Judah learns that Tamar is pregnant, and he insists that she be burned because she clearly prostituted herself (38:24). As she is on her way to be punished, Tamar sends the signet, cord, and staff to Judah and says, "it was the owner of these who made me pregnant" (38:25). Judah acknowledges his role in the situation and notes that Tamar is "more right than I am" since he did not follow through on his promise to give her to Shelah (38:26). Tamar's union with Judah is rewarded with twin sons, and in a trope common in Genesis, the second-born son, Perez, usurps his brother's place as the firstborn.[21] This trope of the younger son being chosen is furthered through Perez's descendants, including King David (38:27–30).[22]

Like the daughters of Lot, Tamar initially appears as a passive character in the narrative in Genesis.[23] She is the wife of Er, and when God—not Tamar—kills him, Judah gives her to Onan. Again, it is God who acts, and Tamar is again left a widow in her father's home, accepting that she will have to wait in this liminal state until Shelah is of age. Tamar's own feelings on the situation—namely, her interest in having intercourse with subsequent brothers—are not at issue in the narrative. This is reflected in scholarly discussions on Tamar's role as protagonist. Scholars like Cowan see Tamar as a heroine who acts with her own agency in order to right the wrong that has

---

Rabbah 85:4). Thus, according to the midrash, both sons were killed by God because of sexual deviance. This is a noteworthy fact, since Tamar herself engages in a form of sexual deviance by joining with her father-in-law but is not portrayed negatively in the midrash.

21. For one interpretation of this trope, see Greenspahn, *When Brothers Dwell Together*.

22. Through Boaz's side rather than Ruth's side, which is how Moab, Lot's eldest daughter's son, is ancestor to the messiah. See Ruth 4:18–22. According to Matt 1:3–16, Perez is also the ancestor of Jesus.

23. Menn, *Judah and Tamar*, 29.

been done to her by denying her children and leaving her in this liminal state between father and husband.[24] Other scholars such as Menn see Tamar as subordinate throughout the narrative and interpret Tamar's independent action as a one-time event, since shortly thereafter Tamar is "covered again in the opacity of the biblical text's depiction of her" through Judah's perspective.[25] Notably, Tamar's pregnancy is controlled by Judah, and in the biblical text the birth of the twins is handled not by Tamar but by a midwife.[26]

Tamar's liminal state, poised as she is between her father's and Judah's households, may be partially to blame for the uncertainty surrounding her role as protagonist. While the NRSV translates Gen 38:14 as "she put off her widow's garments, put on a veil, wrapped herself up,[27] and sat down at the entrance to Enaim, which is on the road to Timnah," the next verse colors the reader's understanding of Tamar's actions: "When Judah saw her, he thought her to be a prostitute, for she had covered her face." Verse 14 in no way suggests that Tamar dresses up as a prostitute and seeks to intentionally deceive Judah into having sex with her. In fact, her intentions are unclear. The narrative itself does not specify what kind of "costume" Tamar put on—all the biblical account tells the reader is that she "put off her widow's garments" and "put on a veil" (38:14). The veil, which is what seems to be causing Judah to interpret Tamar's presence as a harlot-for-hire, held numerous meanings in the ancient world and may or may not have been the standard dress for sex workers in the ancient world.[28] Tamar's use of the veil does not necessarily equate with Tamar dressing as a prostitute in order to deceive Judah; instead, it is Judah's viewpoint ("he thought her to be a prostitute") that colors the reader's interpretation of what Tamar actually did. Schneider argues that Tamar's actions—taking off her widow's garments,

24. Cowan, "Genesis 38," 177. See also Berlin, *Poetics and Interpretation*, 41.

25. Menn, *Judah and Tamar*, 32.

26. Ibid., 35. For a more detailed discussion of these two perspectives, see Blachman, *Transformation of Tamar*, 42–47.

27. Note that Speiser translates this phrase as "disguised herself," suggesting that Tamar intended to deceive Judah, although this is not the plain sense reading of the text (Speiser, *Genesis*, 298).

28. Likely the costume that identified a woman as a sex worker in the ancient world was based in local or regional custom; see Bird, "Harlot as Heroine," 112 n15. Schneider notes that Middle Assyrian Law is clear that wives, widows, and concubines veiled themselves, while prostitutes did not—if prostitutes were veiled, there was steep punishment. Likewise, in other pentateuchal texts, veiling does not equal prostitution. See, for instance, Rebekah in Gen 24:65, who veils before Isaac, as well as Moses in Exod 34:33–35, who veils to conceal his shining face after speaking with God (Schneider, *Mothers of Promise*, 154). However, Bird is quick to point out that one cannot use Middle Assyrian Law for practices in Canaan (Bird, "Harlot as Heroine," 112 n15). Thus, our text remains unclear as to the nature of the veil.

donning a veil that may have been worn for weddings (Gen 24:65), and sitting to wait for her father-in-law—should be interpreted as Tamar actively taking herself out of her father's household and physically reminding Judah—by placing herself in a location where she will encounter him—of his responsibility to her as a daughter-in-law. According to Schneider, Tamar may simply be intending to force Judah's hand into arranging the levirate marriage with Shelah.[29] However, Tamar's veil would suggest otherwise—why would she hide her face if she intended Judah to acknowledge her? Instead, Phyllis Bird suggests that Tamar's actions fulfills two purposes for Tamar: First, to move beyond her liminal state as a widow waiting for her levirate marriage in her father's household, and second, to take revenge on Judah for leaving her in this liminal state in the first place.[30]

The interpretation proffered by *Genesis Rabbah* maintains that Tamar is a pious woman, which undercuts the idea that her actions were for revenge or that they were necessarily and intentionally subversive. Citing Gen 38:13–14, where Tamar sees that Shelah is grown, then covers herself and sits "at the entrance to Enaim," the midrash explains that the interaction between Tamar and Judah took place because Tamar prayed:

> Said Rabbi, "We have reviewed the entire Scripture and have not found a place that is called 'the entrance to Enaim.' What then is the meaning of '*Petakh Enaim*'? This teaches that she set her eyes on the entrance to which all eyes look, and she prayed, 'May it be pleasing that I not leave this place empty-handed.'" (*Genesis Rabbah* 85:7)

Here the midrash explains the meaning of an otherwise unknown place-name, *Petakh Enaim*, which means "entrance" or "gate of the eyes." Tamar turns her eyes "on the entrance to which all eyes look"—that is, toward heaven—and prays to God that some sort of action should take place in order to remove her from the liminal state of a widow in her father's household. The outcome is not what would be expected. She is not given to Shelah in marriage, which would be the logical conclusion, but instead liaises with Judah, which results in her pregnancy. Thus, the rabbis understood the place-name as a reference Tamar's prayers, which were answered by God, albeit in an unexpected fashion.[31]

Likewise, in *Genesis Rabbah* 85:8, Tamar's motives are clarified to eliminate the possibility that Tamar sought revenge against Judah. This is

---

29. Schneider, *Mothers of Promise*, 155–56.
30. Bird, "Harlot as Heroine," 102.
31. Bronner, *From Eve to Esther*, 101.

accomplished through a comparison between Tamar and Potiphar's wife.[32] In this midrash, Potiphar's wife knows through astrology that she is to produce a son by Joseph, but she doesn't know if she herself is to be the bearer or if it will be her own daughter—who, according to the interpretation in *Genesis Rabbah* 89:1, is Joseph's wife Aseneth (Gen 46:20). Potiphar's wife is seen in a more sympathetic light: her failed seduction of Joseph is read as an attempt to secure the lineage prophesied through her horoscope, which she simply misread. Potiphar's wife's actions are thus justified, according to the midrash, because she was attempting to do God's will. Likewise, Tamar's actions, while perhaps performed in a questionable manner, are justified because it is God's will that Tamar achieve motherhood. This comparison between Potiphar's wife and Tamar stresses that Tamar's actions, like Potiphar's wife's actions, are for the sake of their future progeny, all of which are God's will. This is akin to the interpretation we saw of Lot's daughters above. Tamar's actions are justified because her offspring with Judah are necessary for the kingship and messiahship that is to come in Israel: Boaz traces his lineage back to Perez, the younger of Tamar's twin sons (Ruth 4:18–22), and is the great-grandfather of King David.

Unlike the negative depiction of Lot in the *Genesis Rabbah*, Judah is cleared of any serious wrongdoing. In *Genesis Rabbah* 85:8, Judah is said to have ignored Tamar when she was dressed up like a prostitute because a prostitute would not have her face covered, and therefore Judah knew that it was a suspicious situation. The midrash continues:

> Said R. Yohanan, "[Judah] planned to go right on by, but the Holy One, blessed be he, designated for him the angel who is in charge of lust. The angel said, 'Where are you going, Judah? From whence will kings arise, from whence will redeemers arise?' 'He went over to her at the roadside' (Gen 38:16) against his will, not for his own desire at all."

Judah here is exempt from any blame. Judah had no intention of stopping, according to the midrash, but his plans were waylaid by God's purpose. In fact, God causes the entire incident between Judah and Tamar through his angel "in charge of lust." In this interpretation, God is concerned with the future progeny of Judah and Tamar who will eventually lead to King David and the messiah.

Tamar's demand for Judah's signet, cord, and staff are also linked to her progeny and the future of Israel. As in its treatment of Lot's daughters, *Genesis Rabbah* 85:9 intertextually connects each of these items with subsequent

---

32. The midrash links these stories because the story of Potiphar's wife's attempted seduction of Joseph comes immediately after the story of Tamar and Judah in Gen 39.

characters or institutions: the signet is linked to Jer 22:24 and the line of King David, the cord is linked to the Sanhedrin through Num 15:38, and the staff is linked to the messiah through Ps 110:2. Thus, through Judah's transfer of these items to Tamar, she was able to conceive "heroes, like him, and righteous men, like him" (*Genesis Rabbah* 85:9). Judah's signet, cord, and staff represent later biblical and post-biblical characters and institutions that are essential for the royal, messianic, and rabbinic future of Israel.

Conclusion

The biblical accounts of Lot's daughters and Tamar both represent the women as either neutral or at fault in the episodes in which they engage in questionable sexual behavior. Despite the namelessness of Lot's daughters, they, like Tamar, take control of their reproductive options and seek motherhood through what seems to be the only means available. In comparison, the rabbis do not interpret these characters' actions negatively. Instead, their concern with royal and messianic lineage prompts them to reinterpret the stories in a more positive light. The agenda that becomes clear upon analysis of the rabbinic interpretation of Gen 19 and Gen 38 is that *Genesis Rabbah* sought to impose rabbinic ideals of the biblical past onto the stories found in Genesis—in this case, on women who sought to be mothers. These two stories in Genesis portray the women in a potentially negative light, showing how they use guile to secure their offspring. The recasting of their actions into positive deeds in *Genesis Rabbah* supports my argument that the midrash is refashioning the characters who appear in Genesis in a positive light in order to highlight the royal and messianic lineage.[33]

Tamar's offspring, secured through her father-in-law, lead to the birth of Boaz. Lot's eldest daughter's son, who begins the line of Moab, eventually produces Ruth, who leaves her family's Moabite traditions in order to marry Boaz, an Israelite. The descendants of Ruth and Boaz lead to the birth of King David, the pinnacle of Jewish monotheism. According to the rabbis, it is from the lineage of King David that the messiah will eventually arise. Thus, the positive reimagining of these women in the midrash is in line with what we know about the treatment of the larger biblical narrative in *Genesis*

33. "The fact that the commentary in *Genesis Rabba* revolves around certain selected details of the biblical narrative confirms that its primary intention is not to explicate evenly all the words of the text, but to accomplish a broader cultural explication of scripture for contemporary generations" (Menn, *Judah and Tamar*, 295 n14). This explication, according to Menn, includes the "broader program of recasting biblical characters associated with Israel's history in an unambiguously positive light" (ibid., 350).

Rabbah: its concern is to idealize the narrative past of Israel in order to highlight the royal and messianic trajectory of God's people, all of which is in line with God's will. Through this refashioning, *Genesis Rabbah* redeems the stories of Lot's daughters and Tamar specifically because these women seek out motherhood. Their deception should not, according to *Genesis Rabbah*, be interpreted in a negative light because their actions seek motherhood as the ultimate goal. In both cases, motherhood will lead to the eventual messianic redemption of the Jewish nation.

Bibliography

Berlin, Adele. *Poetics and Interpretation of Biblical Narrative*. Sheffield: Almond, 1983.

Bird, Phyllis. "The Harlot as Heroine: Narrative Art and Social Presupposition in Three Old Testament Texts." In *Women in the Hebrew Bible*, edited by Alice Bach, 99–117. New York: Routledge, 1999.

Blachman, Esther. *The Transformation of Tamar (Genesis 38) in the History of Jewish Interpretation*. Leuven, Belgium: Peeters, 2013.

Bronner, Leila L. *From Eve to Esther: Rabbinic Reconstructions of Biblical Women*. Louisville: Westminster John Knox, 1994.

Cowan, Margaret Parks. "Genesis 38: The Story of Judah and Tamar and Its Role in the Ancestral Narratives of Genesis." Ph.D. diss., Vanderbilt University, 1990.

Greenspahn, F. E. *When Brothers Dwell Together: The Preeminence of Younger Siblings in the Hebrew Bible*. New York: Oxford University Press, 1994.

Menn, Esther Marie. *Judah and Tamar (Genesis 38) in Ancient Jewish Exegesis: Studies in Literary Form and Hermeneutics*. Leiden: Brill, 1997.

Neusner, Jacob. *Genesis Rabbah: The Judaic Commentary to the Book of Genesis: A New American Translation*. 3 vols. Atlanta: Scholar's Press, 1985.

Reinhartz, Adele. *"Why Ask My Name?": Anonymity and Identity in Biblical Narrative*. New York: Oxford University Press, 1998.

Schneider, T. J. *Mothers of Promise: Women in the Book of Genesis*. Grand Rapids: Baker Academic, 2008.

Speiser, E. A. *Genesis: A New Translation with Introduction and Commentary*. 3rd ed. Anchor Bible. Garden City, NY: Doubleday, 1985.

Strack, H. L. and G. Stemberger, *Introduction to the Talmud and Midrash*. 2nd ed. Minneapolis: Fortress, 1996.

2

Moses

Mother of Israel?

Anthony Rees[1]

Introduction

There comes a time in every parent's experience when the whingeing[2] and whining of their children becomes hard to bear. Whether the whingeing is to do with what is or isn't for dinner, the length of a car journey, or the insistence on certain base-levels of hygiene, it is a truism that for all of us, at some point, it wears thin. At that point, the moment when we approach the outer limits of our sanity, I suspect it is not uncommon to blame God for our circumstances, to question why we of all people were cursed with

---

1. I would like to express my thanks to the Centre for Public and Contextual Theology at Charles Sturt University, whose generous fellowship allowed a year of concentrated research and writing in 2014.

2. I understand that the word "whingeing" is one that does not enjoy universal use. It derives from the same old Germanic root as "whining" but has a distinct use in Australian and New Zealand contexts. *The Australian Oxford Dictionary* suggests that whining is a "feeble or undignified complaining" and compares it to the wailing of a dog. Whingeing, however, is described as a "peevish grumbling" (Moore, *Australian Oxford Dictionary*, 1472). *The Macquarie Dictionary* has an entry titled "Whingeing Pom," a reference to a term used to describe English people's criticisms and complaints about life in Australia (Delbridge, *Macquarie Dictionary*, 1978). While the dictionary suggests it is a derogatory term, popular usage is more jovial these days. However, this joviality is not extended to a parent's use in relation to children! Under normal circumstances, parents' use of word "whingeing" is prefaced with an imperative "Stop."

this ungrateful whingeing brat, and to wonder how despite all our care and devotion, patience and love, this is how things have worked out.

The "murmuring" motif is a well-attested feature of the people of Israel's wilderness journey from the Sinai Peninsula to the land of Canaan.[3] Never really content with their lot, the people are quick to remember the luxuries they enjoyed in the house of bondage and slow to remember how they had cried out for deliverance. Their murmuring, or more accurately, whingeing and whining, was most commonly directed at Moses, the one responsible for their near-unbearable freedom. Moses, it seems, had a slightly greater tolerance for the whining of the people than Yhwh. In Num 11:1, the complaints of the people reach the hearing of Yhwh, and his response is dramatic: he sends a fire to consume the outer parts of the camp. The people's response is well known to parents. They cried out to the other parent, in this case Moses; Moses negotiated with his co-parent, and the fire abated.

As soon as the fire was out (v. 2), it seems, the rabble[4] decide they are hungry and cry out in a way common to children saying, "I'm starving" in Num 11:4–5. This is followed up by another staple of the whingeing playlist: "I don't want to eat that" (Num 11:6). The Israelites have fond memories of their culinary experiences back in Egypt, where they enjoyed cucumbers, melons, fish, leek, onion, and garlic. They forget that they were state slaves oppressed by impossible work conditions and routinely had their children butchered. At least they weren't hungry. Or, at least they didn't have to put up with this monotonous diet of manna cake, anyway.

It is this complaint that sends Moses to his limit. His placating of Yhwh should have bought him at least a night's peace. Surely the whingeing and whining could stop, even for just a little while. Moses needs some "Mommy time" or perhaps it's "Daddy time." With no one else to vent his frustration to, Moses confronts Yhwh. Up to this point, I have been operating with the assumption that Moses and Yhwh are operating as co-parents, but the specific role of each has not been explicit. Who is father? Who is mother? The exchange that ensues between them does little, if anything, to reveal the answer. Indeed, perhaps as a result of his frustration, it seems that Moses cannot quite articulate the way in which he understands his role in relation to this whingey, whiney group of people. In this chapter, we will use Moses' outburst in our attempt to understand the parental role played by both Moses and Yhwh in regards to the people of Israel, drawing on the

---

3. Coats, *Rebellion in the Wilderness*.

4. The use of the pejorative collective term "rabble" in v. 4 might be a hint that like an exasperated parent, even the narrator is beginning to lose his temper!

paradoxically gendered images that punctuate Moses' outburst and historical understandings of parental responsibility.

Moses' Meltdown

The final words of v. 10 tell us that Moses was displeased. It seems this might be somewhat of an understatement. In v. 11, he gives voice to his complaint. The language begins quite deferentially. Moses refers to himself as Yhwh's servant, even while he asks a series of quite pointed questions: "Why have you treated your servant so badly? Why have I not found favor in your sight . . . ?" If we imagine this as a conversation between parents and assume a patriarchal worldview, then it seems safe enough to picture Moses assuming the historical position of the female partner here, which is to say, the role of the mother. In the biblical world, it is the father of the house who takes the role of leadership, and members of his household all become his "servants." This is the model of the *bet 'ab*, the house of the father.

This also makes sense of the final section of v. 11, "that you lay the burden of all this people on me." Mothering was, and continues to be, an incredibly burdensome task. This is not to say that mothering is without joy or fulfillment, but it is valuable to acknowledge that mothering is hard work. In the ancient world, it was the mothers who were responsible for the care of family plantations, the tending of animals, the preparation of meals, the production of clothing, the education and nurture of children, the production of pottery and baskets for home use, and so on.[5] Thus, the task of mothering was a huge load of work, an incredible burden. Given that Moses is imagining himself as the mother of the entire nation of Israel, emphasized by his repeated use of the expression "the entire people,"[6] perhaps it is no surprise for him to speak of this as a great burden. Furthermore, it is no surprise that he may have reached a crisis point!

However, Num 11:12 immediately problematizes this position. The questions "Did I conceive them? Did I give birth to them?" serve to immediately distance Moses from the people. In effect, Moses is saying, "These are not my children! I am not their mother!" Moses, it seems, does not want to imagine himself as a mother. The questions actually carry a rhetorical weight. Moses seems to be reminding Yhwh that it is Yhwh who has conceived and given birth to these children, and thus the motherly burden lays with Yhwh. That is highly problematic, given that Yhwh is being imagined as the father in this family, and Moses' earlier deferential language

5. Tull, "Mother," 154.
6. Levine, *Numbers 1–20*, 323.

is reflective of that construction. However, images of Yhwh as mother are not unknown in the Old Testament materials. Most notably, Isa 42:14 tells of God's gasping and panting as a woman in labor. However, references to God as Mother and even as father are reasonably rare across the canon. God transcends gender performativity, even while displaying attributes traditionally ascribed to either gender role.[7]

In Num 11:12, Moses questions Yhwh: "Did I conceive all this people? Did I give birth to them, that you should say to me, 'Carry them in your bosom as a nurse carries a suckling child,' to the land that you promised on oath to their ancestors." It seems that Moses feels feminized by Yhwh's action. He rejects the role of birthing mother but indicates that he feels he has been cast into the role of wet nurse. But the traditional English translation serves to smooth out what is actually quite an interesting construction in the original Hebrew. The word translated as "nurse" is '*omen*, a masculine form used to describe a male employee in wealthy Israelite households.[8] The feminine form is the one that would be expected of a wet nurse, but it is not employed here. The confused state of Moses' mind is obvious. Perhaps, like so many other parents, sleep deprivation is catching up with him. How would a male guardian carry a suckling child in his bosom?

Moses and Yhwh: Parental Protocol

Matthews and Benjamin outline a series of protocols that governed the life and activities of mothers in ancient Israel.[9] These protocols allow us to examine whether Moses' function within Israel could appropriately be called "mothering."[10] Some of these protocols are shared in common with the list Matthews and Benjamin suggest for fathers. These similarities will be noted, particularly in relation to the tasks that Moses seems to share with his co-parent, Yhwh. Following this, we will consider the protocols unique to fathers

---

7. Sakenfeld, "Numbers, Book of," 73.
8. Milgrom, *Numbers*, 85.
9. Matthews and Benjamin, *Social World of Ancient Israel*, 22.
10. I am not strictly drawing upon the lists of Matthews and Benjamin but am instead using them as a guide. There are points where it makes sense to collapse two of the suggested protocols into a single section here, due to the nature of the material involved.

Protection, Provision, Management

While the functions of protection, provision, and management are shared by both mothers and fathers, we might imagine a distribution of responsibilities, contingent upon necessity. In terms of Moses and his relation to the Israelites, it is probably easiest to imagine him protecting Israel from Yhwh. As we have seen, it is Moses' intervention that moves Yhwh to abate the fire of judgment that was burning in the outer reaches of the camp. This was not the first time Moses had pleaded with Yhwh to withhold punishment. Most prominently, Moses offers himself in exchange for the wellbeing of the people following the apostasy of the golden calf. Admittedly, Moses' pleas only resulted in a partial protection in that situation: the complete destruction of the nation was reduced to the death of the guilty (Exod 32:33)

As noted, provision is one of the issues the Israelites complained about. With memories of the broad variety of produce available in Egypt, the Israelites quickly become bored with the simple, meager fare of the wilderness. The people blame Moses, so perhaps we might say that Moses has failed in this particular motherly duty. However, we must also bear in mind that manna was a divine provision, given from Exod 16 onwards after the Israelites complained they missed the bread they had enjoyed so much in Egypt. Yhwh provides this bread, not Moses. Indeed, manna comes from Yhwh with no word from Moses at all. This stands in contrast to the quails provided in Num 11 following Moses' meltdown and his asking, "Where am I to get meat to give to all this people?" (Num 11:13). The responsibility for the rationing and distribution of food fell squarely upon the mother's shoulders, under a protocol Matthews and Benjamin label "manager."[11] Thus, this question from Moses in Num 11:13 suggests some self-understanding of his motherly role to Israel as well as a sense of inadequacy—a feeling common to most parents—about his capacity to fulfill it.

Moses is also seen fulfilling this motherly management role in his instructions to the Israelites regarding their daily gathering of the manna in Exod 16, including the double portion required on the sixth day ahead of the Sabbath. Moses' skill is demonstrated when those who gather too much find that their supply rots. Similar to a typical parent, Moses becomes angry that they disobeyed his instruction (Exod 16:20)!

---

11. Matthews and Benjamin, *Social World of Ancient Israel*, 25.

Instruction

In Israelite society, mothers played the primary role in educating children. Once boys became young men, their training would become the responsibility of the father, but until that point, it was the mother who was responsible for instructing the children. For girls, the mother always remained the source of instruction. This instruction included learning songs and stories crucial to the identity of the Israelite people, moral formation, religious instruction, and so on.[12] Importantly, it included the explanation of Israelite practices of diet and dress. It also included domestic instruction and the simple matters of teaching boys and girls to speak, read, and write.[13]

It is not difficult to see Moses fulfilling this role within Israel. While what he taught is presented to us as divinely given, the common expression, "Law of Moses," or even "Moses and the prophets" (Luke 16:29) gives a very clear indication of the reverence paid to Moses' role in instructing his people in the way of Yhwh. This instructive role is no better demonstrated than in Deuteronomy. Presented to us as a farewell discourse, Moses not only reiterates the things he has spent his life teaching Israel, he also urges them to embrace and remember those lessons. His exhortation to "choose life" (Deut 30:19) can be read as the sincere plea of a loving and concerned parent, mother or father. Insofar as the content of what Moses taught is covered by what is listed above, it is reasonable to conclude that in this respect, Moses plays a very motherly role in Israel.

Mediation

One of the important roles the mother played in the family was in the mediation of conflict. This was to ensure that minor matters did not escalate to the point of playing themselves out in the village assembly.[14] There is a degree of expediency evident here, in that minor matters are kept from clogging the centralized system of dealing with disputes. Likewise, family concerns were not brought into the public domain, which was a good thing for all families!

As we have seen already, Moses frequently mediated between Yhwh and the people. In many respects, this was his main role. Imagining Yhwh and Moses as co-parents, we have seen a mediation model suggested here: Moses, the mother, mediating between the father and the child(ren).

---

12. De Vaux, *Ancient Israel*, 49.
13. Matthews and Benjamin, *Social World of Ancient Israel*, 28.
14. Matthews and Benjamin, *Social World of Ancient Israel*, 29.

Another example of this is the people's rebellion in Num 14. The people (children) recommence their whingeing about what they had left behind in Israel. Moses tries to placate them, even as Yhwh hears their moaning and is whipped into another bout of fury. Moses' response is telling. He appeals to Yhwh's ego, pointing to his reputation amid the neighboring countries. This is a play on the masculinity of Yhwh,[15] on the power to protect, provide, and conquer. In some sense, it is a game of flattery, and Moses places himself in the position of woman.[16] Yhwh relents, for the sake of his woman, perhaps? But he maintains his masculinity by promising to wipe out the wilderness generation before they enter the land sworn to the ancestors (Num 14:22).[17]

Moses also acts as a mediator on a broader scale as well. In Num 20, just as the people are hoping to travel through Edom, Moses sends messengers to the king. Interestingly, he describes a historical link between Edom and Israel as one of brotherhood (Num 14:14). This family link casts Moses, the mediator, into the role of a mother attempting—in this case unsuccessfully—to negotiate between estranged brothers.

Designation of Heirs

Typically, the designation of heir fell to the father of the household. Matters of inheritance and so on were his responsibility. However, such matters are complicated and are often the cause of conflict and dissent among families, particularly families where there are many children and, at times, multiple mothers involved. Given also that there was room for inheritance to fall outside the family, this was certainly a very sensitive issue.

It is no surprise then, given this range of complexity, that the mother would also be drawn into these discussions from time to time. Given her skills in mediation and her intimate knowledge of the family dynamics, the mother was well placed to mediate disputes between family members in a more impartial way than the father may have been capable of otherwise.[18]

---

15. To be clear, this is not to suggest that Yhwh is a male, but purely for consistency with the family model I am playing with.

16. This is not to suggest that flattery is a uniquely feminine trait either in the ancient world or ours. Rather, as above, it is a continuation of the model I am suggesting here, taking its cue from the play on Yhwh's masculine pride, which Moses is attempting to flatter here with some success!

17. There is a sense of the divine warrior turning his wrath on his own people, here. It is worth noting that the divine warrior is not exclusively male, with some instances of female divine warriors attested in the Ancient Near East. See Coogan, "Warrior, Divine," 815.

18. Matthews and Benjamin, *Social World of Ancient Israel*, 29.

Moses designated Joshua to be his heir. In this regard, Moses seems to acting as father. There was little dispute regarding this decision, which is a reflection of the authority Moses carried in Israel. Interestingly, Moses' successor was not one of his relatives, following the normal mode of succession (including the office of high priest through the lineage of Phinehas, or the kingship through David).

While Joshua succeeds Moses as Israel's leader, the narrative paints a very different picture of the nation following Moses' death. It is Moses alone who is remembered as meeting with Yhwh "face-to-face" (Deut 34:10). While Joshua leads Israel into the promised land and orchestrates military triumphs, his status never begins to approach that of Moses: he is never mother or father to them as Moses had been.

Adoption and Excommunication

When a child was born in Israel, it was the father who determined whether or not the child would enter the family household. Birth, or arrival, did not guarantee life. Rather, adoption was required for the child to take its place in the family. Unwanted children were discarded at the behest of the father. Likewise, people could be adopted into the family later in life, which is where the tradition of heirs outside the familial line stems from. In a similar fashion, the father had the capacity to excommunicate members of the household for various offenses.

This matter of control also played itself out in the sphere of marriage negotiations, where the father determined who was eligible and ineligible to marry his children. The father was held responsible for the sexual purity of his children, particularly his daughters. He was ultimately responsible for their virginity and chastity, thus ensuring that his daughters maintained the legal compliance necessary for marriage covenants and for producing appropriate offspring within those relationships. Women then often lived very small lives; their movements were restricted in an attempt to control their sexuality and to protect them from attack[19] in order to ensure the most lucrative match when it can time for negotiations. All of this was important, of course, because marriage was far more than the bringing together of two individuals; it was a way of gaining prestige as well as property rights and holdings. A successful marriage should bring financial success to both sides, while an unsuccessful one could bring substantial loss.[20]

---

19. Ibid., 15.
20. Ibid., 15.

This principle may seem hard to reconcile with the idea of Moses' and Yhwh's parenting. However, at the heart of marriage negotiations is covenant making between groups, and here we do have a point of entry. Israel was to remain the "treaty-less" people. They were not to engage in covenants with outside people (on a national scale, but note also the warnings regarding individuals being bound to foreign women, particularly in Num 25). This separatist ideology is exemplified by the prophetic use of "virgin Israel" (Jer 14:17, Jer 18:12). Israel is imagined as the daughter of Yhwh—here, despoiled by her engagement with the nations to whom she has given her virginity. In this matter, Yhwh is seen as the father. During Moses' time, no such arrangements were made, and indeed, Moses' teachings warned of the danger of these arrangements.

Against that lies Moses' own engagements with foreigners, most notably his marriage to the Midianite woman Zipporah and his strong bond with her father, Jethro. Moses' foreign wife[21] was a source of trouble for him through his family, though Yhwh sided with Moses in this dispute (Num 12: 6). We should exercise caution, then, in speaking too strongly about the ban on engagement with foreigners in this early period.

Mother Moses? Father Moses? Or Something Else?

On the basis of the protocols examined thus far, Moses' role can easily be imagined as one of parent, and this role tends towards motherhood. He seems to have fulfilled many of the customary mothering roles expected in the traditional ancient family. However, Moses' question to Yhwh, "Did I conceive these people?" suggests that conception is a major issue complicating matters. The implication of this statement is that Yhwh was responsible for the conception of the people and that, at times, Yhwh likewise participated in some of the mothering roles.

Despite the gender ambiguity of the nursing image Moses mentions, exploring the role of the nurse in Israelite society may contribute to our understanding of the family dynamic we are attempting to sketch. As we saw previously, Moses makes reference to a "male guardian," mistakenly rendered as "nurse" in most translations. For the purposes of this argument, we will adopt the incorrect translation, insofar as it matches with the feminine image of breastfeeding that accompanies it.

In Israelite society, the use of midwives was widespread. They comforted mothers in distress, and from time to time they were even involved

---

21. In Num 12, the wife is identified as Cushite. It is feasible that this reference is to a second wife, in addition to the Midianite Zipporah.

in the naming of infants.[22] This displays the important role they played in the childbirth process. It was also common for the midwife to act as a nurse following the birth of the baby. It was believed that a breastfeeding woman was less likely to fall pregnant again, and so the midwife would take on that responsibility so that the new mother might bear another child.[23] Given that breastfeeding was the primary source of nutrition for children, this role was incredibly important within the household, as the nurse became the primary source of physical development for the child.

This may provide a more accurate image of the role that Moses plays. He is not responsible for the conception of the child, though he is certainly close to those events. Yet, when the child is born, Moses takes on a very significant role in their development, leading and guiding them, and ultimately, sustaining them. Interestingly, Moses seems to reject this position. He does not want the responsibility of care and sustenance. He initially states that if this is how it is to be (that is, without assistance from the other parent), he would rather die (Num 11:15)! It seems Moses is prepared to continue with caregiving on the condition that Yhwh take some of the responsibility.

Conclusion

This is a picture of a family in crisis! Parental roles are split in a way that seems unclear and unhelpful, the child is out of control, and things seem to be unraveling. I guess most families have felt that at certain times! However, despite the dysfunction that appears on the surface, we need to look once more at Moses and his role in Israel.

Moses is a great protector of Israel. Often, at great personal cost, he stands up for them in the face of their abject failure. He speaks at times calmly, then at times quite forcefully, with his co-parent in order to maintain the peace and wellbeing of the family unit. At all times, it is the child(ren) whose interests are being served. Furthermore, Moses takes his responsibility as instructor very seriously. His motivation in teaching the children is love and concern for their wellbeing. He wants to pass on to them things that will help them to grow and develop in healthy ways. As a part of that commitment, he prepares Joshua for the responsibility of taking over when he is gone. Moses has the foresight to recognize that the children will continue to need guidance. For this reason, he schools Joshua on what will be required and how to best continue on his work with the people. All of this speaks of motherhood.

22. Pace, "Midwife," 84.
23. Matthews and Benjamin, *Social World of Ancient Israel*, 74.

And yet we cannot look past the reality that Moses' claim was right! He did not bear this people, he did not conceive them, nor did he give birth to them. His relationship with his people in this sense is much closer to the guardianship he also rejects. But even in his moment of meltdown when he seems to want to walk away, we see a hint of the parental bond that links him to the people: "I am not able to carry all this people alone, for they are too heavy for me." This is the cry of a parent. It is one that I have cried, and I imagine many others have as well. Thus, while we may fall short of calling him Mother Moses, it is right to acknowledge the parental, even motherly role Moses played in Israel and to understand his meltdown here in Num 11 as a natural part of the parenting experience.

Bibliography

Coats, George W. *Rebellion in the Wilderness: The Murmuring Motif in the Wilderness Traditions of the Old Testament.* Nashville: Abingdon, 1968.

Coogan, Michael D. "Warrior, Divine." In *The New Interpreter's Dictionary of the Bible*, edited by Katherine Doob Sakenfeld, 815–16. Nashville: Abingdon, 2009.

Delbridge, Arthur, ed. *The Macquarie Dictionary.* Sydney: Macquarie Library, 1982.

De Vaux, R. *Ancient Israel: Its Life and Institutions.* Translated by J. McHugh. London: Darton, Longman, & Todd, 1961.

Levine, B. A. *Numbers 1–20: A New Translation with Introduction and Commentary.* New York: Doubleday, 1993.

Matthews, V. H., and D. C. Benjamin. *Social World of Ancient Israel, 1250–587 BCE.* Peabody: Hendrickson, 1993.

Milgrom, J. *Numbers: The Traditional Hebrew Text with the New JPS Translation.* JPS Torah Commentary. Philadelphia: Jewish Publication Society, 1990.

Moore, Bruce, ed. *The Australian Oxford Dictionary.* Melbourne: Oxford University Press, 2004.

Pace, S. "Midwife." In *New Interpreter's Dictionary of the Bible*, edited by K. D. Sakenfeld, 4:84. Nashville: Abingdon, 2009.

Sakenfeld, K. D. "Numbers, Book of." In *Eerdmans Dictionary of the Bible*, edited by D. N. Freeman, 974–75. Grand Rapids: Eerdmans, 2000.

Tull, P. K. "Mother." In *The New Interpreter's Dictionary of the Bible*, edited by K. D. Sakenfeld, 4:154–56. Nashville: Abingdon, 2004.

3

The Birthing Spirit, the Childbearing God

Metaphors of Motherhood and Their Place in Christian Discipleship

BETH M. STOVELL

Introduction

Within many Christian circles, much discussion centers on the role of God as Father. Throughout the Hebrew Bible and New Testament, God is depicted frequently with this paternal metaphor.[1] Yet one should not overlook that God is also depicted with maternal metaphors across the biblical canon. Within the Hebrew Bible, these metaphors of God as Mother or God as one giving birth are often juxtaposed with traditionally male metaphors such as God as Divine Warrior, God as Father, God as Artisan, and God as Husband.[2] Within the New Testament, childbearing and mothering metaphors serve an important role in describing the spiritual rebirth (Gal 4:29; John 3:3–8), describing the experience of Jesus' death and resurrection for the disciples (Matt 24:8; Mark 13:8; John 16:21), describing Jesus Christ (1 Pet 1:3, 23: 1 John 2:20; Jas 1:18), and Paul describing his relationship to the Thessalonian church (1 Thess 2:7).

---

1. For a helpful introduction to the theological issues surrounding gender and the naming of God, see Kimel, *This Is My Name Forever*.

2. Dille focuses on these specific maternal and paternal metaphors and provides a helpful look at how recent metaphor theory allows for the examination of such metaphors as they interact with one another. See Dille, *Mixing Metaphors*.

This chapter focuses on two of the passages that describe God using such maternal metaphors. This chapter examines the language of motherhood in terms of Christian rebirth in John 3 and God's self-description as "like one giving birth" in Isa 42 and asks what this language might mean for interpreting the Bible as whole in terms of gender roles and the implications for Christian discipleship. This chapter uses linguistic and literary analysis of the metaphors of God's motherhood to develop new ways of approaching how we understand and apply these metaphors.

Towards this end, this chapter first provides a close reading of the comparison in Isa 42 between God as "a mighty warrior" and God as "a woman in childbirth" (more closely translated, "as one giving birth") and notes the use of parallel structures in these two lines to create resonance between the two metaphors. We then discuss the expectations surrounding the typical Divine Warrior metaphor and how the use of childbirth language provides an interesting twist on expected gender roles while emphasizing a context of crisis. Second, this chapter examines the metaphor of birth in the Spirit as presented in John 3:1–21, identifying the linguistic strategies used to emphasize the centrality of birth in this passage and the means of this birth through the Holy Spirit. After our initial linguistic analysis, we delve into the metaphor of motherhood and its relationship to Johannine theology more broadly. Based on insights gained through our analysis of Isaiah and John, this chapter suggests several possible theological implications of these passages for gender relations within the Christian community and particularly for Christian discipleship.

Caveats and Clarifications

Anytime one approaches an examination of the metaphors (and similes) of God as Mother, one must clearly articulate one's position about the significance of such metaphors in terms of their expression of God's overall nature.[3] The metaphor of God as Mother is a favorite of feminist theologians, as they often compare these mother metaphors to the goddess worship in neighboring ancient Near Eastern cultures when discussing the Hebrew Bible and in neighboring Greco-Roman culture when discussing the New Testament. While such parallels may be helpful at times, such discussions may give rise to assumptions regarding the purpose of these metaphors in their assertions about God's nature that are not always helpful and can, in

---

3. Kimel demonstrates the need for clarity in this area and provides a forum for such discussion in his *This Is My Name Forever*.

more radical forms, lead to pantheism or a form of goddess worship that is inconsistent with orthodox Christianity.[4]

In this chapter, I do not assume that speaking of God in terms of metaphors of motherhood implies that God is thereby to be understood as female.[5] God should not be understood as male or female per se, as God is spirit and thereby without gender. Thus, in this chapter, I am not asserting that God should be understood as a "she"[6] but rather that we should closely examine how feminine metaphors are used in conjunction with male metaphors to describe the full Personhood of God. Thus, the theological position assumed in this chapter follows Stanley Grenz's informative position that God should first be viewed as the basis for sexuality and that our description of gender in relation to God should flow from this knowledge.

Grenz argues that the social Trinity helps us to understand gender rather than gender helping us understand the Trinity. In fact, to begin with gender in speaking of God is to make God in our image rather than seeking to better understand how we are made in God's. Grenz states:

> In this manner, God stands as the foundation for human sexual bonding. The triune God is the "self-grounded prototype," of which Barth speaks, to whom this dimension of human life "corresponds" . . . the foundational connection between the triune God and human sexuality does not occur because God is either male or female or because God is both male and female. Rather, God is the foundation of human sexual bonding, insofar as the dynamic that characterizes the social Trinity (unity-in-diversity, mutuality of distinct persons, the interaction of sameness and

---

4. Several of the scholars in Kimel's *This Is My Name Forever* provide critiques of this element in feminist theology. Two are particularly helpful: Mankowski gives a critique of certain elements of feminist biblical analysis, including analysis by Phyllis Trible and Elizabeth Johnston. The critique is helpful, but it is unbalanced by his assumption of the greater value of masculine metaphor over feminine metaphor for God. See Mankowski, "The Gender of Israel's God," 35–61. For a more balanced approach, see the critiques leveled by Stanley Grenz in Grenz, "Is God Sexual?," 190–212.

5. These are some of the conclusions reached by more radical feminist scholars such as Radford Ruether and Starhawk. See Ruether, *Women-Church*, and Starhawk, *Spiral Dance*. Other feminist scholars have been less extreme in their positions but nonetheless focus on the feminization of God. Examples include Trible, *God and the Rhetoric of Sexuality*, esp. ch. 2; and Johnson, *She Who Is*. Grenz provides a critique of these positions. See Grenz, "Is God Sexual?," 207.

6. Some feminists have encouraged this "she" language for God in reaction to the overwhelming use of masculine pronouns and consequent masculine gendering of God by other scholars. One example is Johnson, *She Who Is*, 241–43. Many have been influenced by Mary Daly's statement: "If God is male, then the male is god" (Daly, *Beyond God the Father*, 19).

difference) is reflected in the dynamic of relationship to which our existence as embodied (and hence sexual) creatures lead.[7]

Grenz argues that this view of the *imago Dei* in our sexuality is also found in Christ and further in the church. Grenz affirms that "in the final analysis, then, the 'image of God' is corporate; the nature of the triune God comes to expression through humans-in-community."[8] Following this theological position allows us to (hopefully) avoid many of the pitfalls of focusing on God's gender and instead lets us examine more deeply how the use of maternal metaphors for God[9] can help us learn more about gender's role within Christian community as "embodied creatures" relating to one another.

Isaiah 42: Mighty Warrior God and Childbearing God

We begin our examination of the maternal metaphors for God with the seemingly opposing metaphors of Isa 42:13–14, where God is depicted, on the one hand, as "like a mighty one . . . like a man of war" in v. 13 and, on the other hand, "like one giving birth" in v. 14. Scholars have struggled with the examination of this passage in several directions. First, there is the question of how the structure of Isa 42 should be read in relation to these verses. Should we read them as part of a shared unit or as disparate? If they are a shared unit, what are the implications of the interweaving of these two metaphors?[10]

In answering the structural question, many scholars have pointed to the convincing evidence put forward by Darr that while v. 13 and v. 14 "do not constitute a discrete unit," they can and should be read in relation to one

---

7. Grenz, "Is God Sexual?," 211–12.

8. Ibid., 212.

9. This is not to say that speaking of God in paternal terms is less informative for our understanding, but simply that this chapter focuses on maternal terms rather than paternal ones.

10. For the purpose of this chapter, I am using metaphor in its more broad sense that includes examples of simile and metonymy for the purpose of simplicity. My goal is not to argue a particular theory of metaphor per se, but rather to use metaphorical analysis to inform other elements of Christian understanding. This is not to argue that metaphor should always be understood as equivalent in all its qualities to these other forms. In fact, much important work has been done on differentiating these distinct figures of speech in literary and linguistic circles. For example, see Stefanowitsch and Gries, *Corpus-Based Approaches to Metaphor and Metonymy*; Fass, *Processing Metonymy and Metaphor*; and Kittay, *Metaphor*.

another in the larger context of v. 10–17.[11] Affirming this view allows the reader to examine the two metaphors of God as "warrior" and God as "one giving birth" as intimately related to one another, while also acknowledging that vv. 13–14 represent a shift in the direction of the passage more generally.

Darr's approach also allows us to see an important overlap between the seemingly inconsistent metaphors of "like a warrior" and "like one giving birth" in vv. 13–14. Verses 10–12 begin with calling forth praise to God from all creation, and v. 13 describes God as "like a mighty one" who "goes out/marches out" and "like a man of war/a warrior" then "stirs up" his "zeal/anger," "shouts," "roars," and "prevails" over his enemies. Verse 14 moves from this image of God as Warrior to God as a Woman in Labor, shifting from a third-person description of God into God speaking in the first person. Verse 14a describes God's silence and reticence,[12] and in v. 14b, God describes himself as "like one giving birth," saying, "I groan; I pant; I gasp."[13] Darr notes that what may initially seem like inconsistent metaphors in v. 13 and v. 14b of the masculine figure of a warrior and the feminine figure of a woman giving birth actually are drawn together, as they "share both profound intensity and a markedly auditory quality." Furthermore,

---

11. See Darr, "Like Warrior, Like Woman." As Darr explains, often such divisions are based on assumptions about what scholars take the two similes of "like a warrior" and "like one in labor" to mean. Scholars who agree with Darr's position in terms of seeing vv. 10–17 as a unity include Oswalt, Gressman, Mowinkel, North, McKenzie, Bonnard, and Merendino. Against Darr's view, some scholars argue for other possible divisions, including considering vv. 10–13 and vv. 14–17 as two separate units. Among the scholars who divide up these verses, see Elliger, Begrich, Westermann, Muilenburg, and Whybray. For a fuller discussion of the reasons for these various positions, see Oswalt, *Isaiah Chapters 40–66*, 122–24. More recently, Dille has argued for reading the unit as vv. 8–17, arguing that vv. 8–9 form a frame to the larger unit and help to explain v. 17. Dille points to George Adam Smith as the only scholar who argues for vv. 8–17 as a unit, but Smith does not provide his reasoning. See Dille, *Mixing Metaphors*, 41–44; Smith, *Book of Isaiah*, II, 136–40.

12. In v. 14, there is a transition to verbs of restraint ("I kept still; I was silent; I controlled myself").

13. This verb has the possible dual meaning of "trample or crush." Whereas Darr sees these three verbs as connected to the metaphor of the woman giving birth, scholars such as Oswalt suggest that only the first verb refers to the metaphor of childbirth, while the following two verbs are of judgment. See Darr, "Like Warrior, Like Woman," 568–70; Oswalt, *Isaiah Chapters 40–66*, 125–26. Here Oswalt follows Joüon, "Notes Philologiques," 195–96. Most biblical translations follow Darr's position associating the three verbs with the woman in labor, including the NIV, TNIV, NRSV, ASV, NET, NKJV, CEV, and NASB, while the KJV and YLT group these latter two verbs with the following section as "destroy and devour" and "desolate and swallow up" respectively.

"the travailing woman simile—like the warrior similes in v. 13—serves to underscore Yhwh's power."[14]

Dille points to Darr's examination as a helpful example of metaphorical coherence.[15] Dille explains that Darr establishes this coherence by "finding a common entailment of the metaphors," namely, "crying out or noisiness."[16] Dille suggests other shared entailments for these two metaphors, including "danger, courage, blood, pain, the threat of death, the preservation of life."[17] Similarly, Bergmann argues that ancient Near Eastern texts commonly join these two military and childbirth metaphors more than we might expect because of several perceived overlapping element:

> Ancient Near Eastern examples show . . . that there was a tradition of comparing women giving birth to warriors in battle. Their experience is similar because both warriors in battle and women giving birth can have experiences on a psychological level (the feeling of chaos and loss of control) and on a physiological level (blood, sweat, and stirring movements back and forth).[18]

Bergmann provides a series of examples from ancient Near Eastern texts, including an Akkadian Sargon legend, a Sumerian lament, and a Middle Assyrian medical text, concluding, "war imagery and childbirth imagery can and do fit together, and one need not assume a break between Isa 42:13 and 42:14 on this basis of a shift in imagery."[19]

---

14. Darr, "Like Warrior, Like Woman," 564. For a fuller discussion of how the auditory elements of this birthing metaphor impact other sensory metaphors in Isa 42, see Stovell, *Mapping Metaphorical Discourse*, 124–27.

15. Though Dille describes Darr's examination of describing "the metaphors of 'YHWH is a Warrior' and 'YHWH is a Birthing Woman,'" Darr strongly distinguishes "like a warrior" and "like a travailing woman" as similes rather than as metaphors. Instead Darr emphasizes that these similes should be seen as ways of describing that God *acts* like a travailing woman rather than understanding that Yhwh is identified *as a* travailing woman. Dille does not make this distinction between simile and metaphor as clearly and instead argues with Janet Soskice that the difference between the two is "a minor grammatical technicality and should not be overemphasized" (Dille, *Mixing Metaphors*, 15–16, 48). See Darr, "Like Warrior, Like Woman," 564–65. For further exploration of gender in Isaiah, see Løland, *Silent or Salient Gender?*

16. Dille, *Mixing Metaphors*, 16.

17. Ibid.

18. Bergmann, *Childbirth as a Metaphor*, 139.

19. Ibid., 138–39. Gruber points to the activity of childbirth as an important key to seeing these images working together. As Gruber states, "what these scholars did not know or forget is that in natural childbirth the woman's role is active rather than passive" (Gruber, "Motherhood of God," 355).

Applying these overlapping metaphorical entailments of "warrior" and "childbirth" to God provides a unique perspective on God's power and intensity within Isa 42. Many see in the metaphor of God as Divine Warrior an evocation of Exod 15:3, yet one can point to the many uses of this Divine Warrior imagery throughout the Hebrew Bible.[20] In Isa 42:13, God as Divine Warrior "acts as a champion on behalf of the oppressed Israelites, as well as the other nations who are oppressed by Babylon."[21] Much work has been done on the Divine Warrior motif in the Hebrew Bible,[22] which will not be rehearsed here for the sake of time, but what is especially important for our purposes is how the Divine Warrior's picture of a triumphant champion over Israel's enemies provides the impetus for a change in the childbirth metaphor. The childbirth metaphor, often associated with fear and possible defeat or death, is "turned on its head to describe Yhwh's power."[23] In this way, God is depicted as a figure of both destructive and creative force through masculine and feminine figures, which allows for the picture of destruction and salvation present in the verses of Isa 42 that follow. This picture highlights the hope of "the coming of a new age or new life for the exiles and Yhwh's own passion or involvement with the situation of the people."[24]

Bergmann adds an additional element to this metaphorical interpretation, suggesting that Isa 42:10–17 is also "a variation or reinterpretation of the Birth Metaphor applied to situations of personal crisis." Bergmann argues that the crisis in the passage is God's inactivity and its resolution is

---

20. Dille points to Exod 15:3 specifically, but also notes the use of the imagery in Pss 24:5, 8; 78:65; Isa 9:6; 10:21; 26:11; 37:32; Jer 20:11; Zech 14:3; and Neh 9:32. See Dille, *Mixing Metaphors*, 46. I have elsewhere made a link between Exod 15 and Isa 40. See Stovell, "Divine Warrior and Shepherd."

21. Dille, *Mixing Metaphors*, 47.

22. Examples include Miller, *Divine Warrior in Early Israel*; and Longman and Reid, *God Is a Warrior*.

23. Here Dille begins with Darr's basic argument and fleshes it out with a fuller depiction of the metaphorical coherence between the military and childbirth metaphors in relation to Yhwh. See Dille, *Mixing Metaphors*, 41–73, esp. 68.

24. Ibid., 73. Here Dille disagrees with Schmidt's suggestion that the image of God as mother is derived from Zion imagery and instead argues, "the imagery here is the product of a very different rhetorical process than what Schmidt suggests." See Schmitt, "Motherhood of God," 557–69. No doubt Dille would also argue against Bergmann's comment that the "only direct comparisons to a woman experiencing childbirth are of an auditory nature" (though Bergmann's work follows Dille's work by four years). One is in fact surprised that Bergmann does not use Dille's work as a source, considering she is focused on many of the same texts as Dille, uses the metaphor theory of Lakoff and Johnson like Dille, and deals with many of the same interacting metaphors generally (Bergmann, *Childbirth as a Metaphor*, 141–42).

giving birth. As Bergmann explains, "now labor can progress and newness, a new beginning, a radically different world, can begin."[25]

Thus, the depiction of God as both a warrior and a woman giving birth in Isa 42 allows for a focus on the intensity of both God's destructive and life-bearing power. Indeed, the overlap of masculine and feminine metaphors allows these metaphors to interact in new ways, creating space for the metaphors to be re-envisioned in a fresh light that leads to universal and personal hope for all of God's people.[26]

John 3: The Birthing Spirit

Just as Isa 42 provides a helpful look at the metaphors of childbirth in the Hebrew Bible, John 3 allows us to examine the metaphor of childbirth in the New Testament. Our discussion first identifies the linguistic strategies used to emphasize the centrality of birth in this passage and the means of this birth through the Holy Spirit, focusing specifically on elements of prominence and cohesion in John 3:1–15 surrounding the childbirth metaphor. We then examine the metaphor of childbirth briefly elsewhere in Johannine theology. In order to analyze the elements of cohesion and prominence in John 3:1–15 in brief, we follow the recommended categories for cohesion and prominence suggested by Stanley E. Porter.[27] The goal is to identify which of these factors play a key role in promoting cohesion and prominence with specific reference to the metaphor of childbirth.

First, in terms of cohesion, the passage demonstrates an interesting shift from Jesus referring to Nicodemus in the second person singular in v. 1–10 to Jesus using the second person plural starting in v. 11. Scholars have often noted that this is also the place where Nicodemus begins to disappear from the narrative as a greater sense of universalization builds in the passage. Accompanying these movements from second person singular to plural, we also note Jesus' frequent use of the third person to create an imagined person (similar to our use of the term "one" in English). This imagined third person is repeated in vv. 3–6, 8, and 13–15. This use of the third person joins

---

25. Bergmann, *Childbirth as a Metaphor*, 141–42.

26. I explore further notions of gender and Isaiah in my contributing voice article "Divine Warrior and Shepherd as an Echo of Exodus in Isaiah 40:10–11" in Carol Dempsey's *Isaiah*.

27. As applicable, these elements include personal reference, verbal aspect, and connectives to analyze cohesion and verbal aspect, word order and clause structure, and redundant pronouns to analyze prominence. See Porter, *Idioms of the Greek New Testament*. Some of the research for this chapter is also referenced in my article, "Seeing the Kingdom of God," 439–67.

the first verses to the latter sections of Jesus' speech. It is noteworthy that this use of the imagined third person frequently coincides with Jesus' use of childbirth metaphors. Verses 3, 5, and 11 are further joined to one another and to the surrounding passage by the use of several key connectives: First, in the repeated emphatic particle in the phrase "truly, truly I say to you,"[28] and second, in the cohesive use of conjunctions in v. 11–15.[29]

These cohesive elements work in tandem with elements of prominence. For example, the repeated use of the particle *amen* in these three verses (v. 3, 5, 11) not only creates cohesion between the various parts of the passage, it also makes these particular verses prominent. Each of the verses relates to the concept of the Spirit's birthing and its importance to Christian life. Verse 3 explains that for one to see the kingdom of God, one must be born again. Verse 5 tells us that to enter the kingdom of God, this birth must be by the Spirit and water. These lead to the highly prominent v. 6, which speaks of two kinds of birth: of Spirit and of flesh.

The prominence of v. 6 comes from the repeated use of the perfect participle of "one who is born" (*gegennēmenon*) as, according to verbal aspect theory, the perfect participle is used to bring verbs to the front of the discourse, thus making them most marked and prominent. In v. 6, this use of the perfect focuses the attention of the reader/hearer on the metaphor of childbirth in the Spirit. This use of the perfect participle of "one who is born" (*gegennēmenon*) is repeated again in v. 8, where we are given another discussion of what birth from the Spirit means. In this case, being born of the Spirit implies a particular kind of experience with the Spirit's unexpected movement compared to the wind. Verse 11 follows up on the ideas of seeing and belief and leads into a discussion regarding eternal life. The concept of eternal life and birth in the Spirit are intimately linked by the use of these cohesive phrases and by the concept of knowledge in relationship to new life (i.e., new life in birth, or new life in eternal life).

These features of prominence and cohesion demonstrate the centrality of the metaphor of childbirth for this passage. The important message that

---

28. Whereas in the Synoptic tradition Jesus' statement "truly I say to you" is always with one amen, the Fourth Evangelist uses two particles to create even great emphasis.

29. In verses 11–15, the author repeatedly uses conjunctions to create cohesion between these verses. Verse 11 uses a *hoti* clause and an "and" (*kai*) to create cohesion within the verse. The conjunctions *ei* and *ean* create cohesion between v. 11 and v. 12 as well as within v. 12 itself. Verse 13 begins with an "and" (*kai*) linking v. 12 to 13 and the conjunction *ei* with the particle *mē* to create cohesion within v. 13. The fronted "and" (*kai*) in v. 14 performs a similar function to the fronted "and" (*kai*) in v. 13, joining v. 13 to 14. In v. 14, the conjunction *kathos*, paired with the adverb *houtos*, joins the two clauses in v. 14. The use of conjunction *hina* makes v. 15 a subordinate clause dependent on v. 14 and thereby joined to the entire complex of v. 11–15.

Jesus wishes to share with Nicodemus (and with his more universal audience) is the necessity of birth from the Spirit. This passage depicts the Spirit as a giver of a second birth. This rebirth leads to seeing and entering the kingdom of God. Such a spiritual birth is set in contrast to our physical birth through two elements in the passage: First, Nicodemus' question to Jesus about returning as an old person to one's mother's womb, and, second, Jesus' differentiation between spiritual birth and birth of the flesh. This differentiation between spirit and flesh is consistent with John's theology elsewhere, and, as is typical of John, this is more than a simple differentiation between spiritual and physical birth. It is a clarification of our need to be born anew through cleansing. Belleville convincingly argues that this is the meaning of the use of "from water and spirit" in v. 5, which Belleville connects to the eschatological hope associated with the presence of the Spirit and the cleansing of the people.[30]

Yet how is this new birth given by the Spirit to be understood in its metaphorical extent? What is included in this second birth? Here the root metaphor of childbirth we established above in Isa 42 helps us to consider a new way of understanding this passage. We have already noted that within the Hebrew Bible the metaphor of childbirth is associated with universal and personal crisis and includes the possibility of pain and death.[31] As Bergmann demonstrates in her study from ancient Near Eastern texts to the Hebrew Bible as well as writings dating from the Second Temple period, the childbirth metaphor continues across time to represent crisis.[32] Scholars often overlook this element of the childbirth metaphor when reading John 3, yet this understanding of childbirth as a metaphor for crisis is present elsewhere in John's Gospel.

Consider the example of John 16:21: Jesus depicts the disciples' experience of his death and resurrection as like "a woman ... giving birth to a child has pain because her time has come" (a phrase that echoes Jesus' references to his own death as "his hour had come") "but when her baby is born she forgets the anguish because of her joy that a child is born into the world." The disciples experience the anguish—indeed, the crisis—of Jesus' death

---

30. Belleville, "'Born of Water and Spirit,'" 125–41.

31. I have pointed out this conception of childbirth in my article "A Mother's Perspective," 278–79.

32. Bergmann's analysis includes a discussion of a Thanksgiving Psalm from the DSS as a means of drawing a picture of the childbirth metaphor across antiquity. Bergmann asserts that "it is a literary convention that runs through texts of the ancient Near East, and the Hebrew Bible, and that continues in postbiblical times" (Bergmann, *Childbirth as a Metaphor*, 218). Here Bergmann cites Blenkinshopp's commentary on Isaiah. See Blenkinsopp, *Isaiah 1–39*, 368.

like the anguish and crisis of a birthing woman, but they also experience the subsequent joy of a new birth at Jesus' resurrection.[33]

The language used in John 16:21 mirrors the language used in the Septuagint (the Greek translation of the Hebrew Bible) of Isa 42:14 in the use of the same verb "to give birth." Just as Yhwh is pictured like "one giving birth" in Isa 42:14, the disciples will experience Jesus' death like a woman who "gives birth."[34] John 16:21 also uses language that echoes John 3's discussion of "birth from the Spirit" with its use of the verb "born." Just as the birth in the Spirit is described repeatedly with the perfect participle or the aorist passive subjunctive referring to "giving birth," so here in John 16:21 we find the aorist active subjunctive form of the same verb used to compare the experience of joy following the resurrection to the joy of when a child is "born."

Understanding the resonances in John 16 to both Isa 42 and John 3 suggests a correction is necessary in our general conception of the birth metaphor in John 3. Many commentaries speak of the childbirth in John 3 as simple and painless because it is spiritual rather than physical, as though a spiritual stork dropped the child off in a nice neat package.[35] Yet it is unlikely an ancient reader would have read the metaphor of birth apart from its original implications of crisis. Within the passage, Nicodemus' response

33. Ruth Sheridan explores John 16 and its impact on our view of birth in more detail in her chapter entitled, "She Forgets Her Suffering in Her Joy: The Parable of the Laboring Woman (John 16:20–22)" in this volume [x-ref].

34. One can, thereby, compare the description of the "one giving birth" in John 16 to the wider tradition of the "yodelah" described by Bergmann and Dille, among others, as the "woman giving birth" metaphor in the Hebrew Bible. See Dille, *Mixing Metaphors*; and Bergmann, *Childbirth as a Metaphor*.

35. For example, Morris differentiates the spiritual birth from the physical birth and does not speak of what the metaphor may entail except for its implications for spiritual regeneration and Christian baptism (Morris, *Gospel According to John*, 184–96). Neyrey characterizes Nicodemus' response as "ridicul[ing] Jesus' teaching by reducing it to literal absurdness," but Neyrey misses what such a literal understanding may entail for the metaphorical understanding of the passage in terms of what he calls "the Johannine double meaning of 'born'" (Neyrey, *Gospel of John*, 78–79). It seems more cogent that to deem John as having a "double meaning" would assume he is playing a metaphorical meaning off of the literal meaning—an action that, according to Lakoff and Johnson, would include an original physical referent for the metaphorical abstraction. Moloney associates the "water and Spirit" with a "human experience 'of water'" in baptism and "a spiritual experience 'of the Spirit'" in spiritual regeneration. But Moloney does not identify any relationship between the typical *human* experiences of childbirth that influence the childbirth metaphor within this passage (Moloney and Harrington, *Gospel of John*, 93). Elsewhere I discuss this squeamishness around birthing in Johannine commentators and provide a further discussion on how this impacts the metaphors of John's Gospel more broadly. See Stovell, *Mapping Metaphorical Discourse*, 217–21, 231–32, 326.

gives us a clue to a partial ancient response. Jesus' clarification that this birth is spiritual and not physical does not necessarily remove the metaphorical implications of possible pain or crisis. As Lakoff and Johnson suggest, our understanding of a metaphor's abstract meaning is often embedded in a physical referent.[36] Two suggestive factors in the passage support the view that part of the metaphor of being "born again" of the Spirit involves just such a physical understanding of crisis and pain.

First, Jesus' reference to the unexpected quality of the Holy Spirit's arrival and departure in v. 8[37] may reflect an overlap with the unexpected quality of childbirth. Verses about childbirth in v. 7 and v. 9 surround v. 8's discussion of the unexpected character of the Holy Spirit. Childbirth is a combination of expectancy and uncertainty. In many ways, birth, like the wind and the Holy Spirit, would have been seen as a mystery in the ancient world. For people in the first century, the exact timing of birth was unknown. Mothers were aware that birth was coming but were uncertain exactly when this would occur. In their final month of pregnancy, expectant mothers today experience this same uncertainty. For ancient mothers, this expectancy of joy at birth would be intertwined with an awareness of the intense pain of childbirth and also the distinct possibility of death for mother or child. Similarly, the Holy Spirit's timing is uncertain; like a baby, it comes whenever it pleases (v. 8), outside of our control. Thus, joining the element of unexpectedness between the Holy Spirit's arrival and birth in the Spirit intensifies this sense of crisis and a lack of control in birth.

Factors of cohesion and prominence also suggest a link between Jesus' death on the cross with the pain and crisis associated with childbirth in John 3. As noted above, vv. 3–5 and 6–8 are joined through cohesion and prominence to vv. 11–15. This means the metaphor of childbirth in vv. 3–8 are linked to the language of the "lifting up" of the Son of Man for the purpose of "eternal life." The "Son of Man" being "lifted up" repeatedly refers to Jesus' death through crucifixion throughout John's Gospel. In John 3:15, the purpose of this "lifting up" is so that "everyone who believes will have eternal life in him." Thus, the experience of birth through the Spirit is linked through cohesive language to eternal life via Jesus' death. Thus, birth and life are interwoven metaphors, but in both cases Jesus' death on the

---

36. See Lakoff and Johnson, *Metaphors We Live By*.

37. Karl Olav Sandnes suggests this idea of "whence and whither" has epistemological implications for explaining the coming and going of Jesus and of the Holy Spirit that connect John 3 with other important discussions of knowing and believing throughout the Gospel of John. Sandnes also notes the connection between birth and knowledge in John 3 and John 9, which may be another interesting foray for later discussion. See Sandnes, "Whence and Whither," 153–73.

cross is necessary for this spiritual rebirth and eternal life. It seems likely that the picture of death, resurrection, suffering, and exaltation that John 16:15 compares to a woman who finds both pain and joy in labor should be understood as part of the underlying imagery of the second birth pictured in John 3.

Implications for Christian Community and Discipleship

In both Isa 42 and John 3, the metaphor of childbirth leads from a moment of crisis to the creation of a new life—indeed, a new hope—with eschatological implications. In Isa 42, Yhwh is like a woman giving birth, struggling and crying out, but for a designated purpose of ultimate restoration and fullness for his people. In John 3, the Spirit provides us with birth characterized by new life. Thus John 3's discussion of birth, while spiritual, should not be understood separately from the crisis, travail, and struggle associated with labor. How does this affect our understanding of spiritual regeneration? Do we think of being "born again" as a happy, specific moment? Perhaps this is a misstep in understanding the metaphor presented in John's Gospel. Perhaps it is better to understand it as depicting the difficulty of Christian transformation, whose struggle and suffering leads to ultimate joy.

This means we need to consider pain and struggle as part of the Christian journey. The journey of second birth and of spiritual regeneration is not painless or without crisis; rather, we journey through the difficulties entailed in this new birth because we know hope and joy is to be found in the struggle. Just as Jesus' death and resurrection is pictured in terms of childbirth, our rebirth likewise entails an experience of death and resurrection. This analogy reminds us that, as Christians living in community, we will be neither without pain, nor without hope. We will walk together as male and female through the struggles and we will grow through this walk. Only together as male and female in community do we fully reflect the *imago Dei* (Gen 1:27). In this way, we will be like Christ in his journey from death to resurrection. In anticipating the final eschatological hope, we may also experience it in part in the presence of the Holy Spirit today.

Further, Isa 42 reminds us that we have a triune God who is the foundation of our embodied and thus sexual being and the foundation of our understanding of what it means to be "humans-in-community," to borrow Grenz's phrase. As Yhwh is depicted in both the metaphor of the warrior and the metaphor of a woman giving birth, we are given a picture of Yhwh's ultimate power and his intense love for his people. This echoes forth in his resounding war-cry, demonstrating his divine protection, and in his resounding wail of childbirth, demonstrating the new creation he provides in the ultimate eschatological hope.

Bibliography

Belleville, Linda L. "'Born of Water and Spirit': John 3:5." *Trinity Journal* 1 (1980) 125–41.

Bergmann, Claudia D. *Childbirth as a Metaphor for Crisis: Evidence from the Ancient Near East, the Hebrew Bible, and 1QH XI, 1–18*. Beihefte Zur Zeitschrift Für Die Alttestamentliche Wissenschaft, Bd 382. Berlin: De Gruyter, 2008.

Blenkinsopp, Joseph. *Isaiah 1–39: A New Translation with Introduction and Commentary*. Anchor Bible 19. New York: Doubleday, 2000.

Daly, Mary. *Beyond God the Father: Toward a Philosophy of Women's Liberation*. Boston: Beacon, 1973.

Darr, Katheryn Pfisterer. "Like Warrior, Like Woman: Destruction and Deliverance in Isaiah 42:10–17." *Catholic Biblical Quarterly* 49 (1987) 560–71.

Dille, Sarah. *Mixing Metaphors: God as Mother and Father in Deutro-Isaiah*. Journal for the Study of the Old Testament. London: T. & T. Clark, 2004.

Fass, Dan. *Processing Metonymy and Metaphor*. Contemporary Studies in Cognitive Science and Technology. Greenwich, CT: Ablex, 1997.

Grenz, Stanley J. "Is God Sexual? Human Embodiment and the Christian Conception of God." In *This Is My Name Forever: The Trinity and Gender Language for God*, edited by Alvin F. Kimel Jr., 190–212. Downers Grove: InterVarsity, 2001.

Gruber, Mayer I. "The Motherhood of God in Second Isaiah." *Revue Biblique* 90 (1983) 351–59.

Johnson, Elizabeth A. *She Who Is: The Mystery of God in Feminist Theological Discourse*. New York: Crossroad, 1992.

Joüon, Paul. "Notes Philologiques Sur Le Texte Hébreu D'isaïe 11, 13; 42, 14; 50, 11; Jérémie 1, 5; 1, 14; 20, 10; 27, 10; 31, 40; 43, 12." *Biblica* 10 (1929) 195–99.

Kimel, Alvin F., Jr. *This Is My Name Forever: The Trinity and Gender Language for God*. Downers Grove: InterVarsity, 2001.

Kittay, Eva Feder. *Metaphor: Its Cognitive Force and Linguistic Structure*. Clarendon Library of Logic and Philosophy. New York: Oxford University Press, 1987.

Lakoff, George, and Mark Johnson. *Metaphors We Live By*. Chicago: University of Chicago Press, 1980.

Løland, Hanne. *Silent or Salient Gender?: The Interpretation of Gendered God-language in the Hebrew Bible, Exemplified in Isaiah 42, 46 and 49*. FAT 2, Reihe 32. Tübingen: Mohr Siebeck, 2007.

Longman, Tremper, III, and Daniel G. Reid. *God Is a Warrior*. Studies in Old Testament Biblical Theology. Grand Rapids: Zondervan, 1995.

Mankowski, Paul. "The Gender of Israel's God." In *This Is My Name Forever: The Trinity and Gender Language for God*, edited by Alvin F. Kimel Jr., 35–61. Downers Grove: InterVarsity, 2001.

Miller, Patrick D. *The Divine Warrior in Early Israel*. Atlanta: Society of Biblical Literature, 2006.

Moloney, Francis J., and Daniel J. Harrington. *The Gospel of John*. Sacra Pagina 4. Collegeville, MN: Liturgical, 1998.

Morris, Leon. *The Gospel According to John*. New International Commentary on the New Testament. Grand Rapids: Eerdmans,1995.

Neyrey, Jerome H. *The Gospel of John*. New Cambridge Bible Commentary. New York: Cambridge University Press, 2007.

Oswalt, John. *The Book of Isaiah, Chapters 40–66*. New International Commentary on the Old Testament. Grand Rapids: Eerdmans, 1998.

Porter, Stanley E. *Idioms of the Greek New Testament*. Sheffield: Sheffield Academic, 1999.

Ruether, Rosemary Radford. *Women-Church: Theology and Practice of Feminist Liturgical Communities*. San Francisco: Harper & Row, 1985.

Sandnes, Karl Olav. "Whence and Whither: A Narrative Perspective on the Birth 'Anothen' (John 3,3–8)." *Biblica* 86 (2005) 153–73.

Schmitt, John J. "The Motherhood of God and Zion as Mother." *Revue Biblique* 92 (1985) 557–69.

Smith, George Adam. *The Book of Isaiah, II*. New York: Harper & Brothers, 1927.

Soeur, Anne-Etienne. "Birth [Biblical Images, Esp Jn 16:16–22]." *Ecumenical Review* 34, (1982) 228–37.

Starhawk. *The Spiral Dance: A Rebirth of the Ancient Religion of the Great Goddess*. 10th anniv. ed. San Francisco: Harper & Row, 1989.

Stefanowitsch, Anatol, and Stefan Thomas Gries. *Corpus-Based Approaches to Metaphor and Metonymy*. Berlin: De Gruyter, 2006.

Stovell, Beth M. "The Birthing Spirit, the Childbearing God: Metaphors of Motherhood and Their Place in Christian Discipleship." *Priscilla Papers* 26 (2012) 9–14.

———. "Divine Warrior and Shepherd as an Echo of Exodus in Isaiah 40:10–11: Contributing Voice." In *Isaiah*, edited and primarily authored by Carol J. Dempsey. Wisdom Bible Commentary. Collegeville, MN: Liturgical, forthcoming.

———. "A Mother's Perspective on the 'Born Again' Theme and the Birthing Metaphor [in John 3]." In *Global Perspectives on the Bible*, edited by Mark Roncace and Joseph Weaver, 278–79. Upper Saddle River, NJ: Pearson Prentice Hall, 2013.

———. *Mapping Metaphorical Discourse in the Fourth Gospel: John's Eternal King*. Linguistic Biblical Studies 5. Leiden: Brill, 2012.

———. "Seeing the Kingdom of God, Seeing Eternal Life: Comparing Cohesion and Prominence in John 3 and the Apocryphal Gospels in Terms of Metaphor Use." In *The Language of the New Testament: Context, History and Development*, edited by Stanley E. Porter and Andrew W. Pitts, 439–67. Early Christianity in its Hellenistic Context 3. Linguistic Biblical Studies 6. Boston: Brill, 2013.

Trible, Phyllis. *God and the Rhetoric of Sexuality*. Overtures to Biblical Theology 2. Philadelphia: Fortress, 1978.

Part II

The New Testament and Motherhood

4

She Forgets Her Suffering in Her Joy

The Parable of the Laboring Woman (John 16:20–22)

RUTH SHERIDAN

Asked to "make sense of motherhood" in relation to a canonical text, my first instinct was to turn to the so-called parable of the woman in labor in the Gospel of John (16:20–22). That parable is connected, in the speech of Jesus, to his own impending suffering, death and resurrection, as well as to the grief his disciples will feel at the imminent loss of his presence.[1] This choice reflects the fact that my area of research specialization has thus far concentrated on the Gospel of John, but also that I happen to find the text of John 16:20–22 to be particularly rich with respect to the topic of motherhood—it is perhaps the only gospel text that expresses a sound familiarity with the anxiety of the experience of childbirth.[2] Indeed, it is Jesus' spoken allusion to the experience of maternal *anxiety* that makes the text of John 16:20–22 supremely valuable in any discussion on the meaning of motherhood in canonical perspectives.

While the parables of the Synoptic Gospels sometimes touch upon quotidian female experiences in first-century Palestine—e.g., a woman kneading dough (Matt 13:33; Luke 13:21) or cleaning the house (Luke 15:8–10)—only the Gospel of John contains a parable about the intimate and

---

1. The parable has received its most extensive treatment in Kathleen P. Rushton's *The Parable of the Woman in Childbirth of John 16:21*.

2. The Gospel of John nevertheless exhibits another "natal" metaphor (cf. 3:1–10); see Rushton, "(Pro)creative Parables," 77–90.

agonizing experience of a woman in childbirth and the feelings that suffuse her first moments of motherhood. Far from the idyll of female domesticity found in the Synoptic parables, John 16:20–22 touches on the kind of suffering a woman experiences as she finds herself on the brink of death in order to bring new life into the world.[3] This fact should open up new avenues for discussion between scholars of the gospel who have personally experienced labor; ideally, fresh, situated readings of the text can emerge that tackle the difficult issue of suffering in childbirth, paired with reflections on the theological dimension of the paschal mystery (Jesus' death and resurrection).

Far from suggesting I am the ideal scholar to perform such a task, I must admit that although I have spent much time researching and writing on the Gospel of John, it is, for me, neither a canonical nor a sacred text (I am Jewish, not Christian). My reflections in this essay will not presume to draw upon the implications a text like John 16:20–22 might have for Christian theology. But I am a mother, and the natural birth of my son five years ago has significantly changed the way I read and understand John 16:20–22. It is this experience that I wish to draw upon here. The method I will employ in my interpretation of the gospel text is slightly unorthodox, but as we shall see, such an approach can be justified as a partial corrective to the overly masculinist interpretations of John 16:20–22 we traditionally encounter in the gospel commentaries.

My method is informed by what feminist literary critic Jane Gallop has called "anecdotal theory."[4] Gallop uses this term to describe the kind of writing that begins by recounting an anecdote and proceeds to interpret "that account for the theoretical insight" it affords.[5] Anecdotes can thereby become, in turn, places where theory is "situated."[6] While anecdotes by definition suggest a brief account of a "humorous incident," they need not be thought of as flippant oral forms (although from the diametrically opposed "grand" position of high theory, they are often thought of in precisely that way). Rather, the anecdote is similar to the "occasional" piece of speech or writing inasmuch as both "[open] predictable discourse to the unpredictability of event."[7] Gallop's anecdotal theory attempts to disturb the tightly bound and apparently mutually opposed categories of "anecdote" and "theory"—it blurs those boundaries in order to produce the kind of theory that "honors

---

3. Paul also employs metaphors of labor in very different contexts. See Gal 4:19 and Rom 8:22.
4. Gallop, *Anecdotal Theory*.
5. Ibid., 2.
6. Ibid., 158.
7. Ibid., 157.

the uncanny detail of lived experience."[8] In written form, the anecdote—or let us say, the recounting of a lived event—becomes "literary," capable of interpretation in and of itself, and capable of shedding light on life itself *and* how we theorize it. Anecdotal theory turns away from the abstractions of theory in order to allow experience to punctuate an academic discourse that is too often "ahistorical" by "looking to the place where the literary is knotted to the real."[9] Gallop does not discount the usefulness or importance of theory—indeed, she recognizes its value in balancing out the "excesses" of anecdotes. Gallop's writings project an appealing honesty as she subjects events of her life to close analysis—particularly those events that lie on the margins of discussion in academe—and thereby discovers something rich and insightful about human and, specifically, female subjectivity.

Feminist scholar Lisa Baraitser has recently applied Gallop's theory to her own original work on maternal experience.[10] Baraitser considers her work to be "a throwback to an era in which feminine autobiographical writing . . . [was] being explored as [a way] to escape the closure of subjectivity."[11] For Baraitser, this kind of writing is a "praxis that does not explore or illustrate the personal, but through which the personal takes place."[12] Maternal subjectivity likewise evolves and takes place through the "details of maternal praxis."[13] Baraitser intertwines anecdotal accounts of mothering her young children with stunning theoretical insights (psychoanalytical, literary, and cultural) and examines the specific maternal subjectivities that emerge in the course of being "interrupted," "encumbered" and "viscous" by virtue of being with, and being constantly responsible for, a child. She understands "the maternal subject as arising out of the paradox of the one who sees the world from the point of view of there being two, which in its turn retroactively produces the one."[14] All of this is presented with the acute awareness of a problematic cultural backdrop: that of the figure of the "mother" in western history and discourse, a figure who has occupied an impossible place between the overly idealized and the viciously disparaged. While Baraitser acknowledges the arguments by theorists and psychoanalysts that maternal identity is crafted in the void of negativity (i.e., loss), she claims that through an understanding of the "ethics of interrup-

8. Ibid., 2.
9. Ibid., 3.
10. See Baraitser, *Maternal Encounters*.
11. Ibid., 11.
12. Ibid.
13. Ibid.
14. Ibid., 13.

tion," something positive can be recuperated in the maternal experience; it is possible for something new to "come back."[15] Baraitser refrains from asking what it *means* to be with a child and asks instead what it is *like* to be with a child.[16] Her work thus seems to be broadly phenomenological, but she insists that her "method" is "tenuous" and undetermined by any specific theoretical commitment.[17] It is the spaciousness and vibrancy of her layered approach that yields such an extraordinary work of depth and vision.

Taking my cue from Gallop and Baraitser, I wish to knit together my personal account of becoming a mother through the process of childbirth with my more "academic" discussion of the gospel text in order to bring to light how the "unpredictability of event" exposes fissures in the standard readings of John 16:20–22.[18] The major difference between my approach and that of Gallop and Baraitser is that my reflections involve the intersection of two distinct "texts"—namely, my autobiographically recounted narrative of childbirth and the parabolic text of John 16:20–22. Gallop and Baraister work through theoretical issues about subjectivity via an analysis of their own textually inscribed anecdotes; they do not weave their anecdotes into the interpretation of *another* text. Thus, the approach I adopt here can only be described as an approximation of the mixture of methods Gallop and Baraitser espouse.

One might reasonably critique my approach by arguing that it imports an unwarranted subjectivism into the interpretation of John 16:20–22. Needless to say, such a critique proceeds from the prejudicial assumption that New Testament interpretation ought to be "objective," historicist, and untainted by situated readings, lest the scholar's bias creep in and compromise his or her attempt at discerning the author's original intention.[19] I call this assumption prejudicial because, being hegemonic, it has stakes to uphold and biases of its own to defend, only these are unconscious, revealed by their very attempt to disguise themselves under the rhetoric of normativity. That interpretation can ever be "objective," however positivistic its presuppositions, is fallacious. In short, I would agree that my approach is "subjective," even "subjectivist," but my interpretation is not thereby invalidated. Indeed, it is the very subjective aspect of my personal reflections that

15. Ibid., 12.
16. Ibid., 13.
17. Ibid., 14.
18. Gallop, *Anecdotal Theory*, 157.

19. The best discussion of the politics of interpretation in biblical studies today can be found in Aichele, Miscall, and Walsh, "Elephant in the Room," 383–404. See also Moore and Sherwood, *Invention of the Biblical Scholar*.

provides me with the ability to describe where "the text" is "knit to the real" with respect to childbirth and the parable in John 16:20–22.

Of course, my experience is only that—my own experience. I do not offer it as representative of all women who have given birth or as something to which other women might relate. It stands, anecdotally, as an intertext that frames my reading of the gospel text. It is simply something that has ineradicably shaped me, for good or ill. It is something that stands out in my memory, something that has indelibly marked my flesh, and, in this chapter, marks my writing. Yet I think motherhood can never be fully understood or reduced conveniently to a formula that would give it meaning or "make sense" of it entirely and for all individuals; it is ever-elusive and ever-changing as it is lived. The same could be said of childbirth in its unexpectedness, its trauma, and its potential as a "limit-experience."[20] It can be simplistic, even grotesque at times, to invest "meaning" in psychological and physical trauma.[21] But, paradoxically, the urge to understand trauma is part of a process of recuperation or healing. In my account, I offer story, not "meaning." I offer my story as something that might stimulate thought and as something that might provide a new lens through which to view the complex parable in John 16:20–22. Following this account, I will establish the text of John 16:20–22 and discuss its critical reception in the scholarship, which will open into a further discussion of the text in relation to my own experience.[22]

Labor as Limit and Trauma

Two weeks before my expected due date, I began to have severe abdominal cramps in the late evening. Speaking with a friend over the phone, I eventually put aside my concern that labor was imminent after being reassured that I was only experiencing "Braxton Hicks contractions." A couple of

---

20. On the "limit-experience" as something the subject confronts at the extremity of an intense life experience, see Batailles, *Visions of Excess*, 236. A good discussion of the concept in the writings of Michel Foucault in relation to theology can be found in Fuggle, *Foucault/Paul*, 53–98.

21. The literature on trauma, memory, meaning, representation, and recuperation is vast. An instructive starting point is Ruth Leys' *Trauma*. An earlier collection of essays worth consulting is Cathy Caruth's *Trauma*. The medical and scientific literature on post-partum depression and traumatic labor is likewise well established: see Ballard, Stanley, and Brockington, "Post-traumatic Stress Disorder," 525–28; and Creedy, Shochet, and Horsfall, "Childbirth and the Development," 104 111.

22. I do not discount the value of reading John 16:20–22 from an historical standpoint, nor do I claim my way of engaging with the text is the only appropriate one. It is simply appropriate to the direction and audience of this book.

hours passed, and the painful cramps turned into sharp abdominal stabs. In the bathroom the so-called "show" confirmed my "hour" had indeed come. I was in labor—at this stage, what is technically called "passive labor." I wasn't overly worried; I figured everything would be over by the next morning. As the hours passed, the pain worsened. After calling the midwives at my local maternity hospital, I was told to be patient and to stay home. I'd opted to have a natural labor, a drug-free labor without medical intervention (perhaps, in hindsight, a mistake). It was now close to midnight, but I couldn't sleep. I began to vomit from the increasing force and frequency of my contractions. My husband drove me to the hospital.

Despite the aggressiveness of my contractions, the midwives told me to go back home. They examined me but found that my cervix had only dilated one centimeter. Thus, I wasn't yet in the stage of "active labor," which would have required more concentrated medical attention. However, a fetal examination also revealed that my baby was in the "posterior" position: he was turned so his back was against my spine—a very difficult position to work with. The midwives told me many labors begin that way, but that eventually the baby turns around in order to gain the proper delivery position. They even reassured me with statistics, saying that 95 percent of labors that begin in the posterior position will resolve with the baby turning to the anterior position; only 5 percent of labors will struggle through to the point where the baby actually exits the birth canal facing around the wrong way. Nevertheless, they warned me that my labor would be complicated, protracted, and more painful than the average labor.

Back at home, as the vomiting and pain continued my apprehension grew. The only medical advice I received was to get on all fours at home and to try crawling on all fours to encourage the baby to turn. Twelve hours of crawling later, we returned to the hospital. Another examination revealed that my baby had still not turned and I was only dilated by another two centimeters. The busy midwives set me up in a small bed, telling me that if the baby hadn't come by morning I would need to return home. This news did not help my apprehension, which was growing by the minute. I remember the fear well. I had no control over when, how, or even if this baby would come into the world. I was told not to push, since my waters hadn't yet "broken." But after six more hours of pointless agony, the midwives broke the uterine sack housing the amniotic fluid. Now it was imperative for the labor to progress. I eventually asked for morphine, since the pain of the contractions was preventing me from sleeping. My labor had gone on for more than two whole days. The baby was still intractable, stubborn in his refusal to turn around and take the pressure off my spine. No one suggested emergency intervention. The midwives continued to "wait and see."

I recall the experience of intense physical pain. It was curious and incomparable. The morphine did not make a difference. The physical pain of labor was a kind of "total" pain. It resounded through my whole body. It was a dense agony, not a sharp, local pain. Together with the all-encompassing, physical agony was the mental apprehension of something going wrong and of this "natural" event turning fatal. I was at the mercy of something else, and I felt alone and helpless. Day three came. I had now been in labor for seventy-two hours. The midwives began to worry. Another fetal examination revealed that the baby had moved down the birth canal, but he still hadn't turned and was "in distress." He wasn't getting the oxygen he needed. I began to feel very strange, like I wasn't in my body any longer. It was then that the midwives moved me to a wheelchair and rushed me off to the emergency room. I was lifted into a bed equipped with stirrups. A doctor was present, telling me I needed an episiotomy and that the baby had to be pulled out with forceps.

From out of nowhere, I felt a burst of adrenaline. I refused to let them use forceps, aware of the potential for complications, even stillbirth. I pushed harder than I had thought it possible to push—and finally, my baby was out of my body and into the world. He had joined that 5 percent of babies who insisted on exiting the birth canal in the posterior position. While my physical pain had abruptly stopped, my baby was not crying—or even breathing. A team of doctors rushed my baby away to give him oxygen. His whole body was blue—the umbilical cord was blue too. He was struggling, and I was frantic. Then he started to cry—and so did I. I'd done it, and we'd both survived.

∼

I had entered the experience of labor thinking that it would unfold as a "natural" event, that it would be painful, but also that the pain would pass and I'd be left holding a healthy baby at the end of it. Yet reality was more complex. It wasn't something one "did" or "experienced"—it was something one had to *survive*. Nor were my feelings simple and easy to understand. Beneath my eventual relief was the fear and guilt that I might not have done enough—that abiding feeling, which is still with me to this day, of "What if?" I had the realization that labor could in fact have proven fatal for my baby, and I would have had to live the rest of my life without him. Coupled with this was my anger that the midwives had been negligent in their standard duty of care towards me. I felt it was impossible for me to even contemplate having a baby again. These complex psychological feelings of pain, anger, and regret were not the immediate outcome of my labor. They set in later and abided for longer. Eventually, doctors diagnosed me with post-traumatic stress disorder (PTSD), which lasted about a year after the birth of my son. When I tried to sleep at night, I'd experience "flashbacks" about being in the labor ward, like a nightmare I couldn't shake.

But straight after giving birth, I felt relief, then amazement and pride in what I had achieved. Hormones played a significant role, for breastfeeding is known to stimulate oxytocin. Within a day of giving birth, I was utterly elated at what I'd accomplished and full of joy about having a beautiful baby of my own. For a short while, this overwhelming feeling of joy did indeed make me forget the agony of the previous three days. Yet this hormonally-induced burst of elation did not completely erase the agony and pain of the labor. It muted the immediate memory of the physical pain for a time. In that respect, the transition from "sorrow" to "joy" was sudden. The elation and joy eventually morphed into a deeper sense of gratitude and accomplishment—a pleasure in being alive and in being a mother that has endured.

And yet, the total experience created a new sorrow and a new fear inside of me that has also endured. This "sorrow" was different from the anxiety confronting me as I faced my "hour" in the advent of my labor. It was not the precondition of my labor but the product of it: the longer-lasting fear of having to go through labor ever again, along with the stark, sad realization that a complicated labor carries a real risk of death and loss, even in our current age of fewer maternal deaths and lower infant mortality.

The Text of John 16:20–22

John 16:20–22 occurs in the context of the gospel's "farewell discourse" (13:1—17:26), a long, sermonic-style speech Jesus delivers to his disciples before his arrest and death. The parable of 16:20–22 is found toward the end of the discourse proper (with 17:1–26 functioning as Jesus' concluding prayer but nevertheless an integral part of the farewell discourse form).[23] In the immediately preceding context, Jesus reassures his disciples that "a little while (*mikron*), and you will see me no longer; and again a little while (*kai palin mikron*), and you will see me" (16:16). This statement of two "little whiles" has baffled commentators, and in the text it baffles the disciples too.[24] Jesus' disciples repeat his words verbatim, asking each other what these mysterious words could mean (16:17–18). Jesus, apparently with pre-

---

23. Segovia, *Farewell of the Word*, 1–48.

24. Cf. Bultmann, *Gospel of John*, 577–80; and Barrett, *Gospel According to St John*, 492.

ternatural knowledge, asks them in turn if they are questioning the meaning of his statement. He then restates his promise about the "little while" (16:19). It is at this point, as a means of clarification, that Jesus says:

> Truly, truly, I say to you, you will weep and lament, but the world will rejoice. You will be sorrowful, but your sorrow will turn into joy. When a woman is giving birth, she has sorrow because her hour has come, but when she has delivered the baby, she no longer remembers the anguish, for joy that a human being has been born into the world. So also you have sorrow now, but I will see you again, and your hearts will rejoice, and no one will take your joy from you. (John 16:20–22, ESV).

Jesus acknowledges the somewhat inadequate means of "clarification" he has just adopted, telling his disciples, "I have said these things to you in figures of speech. The hour is coming when I will no longer speak to you in figures of speech but will tell you plainly (*parrēsia*) about the Father" (16:25). After reiterating his claim to have "come into the world" from the Father and to be on the verge of leaving the world to return to the Father, Jesus' disciples exclaim that he is no longer using "figures of speech"; they believe now that he has come from God (16:29). At this sign of belated belief, Jesus resignedly tells them that the "hour" is nevertheless coming—and indeed has come—when they will be "scattered," leaving him alone (16:31–32a). Yet Jesus is not alone; the Father is with him (16:32b). The farewell discourse proper then concludes with Jesus' words to his disciples, "I have said these things to you, that in me you may have peace. In the world you will have tribulation. But take heart; I have overcome the world" (16:33 ESV).

This fuller context of John 16:20–22 indicates that Jesus' departure will be followed by a return of sorts—one that is obscure at this point in the gospel story. Jesus cannot explain it to his disciples directly: he uses obfuscating language about "little whiles" and proceeds to develop a parable based on the image of a woman giving birth. His subsequent "plain speech" further elucidates the parable by suggesting that the purpose of his departure is tied up with the purpose of his coming into the world in the first place: to fulfill the mission given him by God. The promised happy ending—the joy of the disciples following a period of sorrow—is complicated by Jesus' last prophecy that the disciples will soon abandon him. But even this is counterbalanced by Jesus' statement that everything he has just said is meant to provide his disciples with peace. The "world" may appear to have conquered Jesus and will rejoice in seemingly having done so (16:20); the world will also give the disciples their share of "tribulation"—but Jesus has "conquered" the world (16:33). This is the closure the reader has already anticipated (cf. 2:22–23; 7:38–39), and it prepares the reader for John's crucifixion narrative, in which Jesus figures not as a victim but as a victor.

Turning then to the parable of the laboring woman, we can now probe more carefully the dialectics of sorrow and joy, suffering and forgetting we find therein. John's parable is actually complex and subtle, but its allegorical nature ("you will weep" / "a woman . . . has sorrow" *but* "she forgets her suffering in her joy" / "so . . . your hearts will rejoice") lends a deceptive simplicity to the parable. The laboring woman seems to stand for the disciples' sorrow and subsequent joy in the event of Jesus' death and resurrection. But a closer inspection of the parable reveals that the figure of the laboring woman also stands for Jesus himself. We can break this down by looking at the component parts of the parable—or more specifically, at the two human figures who play a role in the parable. On the one hand, there is the woman (*he gunē*) who anticipates and goes into labor; on the other hand, there is the child (*to paidion*) successfully born of her labor: the one human figure has become two through the process of birth.

It is worth tabulating the levels of metaphorical representation between the parabolic figures and the narrative characters (i.e., Jesus and the disciples). The first parabolic figure, the woman, can represent Jesus (left column) and the disciples (right column) simultaneously:

The Woman

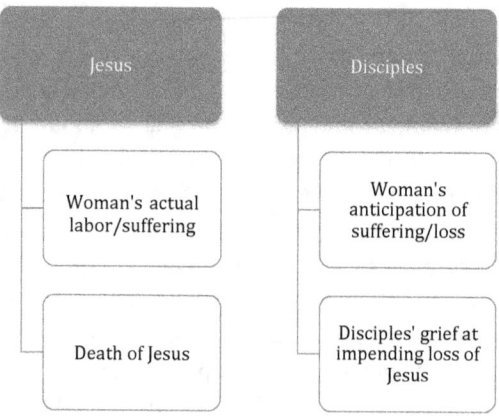

The chart above indicates that the laboring woman in the parable can signify both Jesus *and* the disciples. The left-hand column specifies Jesus as the figure signified in the laboring woman; in this instance, the actual suffering the woman endures in her labor stands for Jesus' approaching death—his "hour."[25] The right-hand column shows how the disciples function as the figure signified by the laboring woman. But in this instance, it is not the *actual* labor of the woman that is in view (*thlipsis*) but rather her *anticipation* of the suffering she will endure in labor (*hē gunē otan tiktē lupēn chei*). In the Greek text, this is denoted by the noun *lupē*, which in itself connotes a multifaceted type of suffering—an anxiety or a physical agony.[26] For the disciples, this is further specified by their "weeping" and "lamenting" (*klausete kai thrēsēte*), verbs that in the NT are used in relation to death or the prospect of death.[27] The disciples' "sorrowing" (*lupēthēsesthe*) over the imminent loss of Jesus through death or departure aligns with the woman's sorrow (*lupē*) about her approaching labor, which might lead to her death. It will be important to keep in mind that there are two types of suffering alluded to in the parable: the woman's anxious anticipation of her impending labor (*lupē*) and the physical pain of labor she suffers (*thlipsis*). It is her physical suffering that eventually gives way to joy (*ouketi mnēmoneuei tēs thlipseōs dia tēn charan*).[28]

The parable's complexity is also notable in that the second figure (the newborn child) dually signifies both Jesus and the disciples. This is represented in the table below:

---

25. Cf. John 2:4; 4:21, 23; 5:25, 28; 7:30; 8:20; 12:23, 27; 13:1; 17:1; and 16:2, 25, 32 (these three referring to the disciples' "hour").

26. Liddel and Scott list *lupē* in its nominal form to denote pain of the body, or pain of mind, a sad plight or condition. As a verb, in the classical literature it could mean "to grieve, vex, whether in body or mind" or "to cause pain or grief" (Liddell and Scott, *Greek-English Lexicon*, 1065).

27. Barrett, *Gospel*, 492. For *klaiō*, Barrett lists John 11:31, 33; 20:11, 13, 15; Luke 7:32; as a noun, *lupē* bears similar connotations; see Rom 9:2; 2 Cor 2:1.

28. Liddell and Scott list *thlipsis* as an intense physical pain, often used in ancient Greek medical tracts to refer to crushing or castration or pressure of the pulse (its literal sense is of a pressing together or a pressure). It also had a metaphorical usage connoting oppression and affliction (cf. LXX Gen 35:3, POxy 939:13, and others) (*Greek-English Lexicon*, 802). In the NT it bears only the figurative meaning referring to great trouble or affliction—an oftentimes apocalyptic kind of suffering brought on by outward circumstances (cf. Rom 5:3; Col 1:24; Mark 13:19; Matt 24:21; Rev 7:14). This sense of great suffering outside of one's control aptly denotes the experience of labor, as here in John 16:20–22.

The Child

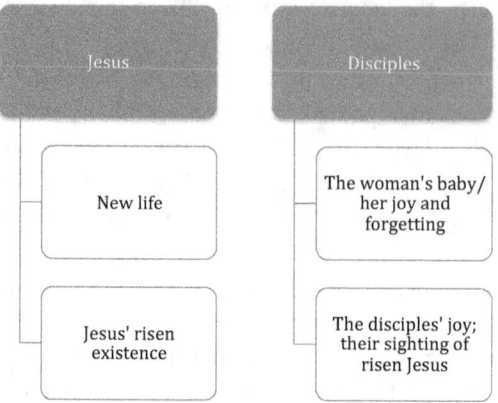

Looking at the left-hand column, the first thing to note is how Jesus can stand both for the laboring woman *and* for the baby she produces. Jesus' death and resurrection constitute a movement in the life of *one person*: Jesus dies, and the same Jesus is resurrected—albeit somehow altered and "new." When a woman goes into labor, she can—and in antiquity, very frequently did—also face her own death, even as her baby is born into "new life."[29] Yet the baby is distinct from the mother; it is not the same life as the life of the mother, but is nevertheless still "part of" the mother. One person has become two. The analogy between a woman giving birth to a child and the death and resurrection of Jesus—where the laboring woman *and* the resulting baby both signify Jesus in two different "states," so to speak—is as curious as it is striking. Yet here, the main point of the left-hand column is that Jesus' risen existence is metaphorically evoked by the birth of the new baby in the parable.

The right-hand column indicates that the figure of the newborn baby signifies the "birth" of the disciples' joy when they see the risen Jesus. Just as the cessation of the woman's labor and the successful birth of her baby leads her—in this parabolic rendering—to "forget" her sorrow and feel complete joy, so too will the disciples forget their grief over Jesus' death and rejoice in being able to see him. We can differentiate between the ways in which the newborn baby signifies Jesus and the disciples respectively, as in the first diagram above. Jesus himself stands for the newborn child, the product of the woman's agonizing labor. But the disciples stand for the woman's altered emotional state after having given birth: after having grieved, their sorrow

---

29. On neonatal mortality in the Greco-Roman world, see French, "Midwives and Maternity Care," 53–62. The same theme in ancient Jewish texts is found in Safrai, "Home and Family," 728–92.

quickly turns to joy, a joy that is so complete that it leaves no trace of the original grief in their memory. The disciples' ability to "see" Jesus once again neatly correlates with the woman's ability to "forget." Furthermore, just as the risen Jesus is the object of the disciples' joy, so too is the newborn baby the object of the woman's joy.

This brief elucidation of the parable, along with its diagrammatic representation, potentially brings clarity to some interpretive issues surrounding it. However, scholars and commentators remain conflicted over the meaning of the parable and its multiple levels of reference. There is no consensus about whether the woman functions as an allegory for Jesus, the disciples, or both. Some of the commentaries on these verses are androcentric and dismissive of the relevance that a woman's labor might have in terms of understanding the death of Jesus *or* the anguish of the (presumably male) disciples. It is to this issue that I now turn.

The Reception of the Parable

John's parable of the laboring woman has not received widespread attention in the scholarship. Apart from one monograph on the parable, the text has only received substantive examination in the gospel commentaries.[30] Yet even the standard commentaries sometimes give scant attention to the parable, or more specifically, to the function of the woman and her child within it. One tendency is for commentators to sideline Jesus' speech about the pregnant woman and concentrate instead on a seemingly more pertinent issue in Jesus' surrounding discourse. Rudolf Bultmann takes this option, focusing significant attention on the meaning of the Greek word *mikron* ("little while") and the eschatological dimensions of Jesus' speech.[31] In Bultmann's commentary, the laboring woman *as woman and mother* holds no significance, metaphorical or otherwise.

Rudolf Schnackenburg likewise denies the interpretive relevance of the woman in the parable, but he is more explicitly dismissive in tone than Bultmann. Schnackeburg doubts that the parable holds "intentional overtones" either with respect to Jesus' departure or to the impending grief of his disciples. Schnackenburg suggests that the parable simply projects an "everyday image of the woman in labour."[32] He later adds, "nor can the word 'hour,' which is used in the image (*her* hour), hardly be related

---

30. See Rushton's monograph *Parable of the Woman in Childbirth*.
31. Bultmann, *Gospel of John*, 5/6–83.
32. Schnackenburg, *Gospel According to St. John*, 2:158.

to Jesus' hour."[33] He offers no compelling evidence to support these assertions. As such, the implication of Schnackenburg's first contention is that the "everyday" image of a laboring woman is simply too mundane a reality to be affiliated with Jesus—a man in the first instance, and as the gospel proclaims, a divinely incarnate man at that. The only reason proffered for Schnackenburg's second objection—that the woman's "hour" cannot allude to Jesus' "hour"—is that such an assertion is based on "the principle, which is certainly open to criticism, that an important word in an author's work always has the same meaning even in different contexts."[34]

Why such a principle should be open to criticism is not immediately evident: I would suggest that the author of the gospel deliberately uses idiosyncratic language that is *supposed* to be read the same way across different contexts—this is what gives his composition thematic coherence. One of the key nouns consistently connected with Jesus is that of his "hour"; it obliquely refers to Jesus' decisive moment (i.e., his death) multiple times across the gospel. The *only* other figure in the gospel who is singularly described as having to face her "hour" is the figurative laboring woman in 16:21. There is, therefore, no reason to exclude the possibility that the woman's "hour" signifies Jesus' own, nor should we deny that, in the context of John 16:20–24, the woman's "hour" can apply to the disciples as they prepare to face their moment of decision (16:25). Yet Schnackenburg is adamant that "the childbearing woman cannot be interpreted allegorically as pointing to the disciples. The only point of comparison is the transition from sorrow to joy."[35]

In similar language, Barnabas Lindars considers it a "mistake" to allegorize the parable as pointing to the disciples; the only relevant detail, in his reading, is also the "sudden transition from grief to joy."[36] There is no way, writes Lindars, that "the woman's pain" is "equivalent to the sorrow of the disciples."[37] The implication is that what belongs naturally to a woman cannot be symbolically predicated of a man. Worse, the suggestion is that the grief of Jesus' disciples is of a comparatively "higher order" than the agony of John's figurative woman—and by extension, of any real laboring woman. When commentators reduce the significance of the parable to the point of the woman's "sudden transition" from suffering to joy, they reinforce the erroneous notion of labor as something inevitably suffered but quickly forgot-

---

33. Ibid., emphasis in original.
34. Ibid.
35. Schnackenburg, *Gospel According to John*, 158.
36. Lindars, *Gospel of John*, 509.
37. Ibid.

ten, as something endured but suddenly transfigured into normalcy again, or as an ordeal that runs its course in the "natural" realm and from which a woman's body quickly recovers.[38]

Such myopic and possibly even misogynistic foci reduce the reach of the parable, as well as the importance of the metaphor of childbirth and of the sorrow and turmoil of labor. Fortunately, other gospel commentators have not been so averse to Jesus' use of the image of a laboring woman, with all its messy, anguished, bloody reality, as a touchstone symbol for the experience of Jesus and/or the disciples. For example, Francis Moloney readily admits the symbolic function of the parabolic woman, reading her as a general symbol of how "joy can be attained through sorrow and anxiety."[39] Rather than insisting on the "sudden transition" as the formative point of the parable, Moloney attends to the *contrast* between what a woman feels *prior* to labor and what she feels *after* labor—and the fact that the experience of both emotional states "cannot be avoided."[40] Perceptively, Moloney understands that this shift is not "sudden"—rather, it is that "the memory of the anguish . . . disappears (v. 21b) because a child . . . has been born to the world (v. 21c)."[41] The memory of anguish gives way to joy because of the child. So also must the disciples accept the inevitability of their experience and of their sorrow as the crucible out of which their joy is to emerge.

Raymond Brown also notes that the parable in 16:20–22 is allegorical, stating that it simultaneously refers to the "present sadness and future joy" of the disciples, as well as referring to Jesus' death and resurrection-victory.[42] Brown hesitates to push the allegory too far, however, questioning claims of earlier scholars that the laboring woman also signifies the "synagogue" converted (triumphantly) to Christianity.[43] Also, C. H. Dodd has no qualms about the parable's signification in his claim that it refers to the disciples' agony.[44] On the semantic evidence, C. K. Barrett makes the same point.[45] Craig Keener comments that the "birth pangs" in the parable refer "especially to Jesus" but also to the "whole people of God."[46] It is therefore

38. Compare, "the parallel is itself a simple one: the short travail pains give place to satisfaction at the birth of a child—the short sorrow of Good Friday and the following day give place to the joy of Easter" (Barrett, *Gospel According to St. John*, 493).

39. Moloney, *John*, 449.

40. Ibid.

41. Ibid.

42. Brown, *Gospel According to John*, 2:732.

43. Ibid.

44. Dodd, *Historical Tradition*, 370.

45. Barrett, *Gospel According to St. John*, 492.

46. Keener, *Gospel of John*, 2:1045.

important to note that some commentators do appreciate the parable of the laboring woman in John 16:20–22 as an allegory referring to Jesus and/or to the disciples, even if other commentators pass over the reality (and representative function) of the figurative woman's agony in order to focus on the point of her "sudden transition" to joy.

Finally, despite the diversity of scholarly views about the allegorical significance of John 16:20–22, commentators are virtually all in agreement on one point, namely, that specific intertexts have shaped the parable. Commentators regularly remark on the fact that texts from the prophetic corpus use the image of a woman in labor to metaphorically evoke extreme psychological or physical anguish.[47] This image is often used eschatologically, either depicting the travails of the future end time (cf. Hos 13:13, Mic 4:9–10) or the realization of the end of the ages in the present (cf. Isa 26:16–21). Imagery and metaphors of labor pains are also used in the post-biblical texts to signify eschatological turmoil, whether future (cf. Mark 13:19, 24; Matt 24:9, 21, 29; Acts 14:22; 1 Cor 7:26; 10:11; 2 Cor 4:17; cf. 1QH 3:3–18; *1 En.* 62:4; *b. Sanh.* 98b; *Shabb.* 118a) or realized (cf. Rev 12:2, 5; Rom 8:22). The consensus position is that John 16:20–22 is indebted to a conflation of two specific prophetic texts—Isa 26:16–19 and Isa 66:7–14.[48] Some also see a parallel with a *Hodayot* text from Qumran, in which an anonymous woman "labours in her pains, [she] who bears the man" (1QH 3:9).[49] The text is clearly messianic (cf. Isa 9:6), but the fuller context of the passage reveals that the birth of a "messianic people" is also in view.

What is so intriguing about the Johannine parable is not only its resonant eschatological flavor, but also its probing perspective on maternal psychology: the woman in John 16 *anticipates* the suffering of her labor, and this very anticipation is the cause of her sorrow. Added to this is the suffering of her actual labor—thus, her agony spans two levels: the psychological and the physical. Set beside this in the parable is the woman *forgetting* her agony once her child is born. This double dialectic of remembering and forgetting, of sorrow and joy, is most interesting and remains under-examined in the

---

47. E.g., Keener, *Gospel of John*, 1045, n154. In addition to the Isaian texts, Keener references Ps 48:6; Isa 13:8; 21:3; 26:17; 42:14; Jer 4:31; 6:24; 13:21; 22:23; 30:6; 31:8; 48:41; 49:22, 24; 50:43.

48. Beginning with Hoskyns, *Fourth Gospel*, 487. Some also cite Isa 9:6, cf. Mihalios, *Danielic Eschatological Hour*, 143–49.

49. See most of the commentators cited above for discussion of the *Hodayot* text in the context of John 16:20–22. However, absent from the Qumran text, unlike the Isaian passages, is a reference to an all-encompassing joy following a period of labor-like suffering.

scholarship. In the next section I will return to my narrative of childbirth and discuss some of these issues in light of it.

Reflections

The correlation that the parable makes between "forgetting" and "joy" suggests, as Moloney has hinted, that its primary meaning resides not in the woman's "sudden transition" from sorrow to joy—as if she merely vacillates from one extreme state to another—but in something subtler. I would suggest that the woman's "sorrow" (*lupē*) refers to her lament-like grief and anxiety at the prospect of her impending labor, alluding to her fears of imminent death or even the possible death of her child. The woman's "suffering" (*thlipsis*) refers to the unendurable pain of her physical labor. Both kinds of agony (the mental and the physical) indelibly mark the woman. Yet the birth of her baby produces a sense of experiential immediacy that enables the woman to "temporarily" forget the agony of her *thlipsis*. Her newborn baby is a tangible reminder that she has survived her labor; her joy and relief coalesce. The woman cannot simultaneously hold in her mind the thought of her recent physical suffering (i.e., she "forgets" it) *and* experience the joy her newborn baby brings. It is not so much that the "transition" is "sudden" but that the two realities—the physical agony and the emotional joy—do not coexist.

The parable does not imply that the woman's transition from sorrow/pain to joy is sudden and complete, and we can glean this understanding from an examination of the allegorical function of the parable with respect to the disciples. In the gospel narrative, their eventual joy at seeing Jesus again follows from their feelings of dejection and loss, but it is clear that some of the disciples nevertheless grappled to believe and understand that it was the risen Jesus they were witnessing (cf. 20:15, 24–29). Their transition to "complete joy" (cf. 16:22) in other words, was not "sudden"; it was complex and progressed in stages—although some disciples did exhibit "joy" (*chairō*) directly when seeing the risen Jesus (20:20). It is the same with the woman in the parable: her eventual joy is indeed "complete," and it is intricately tied to her ability to temporarily forget her pain. But, I would argue, whereas the disciples are able to "forget" their *lupē* in their eventual joy, the parabolic woman retains residual memories of her *thlipsis*, which is what fed into her *lupē* in the first place. In other words, her sorrow and anxiety (her *lupē*) is never altogether erased, nor is it suddenly put away within the postpartum experience.

The dialectic of "forgetting through joy" in the parable (16:21b) is paralleled by a subtler and less directly expressed dialectic of "remembering through sorrow" (16:21a). Via the "anecdotal" hermeneutic I am using in this essay, I would suggest that John's parabolic woman bears a residual *memory* of physical agony—maybe a prior labor, maybe her witnessing of another mother's complicated labor—and the memory of this pain is reawakened as her "hour" approaches. This contributes to her anxiety. The woman's *sorrow* would be therefore intricately tied to her ability to *remember*, and her ability to remember would be bound tightly to her prior experience(s) of suffering; her body has a "memory" of its own, so to speak. The pain of a woman's labor is never "forgotten." It reawakens and is reactivated by the anxiety she feels each time she subsequently faces her "hour" afresh. The woman's "joy" is temporary and contingent upon the successful birthing of her baby, but it does not, indeed cannot, entirely erase her "sorrow."

Now, it is equally possible that the woman's anxiety (*lupē*) is activated not by her memory of past labor(s) but simply by the overwhelming physical pain she feels and by the terror of the unknown. Of course, reading the parable with reference to the figure of Jesus in the gospel, this would make more sense, since Jesus does not "die" recurrently but only once—just so, the parabolic woman faces a "one-time" labor. Nevertheless, from a semantic perspective, the *lupē* of the woman is correlated with the "weeping" and "lamenting" of the disciples in 16:20, where we find verbs that (as already indicated) connote loss through death. The woman's source of anxiety as her "hour" approaches *must* be related to her cognitive awareness ("memory") of some prior complicated labor—whether her own or someone else's. In the beginning of the parable we therefore see that memory and sorrow are intertwined, just as in the parable's conclusion we observe that forgetting and joy are correlated.

I think these nuances are present under the surface of John's parable, but my perception of them does, admittedly, arise from my own experience of labor. Maternal identity emerges out of loss—out of the void of a "limit experience" that threatens to annihilate the woman as a subject and even truly as a living being. The trauma of labor inflicts a kind of psychological loss on the new mother, the loss of a certain innocence that led her to have faith in her control over her body. Childbirth is a *thlipsis*, a suffering that imposes itself from without. In the aftermath of labor and out of the void of negativity, maternal identity is formed complexly: physical agony is temporarily forgotten, but long-term residual memories arising from trauma can persist alongside feelings of guilt. There may be a need to *remember* the initial feelings of joy following the triumph over labor as a form of consolation when a woman's "hour" returns.

If John's parable in 16:20–22 has any basis in observed reality—and his acute understanding of maternal psychology indicates that it might—we can imagine that one of the ways laboring women steeled or consoled themselves was by projecting the outcome of a successful labor and the joy that was to be felt when their child was born into the world. In John's farewell discourse, Jesus uses the metaphor of labor to elicit hope, and he uses that hope as a means of consolation. The impending pain the disciples will feel is thereby assuaged, and their eventual guilt at abandoning Jesus is attenuated in advance.

The joy of birthing a child is real and enduring. The great paradox is that it requires pain and sorrow as its vehicle—indeed, it may even produce a new kind of sorrow as a consequence of complications. The complex emotions that form part of the experience of labor are not easily reducible to simple statements about "sudden transitions" from sorrow to joy. John's parable seems to be saying as much, but it is in fact saying more than that. In the parable, Jesus' death and resurrection, as well as the disciples' grief and joy, is allegorized as an experience of labor and birth. The real experience of (a successful, if complicated) labor and birth is thereby cast as a "death-and-life" redemptive experience—of new life arising from the shadow of death.

Bibliography

Aichele, George, Peter Miscall, and Richard Walsh. "An Elephant in the Room: Historical-Critical and Postmodern Interpretations of the Bible." *Journal of Biblical Literature* 128 (2009) 383–404.

Ballard, C. G., A. K. Stanley, and I. F. Brockington. "Post-traumatic Stress Disorder (PTSD) after Childbirth." *British Journal of Psychiatry* 166 (1995) 525–28.

Baraitser, Lisa. *Maternal Encounters: The Ethics of Interruption*. London: Routledge, 2008.

Barrett, C. K. *The Gospel According to St John*. 2nd ed. London: SPCK, 1978.

Batailles, Georges. *Visions of Excess: Selected Writings, 1927–1939*. Minneapolis: University of Minneapolis, 1985.

Brown, Raymond E. *The Gospel According to John*. Anchor Bible 29a. New York: Doubleday, 1970.

Bultmann, Rudolf. *The Gospel of John*. Translated by G. R. Beasley-Murray et al. Oxford: Blackwell, 1971.

Caruth, Cathy, ed. *Trauma: Explorations in Memory*. Baltimore: John Hopkins University Press, 1995.

Creedy, Debra K., Ian M. Shochet, and Jan Horsfall. "Childbirth and the Development of Acute Trauma Symptoms: Incidence and Contributing Factors." *Birth: Issues in Perinatal Care* 27 (2000) 104–111.

Dodd, C. H. *Historical Tradition in the Fourth Gospel*. Cambridge: Cambridge University Press, 1965.

French, Valerie. "Midwives and Maternity Care in the Roman World." In *Midwifery and the Medicalization of Childbirth: Comparative Perspectives*, edited by Edwin van Teijlingen et al., 53–62. New York: Nova Science, 2004.

Fuggle, Sophie. *Foucault/Paul: Subjects of Power*. London: Palgrave Macmillan, 2013.

Gallop, Jane. *Anecdotal Theory*. Durham: Duke University Press, 2002.

Hoskyns, Edwyn. *The Fourth Gospel*, edited by F. N. Davey. 2nd ed. London: Faber & Faber, 1947.

Keener, Craig S. *The Gospel of John: A Commentary*. Grand Rapids: Baker Academic, 2003.

Leys, Ruth. *Trauma: A Genealogy*. Chicago/London: University of Chicago Press, 2000.

Lindars, Barnabas. *The Gospel of John*. New Century Bible Commentary. London: Oliphants, 1972.

Mihalios, Stefanos. *The Danielic Eschatalogical Hour in the Johannine Literature*. Library of New Testament Studies 436. London: T. & T. Clark, 2011.

Moloney, Francis J. *John*. Sacra Pagina 4. Collegeville, MN: Liturgical, 1998.

Moore, Stephen D., and Yvonne Sherwood. *The Invention of the Biblical Scholar: A Critical Manifesto*. Minneapolis: Fortress, 2011.

Rushton, Kathleen P. *The Parable of the Woman in Childbirth of John 16:21: A Metaphor for the Death and Glorification of Jesus*. Lewiston, NY: Mellon, 2011.

———. "The (Pro)creative Parables of Labour and Childbirth (John 3:1–10 and 16:21–22)." In *The Lost Coin: Parables of Women, Work and Wisdom*, edited by Mary Ann Beavis, 77–90. Sheffield: Sheffield Academic, 2002.

Safrai, S. "Home and Family." In *The Jewish People in the First Century: Historical Geography, Political History, Social, Cultural and Religious Life and Institutions*, edited by S. Safrai and M. Stern, 2:728–92. Assenm, the Netherlands: Van Gorcum, 1974–1976.

Schnackenburg, Rudolf. *The Gospel According to St. John*. Translated by K. Smyth et al. Vol 2. London: Burns & Oates, 1980.

Segovia, Fernando F. *The Farewell of the Word: The Johannine Call to Abide*. Minneapolis: Fortress, 1991.

5

The Inward Groaning of Adoption (Rom 8:12–25)

Recovering the Pauline Adoption Metaphor for Mothers in the Adoption Triad

Erin M. Heim

In academic writing, I rarely have the opportunity to write from personal experience, and even when the opportunity presents itself, as an academic I am usually reluctant to take it because it seems to sneer at conventions such as objectivity and passive observance. So when I was presented with an opportunity to write about the Pauline adoption texts and mothers in the adoption triad in a North American context[1] (i.e., adoptive mothers, biological or first mothers,[2] and adoptees) my first instinct was to try to approach the topic as an outsider. However, as Hilbrand Westra of United Adoptees International observes, "adoption is something you take with you your whole life. You can try to run from it, but it runs faster than you."[3] In the process of writing this article, my adoption has "caught up" to me. As

---

1. The research used in this chapter is primarily written for and from within the United States and thus assumes the cultural norms of the United States regarding adoption.

2. In this essay I will use the terms "biological mother" or "first mother" rather than "birthmother" to refer to a woman who has relinquished a child for adoption in order to respect the ongoing biological connection between a biological mother and her child and also to resist language that reduces her role in the adoption triad to the birth of her child.

3. Hilbrand Westra, qtd. in Knowlton, *Somewhere Between*.

an adoptee myself, I cannot write about mothers in the adoption triad as a disinterested outsider. I cannot run from the story of my own adoption, nor can I bracket it out in order to produce an "objective" look at adoption in Rom 8 and its relevance for contemporary practices of adoption. I cannot claim that my own adoption story, this narrative that I inhabit, has not affected how I think and feel about the Pauline adoption texts. The story of my own adoption causes me to search for the complexities of adoption in the Pauline text and to embrace the existential tension that Paul intimates is inherent in the narrative of adoption (Rom 8:15–23). Nor can I claim that my own identity as an adoptee who is now also a mother has not colored how I view motherhood or influenced how I view other mothers in the adoption triad. Rather than assuming a posture of objectivity or dispassionate observation, the exposition of Rom 8 that I offer below is the result of a deeply personal wrestling with the Pauline adoption texts and with my own story as an adoptee. In the exposition below, my goal is not to explain or uncover what Paul meant when he wrote Rom 8. Rather, below I will use the adoption narrative in Romans 8 as a conversation partner with narratives from mothers in the adoption triad of contemporary adoptions in order to illuminate their complex stories and give voice to the paradoxes these mothers experience as they inhabit a narrative that, in many ways, feels "caught between" and "neither here nor there." Moreover, what I offer below is not meant to be an exhaustive account of the stories of mothers in the adoption triad, but rather it is a roughly sketched theological reflection on the intersection between contemporary adoption narratives and the Pauline narrative in Rom 8.

When the Pauline adoption texts are put into conversation with contemporary practices of adoption, it is often overlooked that these texts do not actually deal with the experience of motherhood at all. In both Greek and Roman law, fathers adopted adult males as their sons in order to insure the continuation of the *familia* and to perpetuate patrilineal descent.[4] In keeping with the dominant first-century practice of adopting sons, Paul too speaks of the Father extending the "adoption to sonship (*huiothesia*)" to believers, requiring his female readers to perform one more interpretive move and assume a male identity before the Pauline metaphor can apply to them.[5] When this narrative is re-inscribed in contemporary contexts, authors often employ it to speak of adoption as a solution for "fatherless" children.[6] The

---

4. For a good overview of the social norms and legal practices of adoption in the first century, see Walters, "Paul, Adoption, and Inheritance," 42–76.

5. For an extended treatment of the issue of gendered language in Rom 8, see Corley, "Women's Inheritance," 117–21.

6. E.g., Russell Moore exhorts Christians to "prioritize the need for families for

mothers in the triad lurk in the background, silent partners to the adoptive fathers, silent suppliers of children surrendered for adoption, and silent daughters who themselves grow up to mother children. Their narratives are often not the "Cinderella story" that adoption advocates extract from the Pauline adoption texts; rather, they express a dialectic of displacement and belonging, of suffering and hope, and of existential groaning for answers that may never come. Though they are often ignored, these themes also loom large in Paul's adoption narrative in Rom 8, making this text a valuable dialogue partner for triad mothers as they wrestle with the elusive and often paradoxical emotions and experiences that accompany the adoption narrative.

Boundary Ambiguity, Belonging, and Displacement

Paul's narrative in Rom 8 shares much in common with another story rife with themes of displacement and belonging: Virginia Woolf's "A Haunted House." In Woolf's story, where past and present intermingle through a ghostly encounter, the narrator speaks the refrain "my hands were empty," while the house insistently replies, "safe, safe, safe."[7] The women in Woolf's short story each exist on the periphery of the other's world, yet they occupy a communal space. Likewise Paul, by insisting that those adopted by God the Father exist in the present age and yet still groan for the full expression of their adoption in the age to come, creates a third, liminal space where members of the Christian community play out their adoption narrative. In Woolf's story, the women are present yet absent, tangible yet illusive, eerie yet reassuring ghosts to one another; they are cautious and wary of each other, yet their house, as their co-inhabited space, chants "safe, safe, safe." Similarly, Paul's Christians must negotiate ambiguous boundaries between belonging and displacement, causing deep existential unrest that irrupts into sighs and groans (Rom 8:23). Like the characters in Woolf's story and like Paul's Christian community, as uneasy members in a shared narrative, mothers in the contemporary adoption triad must negotiate the complex and ambiguous boundaries and relationships between persons joined and separated by adoption. These women—one whose "hands are empty," another whose "hands are full," and one, the adoptee, who must make sense

---

the fatherless" and adoption as "representing Christ to the fatherless" (Moore, *Adopted For Life*, 156, 217), while Jason Kovacs writes, "Adoption and our care for the fatherless provide a visible demonstration of the gospel. Our adoption of children serves as a window into Christ's rescue of us" (Kovacs, "Adoption and Missional Living," 86).

7. Woolf, "Haunted House," 122–23.

of her life in the tension between "emptiness" and "fullness"—live in the confines of society's insistence that their shared story of adoption is "safe, safe, safe."

Romans 8 does not present a "safe" narrative of adoption. As in Woolf's story, belonging comes at the expense of displacement, and Paul's adoptees groan at the feeling of being neither here nor there (Rom 8:23). In Rom 8 the reception of the Spirit brings with it the mindset of the Spirit (Rom 8:5–7), which creates awareness of the change in identity from slave to son and of the transference into the family of God by the act of adoption (Rom 8:15). By the Spirit, Paul's adoptees are true members of God's family, declaring their belonging through their cry, "*Abba*, Father!" Through adoption, they have achieved belonging to God's family within the community of believers, where God is Father and Christ is the firstborn of many brothers and sisters (Rom 8:29). As a result of their adoption, Paul's adoptees encounter the world from a new perspective. They are aware of their displacement, caught in the liminal space between the "now" and "not yet." They perceive the fallenness and bondage of creation for the first time (Rom 8:20–21). They perceive that they have not yet experienced the fullness of redemption (Rom 8:23). They perceive their existence as a state of in-between, belonging to God's family yet still displaced as occupiers of a new space created by the Father's act of adoption.

Likewise, the narratives of mothers in the contemporary adoption triad do not occupy conventional cultural spaces but are instead formed through their interaction in a shared liminal space, much like Woolf's haunted house and the space Paul creates through the tension between the "now" and "not yet" of adoption in Rom 8:15–23. For biological mothers who have given children up for adoption, their children are most often physically absent, yet these children continue to be present in their mothers' thoughts, subtly and sometimes overtly influencing their perceptions and actions.[8] Adoptive mothers struggle in a complementary fashion. They are mothers yet not mothers, at least not in the culturally defined acts of motherhood.[9] They struggle to forge their own narrative of motherhood apart from the experiences of pregnancy and giving birth, while also recognizing that these experiences have joined their child with another mother. Caught between biological mothers and adoptive mothers, adoptees narrate their own stories in the midst of the tension wrought between the conflicting narratives of the woman whose "hands are empty" and the other whose "hands

---

8. Fravel, McRoy, and Grotevant, "Birthmother Perceptions," 425–33.

9. Priel, Melamed-Hass, Besser, and Kantor, "Adjustment among Adopted Children," 389–96.

are full."[10] Belonging comes at the expense of displacement, and adoptees sometimes feel as though they are "neither here nor there." Romans 8, with its ambiguous boundaries and tension between displacement and belonging, shares much in common with the stories of mothers in the adoption triad; in both narratives, the picture of adoption that emerges is anything but "safe, safe, safe."

Boundary Ambiguity, Belonging, and Displacement for Biological Mothers

In Rom 8:22–23 Paul curiously asserts that "creation has been groaning in the pains of childbirth," and yet the birthing creation does not bring forth children of its own (Rom 8:22). The only children in view in Rom 8 are children adopted by God the Father; like the culturally-sanctioned contemporary adoption narrative in North America, Paul's narrative leaves no room for the birthing mother to bring forth her children.[11] Too often, the stories of biological mothers go unexpressed or unheard by society at large, leaving no space for these mothers to grieve and process the loss of their children or negotiate the complexities of having connections to a child who is physically absent yet psychologically present. They have groaned in labor, and yet their hands remain empty. They have groaned in labor, and yet society does not honor them with the designation "mother."

Because their children are psychologically present—existing in their minds and memories—yet most often physically absent, biological mothers experience high degrees of boundary ambiguity.[12] Boundary ambiguity, which is an incongruence between physical and psychological presence, makes it difficult for biological mothers to determine whether the children they relinquished are "inside or outside" of their concept of family.[13] As one biological mother poignantly states, "She is my daughter, but she is their daughter too."[14] Unsurprisingly, biological mothers experiencing the effects of boundary ambiguity, especially mothers in closed adoptions, report higher levels of stress, increased family dysfunction, and poorer emotional health.[15] For many biological mothers, the lack of a socially institutional-

10. Kranstuber and Kellas, "'Growing Under Her Heart,'" 179–99.
11. Harris, "Re-defining the Family Post-Placement," 27.
12. Fravel, McRoy, and Grotevant, "Birthmother Perceptions," 431–32.
13. Ibid., 425.
14. Elle, a biological mother, qtd. in Harris, "Re-defining the Family Post-Placement," 29.
15. Fravel, McRoy, and Grotevant, "Birthmother Perceptions," 425–26.

ized role for her in the life of her child makes the resolution of boundary ambiguity a difficult process. Socially conceived, adoption is a zero-sum relationship. One mother's hands are full at the expense of the empty hands of another.

Sadly, instead of providing space to express the groaning and grief that results from relinquishing children for adoption, the Pauline adoption texts are often used in ways that further suppress the stories of biological mothers; their empty hands continue to go unrecognized by those who do not see the loss that adoption inevitably involves. In their desire to minister to orphans and vulnerable children, evangelical Christians in the United States are often among the chief culprits in perpetuating a narrative of adoption that excludes the plight of biological mothers or diminishes the psychological and emotional impact that relinquishing a child has on these women.[16] Instead, the elements of transfer in the Pauline narrative are mapped onto contemporary adoptions, perpetuating the same "zero-sum" schema that produces high levels of boundary ambiguity in biological mothers.

Perhaps the Pauline adoption texts have been used in such damaging ways toward biological mothers that there is little hope of redeeming them. Perhaps the best course of action is to resist drawing parallels between the biblical text and contemporary adoption narratives altogether. But the text in Rom 8 need not be read as a neat, clean, zero-sum narrative of adoption. The text beckons us to consider the groaning and travail of creation—groaning that results from futility and frustration. This kind of groaning embodied by biological mothers as they birth their children, groaning in labor, groaning in futility, groaning in frustration as they navigate the ambiguous boundaries in their role as the "birth mother" with empty hands. Like Paul's ambiguous boundary between the "now-and-not-yet," biological mothers wrestle with the tension between their children's belonging-yet-displacement, their children's identity as family-yet-not-family, and their child's presence-yet-absence in their own narratives of adoption. Perhaps there is hope that by listening carefully to the groaning that results from ambiguous boundaries and feelings of displacement in the Pauline texts, the Christian community can become a safe space for biological mothers to process, grieve, and heal.

---

16. For examples of pro-adoption literature that diminishes or excludes the biological mother and her family, see Moore, *Adopted for Life*; and Cruver, *Reclaiming Adoption*. For a brief critique of the evangelical orphan care movement and its exclusion of the stories of biological mothers, see Smolin, "Thinking about Adoption," 4–5.

Boundary Ambiguity, Belonging, and Displacement for Adoptive Mothers

As the mothers whose "hands are full," one might be tempted to conclude that adoptive mothers do not struggle with feelings of belonging and displacement or with the boundary ambiguity that adoption brings. But adoptive mothers, even with their "full hands," struggle with the knowledge that they parent children they did not carry, children that once belonged to a woman whose hands are now empty.[17] The biological mothers of their children are their silent companions through their journeys of motherhood—they are ghosts lurking in the background, sharing their children's milestones, wordlessly casting their approving or disapproving glances. In Rom 8, Paul describes adoption as both a completed action (Rom 8:15) and yet one still in process (Rom 8:23). Likewise, contemporary adoptive mothers possess an intuitive and experiential knowledge that adoption is never a completed transaction; rather, it forms relationships that are continuously in process.

In addition, adoptive mothers struggle with the social stigma that adopted children are less desirable than "children of their own," a stigma that most Americans "appear to go to extraordinary lengths to avoid."[18] Although the majority of adoptive families manage quite well, adoptive mothers are far more likely to struggle with their own identity and role as "mother" than their biological counterparts.[19] American society simultaneously lauds adoptive mothers and stigmatizes their relationship with their adoptive children. These mothers are praised for their selflessness, yet "society still sees it as second best"[20] because of the lack of biological connection with their adopted children. Though most adoptive parents have overwhelmingly positive experiences with adoption, the remaining social stigma can subtly taint the sense of belonging within an adoptive family.[21] However, in answer to this stigma, Paul's adoption narrative in Rom 8 presents adoptive relationships—despite being "in process"—as forging deep familial connections between members of an adopted family. In contrast to the social stigma in American society, in Rom 8 adoptive relationships are

---

17. Fravel, "Boundary Ambiguity Perceptions."

18. Fisher, "Still 'Not Quite As Good,'" 353.

19. Priel, Melamed-Hass, Besser, and Kantor, "Adjustment among Adopted Children," 394.

20. Fisher, "Still 'Not Quite As Good,'" 355.

21. Ibid.

not "second best" and adoption in no way diminishes the level of belonging within a family.[22]

Boundary Ambiguity, Belonging, and Displacement for the Adoptee

In the zero-sum story of adoption, adoptees are taken from the hands of one mother and placed in the hands of another. They often have little or no access to information regarding the circumstances that led to their relinquishment. They often had no control or say in either their relinquishment or their adoption. Like creation in Paul's narrative, adoptees were created and then "subjected to frustration" (Rom 8:20). This frustration is wrought from their displacement from their families of origin—frustration at their lack of access to their family histories, frustration at their lack of control over their own circumstances, and frustration at the lack of socially sanctioned space to grieve the losses adoption brings. Adoptees are subjected to these, and many other frustrations, "not by [their] own choice" (Rom 8:20). Their stories are marked by shadowy beginnings; their histories and origins are often unknown. They forge their narratives in the tense intersection between displacement and belonging as lonely inhabitants of a third liminal space.

Displaced from their families of origin yet aware of their biological parents, adoptees also suffer from the effects wrought by boundary ambiguity. Despite their feelings of displacement, adoptees also "belong" in their adoptive families. For some, the feeling of belonging comes naturally, and they blend seamlessly into their adoptive families. For others, belonging is in name only, and they struggle to fit into families that never quite feel like home.[23] In my own adoption narrative, the effects of boundary ambiguity and the tension between feelings of belonging and displacement were never more strongly present than in the nine months of my pregnancy with my own firstborn daughter. As my daughter grew inside me—a child longed for and cherished—I wondered what the experiences of pregnancy and birth had been like for my biological mother, who carried me inside her only to give me away to another family. As a woman groaning in labor with a child

---

22. I acknowledge that there are differences between the practice of adoption in view in the Pauline text, in which adult males were adopted by other adult males, and the contemporary practice of adopting children in the United States. However, I point out that both types of adoption create, or at least purport to create, permanent familial ties.

23. Grotevant, Dunbar, Kohler, and Esau, "Adoptive Identity," 383–84.

destined for adoption (Rom 8:22–23), she too carried me, felt me move and grow, birthed me, and yet her hands are now empty.

For the first time, I began to wonder if she still thought of me as "hers" or if adoption had irreparably erased my place in my family of origin. For the first time, I wondered if my daughter would bear traces of my own shadowed biological history, and I grieved that she would not share the DNA of my adoptive family. For the first time, I wondered at the ease with which my adoptive mother seemed to assume her role as "mother" without the formative experience of pregnancy and birth that gives so many women the confidence to parent, as it did for me. My own entrance into motherhood made me simultaneously grateful for the overwhelming sense of belonging I feel in my adoptive family, yet also acutely aware of the "unnaturalness" of adoption that separates a mother from her child. My journey into motherhood carried me further into my lonely liminal space of belonging-yet-displacement as the daughter of two women yet also of neither, and for the first time I became acutely aware of the "otherness" of my story of birth and adoption.

Suffering and Hope

In his adoption narrative in Rom 8:15–23 Paul intertwines the dialectic of suffering and hope as a hallmark of the existential experience for the Christian who has received adoption in Christ.[24] In Paul's narrative, suffering is an integral part of the adoption story, as seen through his interspersion of terms like *sympáschō* ("to suffer with"), *páthēma* ("sufferings"), *sustenázō* ("to groan together"), and *sunōdínō* ("to be in travail together"). For Paul, these sufferings are evidence of belonging; they are evidence of a cruciform existence brought about by adoption into the family of God.[25] In Rom 8, the source(s) of suffering are unclear, but it is clear that Paul sees suffering (and indeed co-suffering) with Christ as an inherent part of his narrative of adoption.[26] Yet alongside the motif of pain is Paul's insistence that adoption in Christ brings hope and eager expectation for future redemption (Rom 8:20–23). This hope is unseen (Rom 8:24–25), but it is grounded in the assurance that just as Christ was raised and glorified, adoptees in Christ will be raised and glorified on the last day (Rom 8:29–30). This hope is founded

---

24. On this Pauline theme, see especially Beker, "Suffering and Triumph," 105–119; Hooker, "Interchange in Christ and Ethics," 3–17.

25. See Dunn, *Romans*, 486–87.

26. On the Christians' experience of suffering and the sovereignty of God, see Emerson Powery, "'Groans of 'Brother Saul,'" 315–22.

in the goodness of God and the goodness of adoption into God's family as a co-heir with Christ. In Rom 8, the goodness of God and his adoption of Christians far outweighs the sufferings of the present time, and yet the experience of suffering is an integral part of adoption.

Hope and Suffering in the Story of Biological Mothers

However, for mothers in the contemporary adoption triad the dialectic between hope and suffering is not quite so clear-cut. Adoption is not a universal good but can only ever be a relative good,[27] and the tension between hope and suffering is often acute. Contemporary adoption, in all circumstances, involves some degree of loss. Unlike loss resulting from death, which is natural and socially acknowledged, loss resulting from adoption is often endured silently, even secretly.[28] Biological mothers cannot grieve because there is no socially acceptable model of grief for mothers who have relinquished children. Yet for a biological mother, adoption is an experience akin to amputation.[29] One biological mother explains adoption loss as "kind of like being in a black hole somewhere . . . It's like suddenly you got cut in half."[30] Pain accompanying the death of a loved one fades with time, but the pain associated with adoption loss does not subside: "Nothing takes away that black hole."[31] For some, there is no relief from the "sufferings of the present time" (Rom 8:18). Biological mothers continue to suffer and grieve long after their children have been placed for adoption.[32] They do not forget, and they carry their pain with them through future experiences of motherhood.

For biological mothers, the suffering brought about by the loss of their children and by the shame associated with relinquishment and their "second-class" status as "birth mothers" often outweighs or taints their hope for any good to be brought out of relinquishing their children. Biological mothers who do hope often root their hope in future reconciliation and reunification with the children they surrendered. Wendy, a biological mother, remarks, "When you give up a child, you certainly hope that they get better than what you could have done."[33] Others place their hope in the prospect

27. Smolin, "Thinking about Adoption," 4–5.
28. Fravel, McRoy, and Grotevant, "Birthmother Perceptions," 431.
29. Lifton, *Twice Born*, 169.
30. Ann, a biological mother, qtd. in Fessler, *Girls Who Went Away*, 207.
31. Ibid.
32. Askren and Bloom, "Postadoptive Reactions," 395–400.
33. Qtd. in Fessler, *Girls Who Went Away*, 182.

of a better future for their children—a hope that may or may not have been realized in the life of the adoptee. These mothers "hope for what they do not see" (Rom 8:25). For some, it is a hope that they may never see. In instances of reunification, the dialectic of suffering and hope collide, sometimes volatilely, when the reestablishment of relationship brings both restoration and healing but also an acute awareness of their child's absence for many years prior. Then both mother and child must work to build a new narrative. This new narrative includes, redefines, and expands cultural notions of a parent-child relationship—a relationship whose foundation is built upon a shared lineage but an unshared past.

Hope and Suffering in the Story of Adoptive Mothers

In many ways, hope is the dominant voice in the narrative of adoption society pitches to adoptive mothers. Adoptive parents enter into adoption with the hope that it is a "win-win-win" situation for adoptive parents, adoptees, and biological parents. Mothers adopt with the hope that they can provide their adopted children with a sense of belonging, with family, and with a new future.[34] Mothers adopt with the hope that adoption will fill the void left by infertility.[35] Mothers adopt with the hope of finding fulfillment in caring for "the least of these."[36] However, for adoptive mothers, hope that is untempered by an awareness of the suffering inherent to the adoption narrative can have disastrous and damaging results for the other members of the adoption triad. Adoptive mothers must come to terms with the suffering, grief, and loss that always accompanies the process of adoption, and hope must be forged in the midst of the suffering, not applied as a veneer coating that can smooth over difficulties.

Since adoption always involves some degree of loss, suffering is a constant companion to adoptive mothers—at times lying dormant and at times the dominant voice in their motherhood narrative. For these mothers, suffering and grief can come from many and diverse places. Some adoptive mothers have experienced the suffering and grief of being unable to bear biological children. Some adoptive mothers experience the grief of having a child placed for adoption returned to his or her biological family before the adoption is complete. Some adoptive mothers experience rejection from their adoptive children. Adoptive mothers suffer the stigma of being

---

34. Tyebjee, "Attitude, Interest, and Motivation," 685–706.
35. Malm and Welti, "Exploring Motivations to Adopt," 185–208.
36. Cruver, "Adoption and the Incarnation," 32.

perceived as having "second-rate" families because of the lack of biological connection.

In addition to these external sources of suffering, adoptive mothers also suffer in intangible and existential ways. Mothers of adopted children are far more likely to suffer from insecurity in their own identities as mothers. Although the state recognizes their absolute role as mothers to their adoptive children, the lack of a biological connection can undermine their own confidence in their mothering abilities.[37] Moreover, some adoptive mothers suffer a rift in their relationships with their adopted children as adoptees struggle with questions of their past. For some adoptive mothers, suffering is a constant theme in their adoption narrative, weaving itself inextricably into the fabric of their family as they attempt to navigate the difficult parenting situation adoption often brings. For others, including my own mother, suffering lurks quietly in the background, called to mind only in vague recollections of events long since past. But whether suffering is acute or latent, its inherence in the narrative of adoption accentuates the difference between adoptive mothers and mothers of biological children, reminding them that their family story is not the one sanctioned and celebrated by society at large.

Hope and Suffering in the Story of Adoptees

For adoptees, the sources of suffering in their adoption narrative are often as illusive as the truth about their biological families and the circumstances leading to their relinquishment. Suffering can come not only from tangible experiences—such as being visibly different from their adoptive families or being subjected to rude questions regarding their adoption and other violations of their privacy —but also from the difficulty of processing what they are "missing" as an adoptee (e.g., biological parents, siblings, extended family, family history, and so on).[38] In my own adoption narrative, the experience of motherhood acted as a catalyst to examine these feelings of pain, grief, and loss. The act of carrying my children inside me, feeling them move and grow, giving birth to them, touching them, holding them, smelling them, and feeding them at my own breast has brought an acute awareness of my own losses at the hands of adoption. As a mother, it is difficult for me to understand how mothers are brought to the point of relinquishing their children. It pains me to think that my biological mother had to suffer

37. Priel, Melamed-Hass, Besser, and Kantor, "Adjustment among Adopted Children," 389–96.

38. Ballard, "Narrative Burden," 229–54.

the agony of surrendering a child. As an adoptee, I'm afraid that my mother rejected me in a way that feels incomprehensible to me when I look at my own children. The intersection of "adoptee" and "mother" produces within me "groans that are too deep for words" as I ache for answers in the paradox of adoption.

And yet there is hope in the midst of suffering and grief. Hope begins in finding my identity not in the neat, clean version of the adoption narrative where my past begins the moment I entered my adoptive family, but by embracing the silences in my narrative, searching for origins, being open to future reunification with my biological parents, and finding continued belonging in my adoptive family. In Rom 8, Paul speaks of hope as an attitude, even a choice. Hope is the posture of those who have received the "Spirit of adoption" (Rom 8:15). Adoptees often had no input or control in their relinquishments or adoptions; relinquishment and adoption occurs when children are most vulnerable. But adoptees can choose to navigate their narratives with a posture of despair or a posture of hope. For some, hope might look like severing ties with their adoptive families and pursuing reunification. For some, hope appears in the prospect of enacting legislation for adoption reform that better protects vulnerable children and mothers. For some, hope appears as a complete severance from their abusive pasts and being embraced wholly by their new adoptive family. For some, a posture of hope seems impossible. For many, hope is finding the delicate balance between their biological and adoptive families so that healing for all triad members becomes possible.

Paul's narrative in Rom 8 presents a complex and multifaceted view of adoption punctuated by suffering and postured in hope. In the midst of their spiritual adoptions, contemporary Christians likewise live in the tension between suffering and hope. However, the multivalence of Paul's text is often smoothed over, while the Christian community instead rushes to the reassuring refrain of 8:28 that "in all things, God works for the good of those who love him." Their spiritual adoptions are "safe, safe, safe." Yet mothers in the adoption triad cannot so easily escape the complexities of Paul's narrative. They inhabit them, filling them with their own flesh, blood, and tears. They embody Paul's themes of suffering and hope, living in the tension created by the paradox, and finding their identities in the intersection of the narrative complexities.

Groaning and Growing in Adoption

Paul's narrative in Rom 8 does not shy away from or gloss over the complexities inherent in adoption. For Paul, the act of adoption creates tension between belonging and displacement, graying boundaries and forging liminal spaces where Christians live out their identities as individuals caught between the "now" and the "not yet." Living on the margins in the midst of the existential tension created by the Father's act of adoption, the Christians in Paul's community inhabited a narrative marked by a dialectic of suffering and hope. Paul's community groans and grows together in the shadow of their adoption, suffering in their displacement, yet resting in their belonging and hoping for the time when their adoption journey will end in glory.

In Rom 8 Paul uses the vocabulary of groaning to describe birthing creation (Rom 8:20) and Christians as they groan in their adoption (Rom 8:23). He also describes the Spirit as groaning for words as he searches the hearts and knows the minds of those who themselves groan in the midst of their adoption journeys. In Paul's narrative, groaning expresses deep emotive elements—emotions that words cannot express. The groaning of creation signals expectancy and hope for the adopted sons of the Father, as well as for its own liberation from bondage (Rom 8:22). The groaning of the sons expresses the paradoxical feelings of belonging and displacement that accompany their adoption journey (Rom 8:23). The groaning of the Spirit signals the recognition that adoption has brought about good, yet Paul's adoptees still struggle in the midst of brokenness (Rom 8:26). Paul's narrative in Rom 8 promises the adoptees wholeness and belonging, though these come at the expense of suffering and are delayed until the *parousia* of Christ. Yet the love of God goes with them as they journey through the liminal space created by their adoption (Rom 8:37–39).

Paul's adoption narrative, though marked by suffering, has a happy ending. The adoptees will be received wholly—body and spirit—into the family of God at the end of the age (Rom 8:23, 37–39). For members of the contemporary adoption triad, their narrative of adoption lacks this neat and clean ending. The groans of mothers in the contemporary adoption triad are persistent, and they resist simple or trite resolution. Wholeness and healing are possible, however. Both can be found in embracing the complexities, in telling the truth about the grief, loss, and difficulties adoption brings, and in expanding our socially sanctioned understanding of family to make space for all the triad members. In my own adoption narrative, motherhood has become the catalyst for acknowledging adoption-induced loss, for seeking wholeness, for seeking answers regarding my own history, and for accepting the complex reality that adoption has brought to my own story. By peeling back layers long ago papered over, motherhood has called me to embrace the suffering and displacement in my narrative; to embrace my biological mother, whose hands have been empty for so many years; to embrace my adoptive mother, whose hands and heart are full of love for me; and to inhabit my narrative with a posture of hope. Healing can only begin when triad members come to terms with suffering, finding hope for restoration in the midst of the complex stories of their past and moving with hope toward the unwritten narratives of their futures. If healing is to begin, then we must do away with narratives that present adoption as a zero-sum action. If triad members are to work toward wholeness, then there must be room for both biological mothers and adoptive mothers in the lives of their adoptive children. Then there can be wholeness marked by the full hands and open hearts of mothers in the triad embracing each other as fellow pilgrims on the adoption journey, affirming each other's motherhood, and honoring each other's story.

Bibliography

Askren, Holli A., and Kathaleen C. Bloom. "Postadoptive Reactions of the Relinquishing Mother: A Review." *Journal of Obstetric, Gynecologic, and Neonatal Nursing* 28 (1999) 395–400.

Ballard, Robert L. "Narrative Burden: A Qualitative Investigation of Transnational, Transracial Adoptee Identity." *Qualitative Communication Research* 2 (2013) 229–54.

Beker, J. Christiaan. "Suffering and Triumph in Paul's Letter to the Romans." *Horizons in Biblical Theology* 7 (1985) 105–119.

Corley, Kathleen. "Women's Inheritance Rights in Antiquity and Paul's Metaphor of Adoption." In *A Feminist Companion to Paul*, edited by Amy-Jill Levine, 117–21. Cleveland: Pilgrim, 2004.

Cruver, Dan. "Adoption and the Incarnation." In *Reclaiming Adoption*, edited by Dan Cruver, 33–48. Hudson, OH: Cruciform, 2011.

Dunn, James D. G. *Romans*. Vol. 1. Dallas: Word Books, 1988.

Fessler, Ann. *The Girls Who Went Away*. New York: Penguin, 2006.

Fisher, Allen P. "Still 'Not Quite as Good as Having Your Own'?: Toward a Sociology of Adoption." *Annual Review of Sociology* 29 (2003) 335–61.

Fravel, Deborah Lewis. "Boundary Ambiguity Perceptions of Adoptive Parents Experiencing Various Levels of Openness in Adoption." PhD diss., University of Minnesota, 1995.

Fravel, Deborah Lewis, Ruth G. McRoy, and Harold D. Grotevant. "Birthmother Perceptions of the Psychologically Present Adopted Child: Adoption Openness and Boundary Ambiguity." *Family Relations* 49 (2000) 425–33.

Grotevant, Harold, Nora Dunbar, Julie K. Kohler, and Amy M. Lash Esau. "Adoptive Identity: How Contexts Within and Beyond the Family Shape Developmental Pathways." *Family Relations* 49 (2000) 379–87.

Harris, Stephanie. "Re-defining the Family Post-Placement: Birthmothers and Kinship through the Adoption Lens." *North American Dialogue: Newsletter of the Society for the Anthropology of North America* 14 (2011) 23–30.

Hooker, Morna. "Interchange in Christ and Ethics." *Journal for the Study of the New Testament* 25 (1985) 3–17.

Knowlton, Linda Goldstein. *Somewhere Between*. DVD. New York: Long Shot Factory, 2011.

Kovacs, Jason. "Adoption and Missional Living." In *Reclaiming Adoption: Missional Living through the Rediscovery of Abba Father*, edited by Dan Cruver, 83–94. Hudson, OH: Cruciform, 2011.

Kranstuber, Haley, and Jody Koenig Kellas. "'Instead of Growing under Her Heart I Grew in It': The Relationship Between Adoption Entrance Narratives and Adoptees' Self Concept." *Communication Quarterly* 59 (2011) 179–99.

Lifton, Betty Jean. *Twice Born: Memoirs of an Adopted Daughter*. New York: McGraw-Hill, 1977.

Malm, Karin, and Kate Welti. "Exploring Motivations to Adopt." *Adoption Quarterly* 13 (2010) 185–208.

Moore, Russell. *Adopted for Life: The Priority of Adoption for Christian Families and Churches*. Wheaton, IL: Crossway, 2009.

Powery, Emerson. "The Groans of 'Brother Saul': An Exploratory Reading of Romans 8 for 'Survival.'" *Word and World* 24 (2004) 315–22.

Priel, Beatriz, Sigal Melamed-Hass, Avi Besser, and Bela Kantor. "Adjustment among Adopted Children: The Role of Maternal Self-Reflectiveness." *Family Relations* 49 (2000) 389–96.

Smolin, David. "Thinking about Adoption." *Journal of Christian Legal Thought* 2 (2012) 4–5.

Tyebjee, Tyzoon. "Attitude, Interest, and Motivation for Adoption and Foster Care." *Child Welfare* 82 (2003) 685–706.

Walters, James C. "Paul, Adoption, and Inheritance." In *Paul in the Greco-Roman World: A Handbook*, edited by J. Paul Sampley, 42–76. Harrisburg, PA: Trinity, 2003.

Woolf, Virginia. "A Haunted House." In *The Complete Shorter Fiction of Virginia Woolf*, edited by Susan Dick, 122–23. Orlando: Harcourt, 1989.

6

Pater Nutrix

Milk Metaphors and Character Formation in Hebrews and 1 Peter

ALICIA D. MYERS

Several passages in the New Testament epistles make use of the metaphor of breast milk (*gala, galaktos*) to describe their addressees' reception of the gospel message. While perhaps the most memorable of these passages is Paul's admonition in 1 Cor 3:1–3, the imagery is also employed in Heb 5:12–14 and 1 Pet 2:1–3. To explain these passages, scholars regularly note parallels between these milk metaphors and those found among other philosophic and educational works to describe levels of understanding (Quintilian, *Inst.* 2.4.5–6; Epictetus, *Diatr.* 2.16.39).[1] Only recently, however, have scholars such as Philip Tite begun to explore the broader cultural assumptions surrounding milk and breastfeeding that make them ideal metaphors for educational and philosophical development.[2] Ancients believed breast milk to be *part of the educational process* of character formation, effectively shaping newly born children as they matured into their place in society. This conclusion follows from understandings of gender, pregnancy, and lactation that undergirded cultural constructions of mothers and motherhood in the Greco-Roman era. Crafted and reinforced by the male voices preserved in the extant literatures, motherhood was the assumed *telos* for every female. This ideal extended to an exaltation of ma-

---

1. Attridge, *Hebrews*, 308–11; Thompson, *Hebrews*, 120–22, 128–33.
2. Tite, "Nurslings," 371–400; Myers, "Father's Bosom," 481–97.

ternal breast milk as the best character-forming nutrition for an infant, even though the widespread use of wet nurses (*nutrices*) throughout social strata is well documented. By employing milk metaphors, then, New Testament authors use language and concepts familiar with their cultural context, whether to encourage their audiences to continue consuming milk (1 Pet 2:1–3) or progress onward toward "solid food" (*stereas trophēs*, Heb 5:12). The breast milk enjoyed by these audiences is a character-forming substance that enables fuller imitation of the ideal Son, Jesus. Nursed in this way, the addressees share a special intimacy with their fellow nurse-mates, including Jesus, which the authors insist should carry them through various trials.

Contextualizing a Metaphor: Breast Milk in Greco-Roman Perspective

Person-making: Constructing "Woman" and "Man"

The story of milk in the Greco-Roman world begins in utero, intimately associated with ideas concerning conception, generation, and childbirth along with larger constructions of masculinity, femininity, and effeminacy. Recent studies on gender in the Greco-Roman world have emphasized the permeation of assumed male normativity. Male normativity—and its accompanying equation with superiority over all things "un-male"—creates a scale not just of maleness, but also of humanness in the Greco-Roman world.[3] Maleness, recognized by that which is "masculine," is aligned with full personhood, orderliness, harmony, and perfection. To be a man is nothing less than to be unchanging, rational, and supremely in control of one's self (body, emotions, speech, dress, mannerisms) and others (wife, children, slaves, subordinates). Rightly (i.e., "masculinely") ordered physically and mentally, a man was an "impenetrable penetrator" able to "defend [his] own body" against attack and assert the right to penetrate others.[4] He was able to discern right order and right behavior in any situation, was rightly acknowledged as the leader of others, and was depended upon for protection but

---

3. Flemming, *Medicine*, 180–83. The freeborn, elite, and socially secure male was pictured as the "norm" for humanity in ancient literature because it was precisely these sort of men who were writing to one another as the primary agents in society.

4. Walters, "Invading the Roman Body," 30, 44; Conway, *Behold the Man*, 21.

also due honor for his pains.[5] If being a man was to be fully human, then to be an ideal man was to approach the divine.[6]

Demonstration of masculinity was a constant preoccupation of Greek and Roman elite males—described in terms of following a *vir*tuous life.[7] Females, however, were at a supreme disadvantage in this pursuit. Inverted and ill-equipped to penetrate others, females were presented by ancient men as made for penetration.[8] Beyond this physical handicap, females were understood to be deficient in *logos* ("reason" or "rationality") and thus naturally weak and literally open to vice in the form of various excesses—emotional, material, and physical.[9] Females, therefore, were in need of a man's control to prevent them from bringing disaster upon themselves, families, cities, the empire, and even the cosmos.[10] Only when properly controlled could a female reach her own *telos*—becoming a woman (*gunē*) as a wife and mother whose womb and breasts made possible a sort of "immortality" for the male in the reproduction of his (ideally male) offspring. In such a world, female "specificity" or "difference" is dangerous, but also purposeful and even useful when tamed and ruled with the *logos* inherent to the masculine norm. As a result, motherhood was intertwined with womanhood as a natural and inevitable consequence of her femininity unless unusual circumstances intervened.[11] Moreover, motherhood opened an avenue of a

---

5. Plato, *Resp.* 4.443d–e; Aristotle, *Eth. nic.* 1.7.15; 1.10.11; 2.6.11; 4.9.1–8; Quintilian, *Inst.* 11–12.

6. Conway, *Behold the Man*, 36–39.

7. *Vir* is the Latin word for "man" (Conway, *Behold the Man*, 22–24).

8. As Aristotle explains, a woman is supposed to be "soft" (*malakos*, "feminine"), which he equates with being "passive and not active in sexual intercourse" (Aristotle, *Eth. nic.* 7.5.4 [Rackham, LCL]; cf. 7.7.6). Please note that "LCL" refers to the Loeb Classical Library throughout.

9. Aristotle argues, "A woman [wife] is more compassionate than a husband, more given to tears, at the same time is more jealous and complaining, more apt to scold and strike. The female is also more dispirited and despondent than the male, more shameless and lying, is readier to deceive and has a longer memory. She is also more wakeful, more afraid of action, and in general less inclined to move than the male and takes less nourishment" (Aristotle, *Hist. an.* 9.1.608b8–15 [Thompson]). Philo offers a similar opinion in *QG*, 1.33.

10. A review of developing mythologies surrounding the creation of women during the Hellenistic age demonstrates the assumed chaotic power of unfettered femininity. See Hesiod, *Theogyny*; ibid., *Works and Days*; Philo, *Creation*; ibid., *QG*; and *Life of Adam and Eve* as well as analyses of these texts by Zeitlin, *Playing the Other*, 53–86; King, *Hippocrates' Woman*, 21–26; Arbel, *Forming Femininity*, 33–37; Solevåg, *Birthing Salvation*, 43–49.

11. Solevåg explains, "The ideal for free women, then, was to assume the role of motherhood and produce legitimate heirs. Any deviation from this role could be met with accusations about sexual degeneracy and un-womanly behavior" (*Birthing*

sort of "redemption" for the female who would submit and use her inferiority for its only positive function: the production of legitimate sons.

These gender constructions dominate Greco-Roman culture, including the medical literatures of both Greece and Rome, and they lead to surprisingly consistent constructions of the female body and its association with—and indeed *need* for—motherhood. Ancient medical authors are utero-centric in their view of the female body: they define the female body primarily by the uterus, especially the menstrual blood that flows to and through it. Considered to be composed of loose flesh, the female body is thought to absorb and retain more moisture than its male counterpart, resulting in and contributing to her colder nature.[12] Accordingly, woman's collection of excess moisture manifests each month in her menstrual cycle. To ensure her health, therefore, most ancient physicians agree that she should have a regular (and rather heavy) menstrual flow, demonstrating clear passageways and enabling her body to be unburdened of its excess moisture.[13]

Marriage was also a prescription for female health, since male penetration was thought to widen the vagina and, ideally, put a female's blood to work in the construction of a fetus. According to the dominant embryologies of the ancient world, menstrual blood does not evacuate during pregnancy *not* because it no longer collects, but rather because the growing fetus consumes it.[14] Only a faulty womb "gaps open" and allows blood to escape, thus depriving the growing child of food and impairing its development (Hippocrates, *Genit.* 9.483). When a fetus no longer receives sufficient blood from its mother, *the fetus* initiates childbirth and continues

---

Salvation, 59–61). See Seneca, *Helv.* 16.3–4; Juvenal, *Sat.* 6.592–601; Ovid, *Am.* 2.14).

12. Hippocrates, *Glands*, 16.573; Aristotle, *Part. an.* 2.1.646b21—2.3.650b13. The Hippocratics emphasize the looseness of female flesh as the cause for its retaining moisture, while Aristotle focuses on its "colder" composition he claims prevents female bodies from being able to "concoct" blood into its final form: seed (*sperma*; see n196 [x-ref]). On the persistence of the cold/wet view for female bodies and their resulting instability, see Dean-Jones, *Women's Bodies*, 41–65; and Flemming, *Medicine*, 185–249.

13. Among those endorsing the need for menstruation (and pregnancy) include the Hippocratics, Aristotle, Rufus of Ephesus, Pliny the Elder, Plutarch, Celsus, as well as Galen. Soranus, however, suggests that menstruation (as well as pregnancy and lactation) has the potential to rob some females of needed nourishment (*Gyn.* 1.4.19–23). Nevertheless, Soranus encourages marriage and reproduction for the sake of humanity and *not* for the sake of female health.

14. *Pangenesis* and *epigenesis* were the dominant embryologies of the ancient world. According to *pangenesists*, the more popular view, both males and females contribute seeds to the construction of a fetus (Hippocrates, *Gen.*; ibid., *Nat. puer.*). Aristotle, as an *epigenesist*, did not think women contribute seed but only menstrual blood, which is the material shaped and given life by the *logos* and heat of male seed (Aristotle, *Gen. an.* 2.4.740a35–6.745b21).

the healthful process of widening female passageways—even though many died in childbirth.[15] It was through this event that a girl completed the process of becoming an adult: from virgin (*parthenos*) to woman-wife (*gunē*).[16] Marriage and motherhood, therefore, were not only beneficial to males, but also for females, who were formed for this purpose. Without marriage and childbirth, females remained constricted, susceptible to suffocation by their excess blood or insanity as a result of their un-inseminated, wandering wombs.[17]

From Female Excess to Tempered Treasure: Breast Milk

Of particular importance for this present chapter is the association between blood and milk that follows from the embryological discussions outlined above. While in the womb, a fetus consumes excess blood. Upon birth, the newborn child continues to receive this same nourishment, conveyed no longer through the umbilicus but through a woman's breasts (Plutarch, *Am. prol.* 3.495d–496a; Aristotle, *Gen. an.* 2.7.746a2–4; Hippocrates, *Carn.* 6.594). In other words, breast milk is extra menstrual blood, pressed upward into the breasts by a growing fetus (Hippocrates, *Glands*, 16.572; *Lev. R.*, 14.3). In addition to fetal pressure, Aristotle argues that male semen also contributes to the creation of breast milk by adding the necessary heat to create something useful from the woman's cold excess. He writes:

> The material which supplies the nourishment and the material out of which Nature forms and fashions the animal are one and the same. And this material, in the case of blooded animals, is the blood-like liquid (i.e., menstrual blood), since milk is *concocted*, not *decomposed* blood.[18]

This heating and infusion with *pnuema* results in milk's white color—just as such heat and *pneuma* ("breath" or "spirit") explains the color of male semen.[19] Soranus likewise describes breast milk as cooked blood, writ-

15. Hippocrates, *Mul.* 1.33–34; ibid., *Nat. puer.* 19.532, 30.2–9; Aristotle, *Gen. an.* 4.8.777a22–26.

16. Demand, *Birth, Death, and Motherhood*, 17; King, *Disease of Virgins*, 50–51.

17. Hippocrates, *Peri Parthenión*. See also Demand, *Birth, Death, and Motherhood*, 102–107; and King, *Hippocrates' Woman*, 76–85.

18. Aristotle, *Gen. an.* 4.8.777a6–8 (Rackham, LCL).

19. On the color of semen, see Aristotle, *Gen. an.* 2.2.735b33–35; and the discussion in Seim, "Motherhood," 102–103. Favorinus of Arles uses the same language to describe the color of milk, explaining, "Is the blood which is now in the breasts not the same that it was in the womb, merely because it has become white from abundant

ing that "raw" milk is "red-yellow [in color]" and when it is "not brought to perfection" (i.e., cooked) it "displays a blood-like color" (*Gyn.* 2.13.12 [Temkin]). A mother's milk collects throughout her pregnancy, but it is only "serviceable" in either the seventh or eighth month, when the fetus was nearly formed (Aristotle, *Gen. an.* 4.8.776a31–776b4).

Breast milk, therefore, is a semen-infused concoction that enables the creation, restoration, and completion of life. In contrast, menstrual blood is depicted as defiling and even "monstrous"—killing crops (especially gourds and cucumbers!), putting pests to flight, clouding mirrors and tarnishing metal, or even causing sterility in livestock. Breast milk, however, has medicinal qualities for any who partake of it.[20] According to Pliny the Elder, "Mother's milk is the most useful thing for anybody . . . Moreover, human milk is the most nourishing for any purpose" (*Nat.* 28.123).[21] Such "uses" include fertility tests, fumigations, and salves—especially when treating eyes—as well as for the elderly, whom Galen prescribes drinking milk directly from a woman's breast if possible.[22] Larissa Bonfante argues that Roman tradition in particular "preserved features of [the] protective mother figure" with stories of life conferred through the breast milk of goddesses (acknowledged with the epithet *nutrix*, or "wet nurse") and life restored through the milk of mothers, nurses, and even daughters.[23] Anthony Corbeill suggests that these connotations might also explain the baring of breasts in mourning practices in ancient Rome. Just as a woman's breasts nourished new life on earth, so too they are offered before the newly deceased entering into the afterlife. As a symbol of past comfort and affection, they inspire remembrance as well as hope for a new birth into the realm of the dead.[24] As conveyers of milk, breasts themselves are evocative images and are wielded with substantial *pathos* by the great mothers of tragic tradition.[25] The key to their power, however, lies in the transformation of menstrual blood by the addition of male seed, which transforms feminine excess into masculinely-purposed nourishment. Chaotic menstrual blood becomes useful—even the "most useful thing"—in the form of breast milk.

---

air and width?" (Aulus Gellius, *Noct. att.* 12.12 [Rolfe, LCL]). See the discussion of Favorinus' comments below.

20. Richlin, "Pliny's Brassiere," 202–204.
21. Ibid., 205.
22. Galen, *de Marcore*, 9; Laskaris, "Nursing Mothers," 460–62.
23. See Bonfante, "Nursing Mothers," 183, 180–88.
24. Corbeill, *Nature Embodied*, 67–106.
25. Homer, *Il.* 22.77–90; Aeschylus, *Chor.* 523–50, 897–930; Euripides, *El.* 969, 1206–1207; ibid., *Or.* 527–30.

The combination of male and female contributions in breast milk also had ethical implications for those who partook of it, especially newborn infants and young children vulnerable to continued influence of the seed(s) transmitted through the milk. In his defense of maternal breastfeeding, the philosopher Favorinus of Arles makes the connection between breast milk and character formation explicit:

> Is the blood which is now in the breasts not the same that it was in the womb, merely because it has become white from abundant air and width? Is not wisdom of nature evident also in this, that as soon as the blood, the artificer, has fashioned the whole human body within its secret precautions, when the time for birth comes, it rises into the upper parts, is ready to cherish the first beginnings of life and of light, and supplies the newborn children with the familiar and accustomed food? Therefore it is believed not without reason that, *just as the power and nature of the seed are able to form likenesses of body and mind, so the qualities and properties of the milk have the same effect* . . . [T]here is no doubt that in forming character the disposition of the nurse and the quality of the milk play a great part; for the milk, although *imbued from the beginning with the material of the father's seed, forms the infant offspring from the body and mind of the mother as well.*[26]

By drinking breast milk, children consumed the same substance from which they were formed, continuing the formation process outside of the womb either at their mother's breast or at the breast of a wet nurse. For this reason, ancients regularly emphasize the need for quality breast milk. Philosophers and moralists such as Favorinus address other elites and repeat the trope of the ideal mother who nurses her own children "on her lap."[27] Not only would maternal breast-feeding ensure continued communication of parental traits, it was also believed to reinforce affection between mother and child. Suzanne Dixon aptly demonstrates the importance of maternal relationships with children, particularly as they matured.[28] For moralists, the foundation for such a relationship should be breastfeeding, which encourages the natural bond that exists between parents and children.[29]

---

26. Aulus Gellius, *Noct. att.* 12.12–15, 20 (Rolfe, LCL), emphasis added.

27. Tacitus, *Dial.* 29; ibid., *Agr.* 4; ibid., *Ger.* 20; Cicero, *Brut.* 210–12; Plutarch, *[Lib. ed.]* 5 (3c–d); ibid., *Am. prolis.* 3.496b–c; Juvenal, *Sat.* 6.592–94.

28. Dixon, *Roman Mother*, 168–209.

29. Aulus Gellius, *Noct. att.* 12.21–23; Plutarch, *Am. prolis.* 3.496a–496c.

Yet hiring wet nurses was a well-established practice, even the norm, throughout social strata in the Roman world. Wet nurses could be employed for the sake of convenience (a practice maligned by the aforementioned moralists) but also out of necessity in cases of maternal death, physical inability, or even compulsion by an employer or owner who retained the mother's services and prevented her from nursing.[30] As a result, instructions on how to select a wet nurse are abundant in the ancient world. The Roman physician Soranus of Ephesus catalogues common recommendations, writing that a nurse must be "self-controlled, sympathetic, and not ill-tempered, a Greek, and tidy." She should also "abstain from coitus, drinking, lewdness, and any other such pleasure or incontinence" since, according to Soranus, sex "cools the affection toward the nursling" and threatens the supply of milk if pregnancy should result (*Gyn.* 2.19.88 [Temkin]). Soranus continues with strict guidelines on a nurse's daily regimen of food, drink, exercise, and bathing, offering advice on how and when to suckle the child as well as when to wean (*Gyn.* 2.20.89–40.109). After encouraging maternal breastfeeding, Plutarch likewise offers what he deems essential advice on selecting wet nurses. "First of all," he writes, "in character they must be Greek" since "just as it is necessary, immediately after birth, to begin to mould the limbs of the children's bodies in order that these may grow straight and without deformity, so, in the same fashion, it is fitting from the beginning to regulate the characters of children" (Plutarch, *[Lib. ed.]* 5 [3e] [Babbitt, LCL]).[31] The close contact between a mother or wet nurse and child during the early years of life meant that a child was not only formed by the milk imbibed, but also that such forming was reinforced by the language and behavior the child was exposed to while in her care (Plutarch, *[Lib. ed.]* 5 [3f]; Tacitus, *Dial.* 29). In this way, women played a significant role in forming children while still in their most malleable state. It is fitting, then, that milk and wet nursing, in addition to pregnancy, were used in ancient educational literature to describe the formation of children toward ideal man- or woman-hood.

---

30. Bradley, *Discovering the Roman Family*, 13–36.

31. For additional sources and discussion, see Leftkowitz and Fant, *Women's Life*, 187–88; Tite, "Nurslings," 380–83; Myers, "Father's Bosom," 483–92.

Interpreting a Metaphor: Breast Milk and New Testament Pedagogies

Breast Milk in Greco-Roman Paideia

The topics of nurses, mothers, breast milk, and pregnancy fold into the main goal of ancient education (*paideia, artes liberales*): that is, the production of ideal "men" as described above.[32] The pursuit of manliness was a lifelong process and required continual performance in a "world where one's adequacy as a man was always under suspicion and one's performance was constantly being judged."[33] While pedagogues, professional tutors, fathers, and other adult influences contributed to the formation of a "man," their contributions did not begin in earnest until at least the third or fourth year of life, after a child was weaned. The formation of "men," therefore, begins in the womb and continues in the reception of breast milk and early childcare—largely by wet nurses, but also by mothers who conformed to the philosophic ideal.

Whether mothers or hired nurses, then, these women were the primary educators of small children in the early years of their lives, providing milk and general care by keeping children clean, safe, and preventing the development of poor speech and bad habits.[34] Mothers continued their educational role long after weaning, acting as "transmitters of cultural memory and guardians of the *mos maiorum* [ancestral customs]" by embodying ideal femininity, procuring good teachers, and preventing children from inappropriate pursuits.[35] Yet Keith Bradley argues that a wet nurse's influence also extended throughout a child's life, particularly in upper-class households. He explains, "in her developing role as a provider of extended child care the *nutrix* became the equivalent of the *educatrix* or *pedagoga*" before a child was sent to grammar school or established under the instruction of a tutor at age seven.[36] Moreover, epigraphic and other written evidence dem-

---

32. Plutarch, *[Lib. Ed.]*, 1; Quintilian, *Inst.* 1.1.1–9; Theophrastus, *Char.* proem.; Aristotle, *Eth. nic.* 1.3. It should be noted that aristocratic girls also received some education, particularly in the Roman Empire, in order to be suitable partners (Hemelrijk, *Matrona Docta*).

33. Gleason, *Making Men*, xxii.

34. McWilliam, "Socialization," 275.

35. Ibid., 270.

36. Bradley, *Discovering the Roman Family*, 27. An *educatrix* (Latin) or *pedagoga* (Greek) was a female—often but not always a slave—charged with attending children in a household. She was often considered a "foster-mother" to her charges. These women could have served as a wet nurse (*nutrix*) prior to her role as the *educatrix* or *pedagoga*, but not necessarily so. An *educatrix* or *pedagoga* was responsible for the physical care

onstrates that such relationships often continued long after this age, with nurses acting as clients to their charges-turned-patrons. Pliny the Younger famously provided a farm and income for his nurse in his adulthood (*Ep.* 6.3), and Nero took special care for his nurse's burial (Suetonius, *Nero* 50). Wet nurses feature as a trope for affection and patience and were often considered more doting and indulgent than a child's mother, potentially to a fault. For this reason, Cicero explains the changing relationship between a charge and nurse as the child grows (*Amic.* 74). Even though childhood affection for nurses remains strong, the relationship must change to one of inequality, lest the adult should continue to heed her as he (or she) did as a child. The temptation for such a relationship to continue, however, demonstrates the lasting impact nurses had on children in their care.

Criticisms for nurses and mothers, therefore, often focus on the quality of their care and their inability to maintain proper boundaries with growing children. As we have seen, ancients believed poor milk could impact the character of one who drank it. Soranus warns that an ill-tempered nurse would craft an ill-tempered child since "by nature the nursling becomes similar to the nurse" (*Gyn.* 2.19.88 [Temkin]). Yet the real target for admonishment (or explanation) is the deficiency of the one reared, whether still a student or the most powerful man in the empire. Commenting on general moral malaise, Cicero complains about the corruption of nature's "innate seeds of the virtue (*semina innata virutum*) . . . As soon as we are brought forth into the world and raised up at birth," he writes, "straightaway we are caught up in a never-ending whorl of evil practice and the worst possible principles, so that we seem to have drunk in error virtually with our nurse's milk (*lacte nutrices*)" (*Tusc.* 3.1.2).[37] Furthermore, those who remain dependent on milk for too long—even if it is good milk—are stunted in their development; they never mature into full men who exercise proper control over their emotions, minds, and behavior. Epictetus uses the milk metaphor to complain against those who pretend to be "men" but remain infantile because they do not practice what they have supposedly learned (*Diatr.* 2.16; 3.24). Instead, consumed by fear and passions, they cry for their mothers and nurses, and refusing to be "weaned," they stay at home being fed rather than searching for truth (*Diatr.* 2.16). Yet, given the larger context,

---

of children and guiding their earliest moral development. There are also masculine forms of these words and occupations: *educator* and *pedagogos*. The masculine form for "nurse"—who clearly could not "suckle" a child but who could provide physical care—is *nutritor* or *nutricius*. These terms are often translated as "foster-father." Bradley's point is that wet nurses often continued their influence over children as guides and informal teachers long past weaning.

37. Translation taken from Dixon, *Roman Mother*, 115.

the charge of milk-dependence is not just one of immaturity. According to Soranus, children become "moist and delicate if fed on milk for a long time" (*Gyn.* 2.21.46 [Temkin]). The reliance on milk for too long, then, means one takes on traditionally feminine qualities, making them vulnerable to vice.[38] In other words, it is a charge of effeminacy.

In contrast, when milk is discussed positively, it is because it contributes to proper, generally "masculine," development. Having partaken of good milk—for the appropriate length of time—children are properly formed and continue to develop. Thus, Soranus describes the "firming" of the infant's body as an indication that he or she is ready for solid food (*Gyn.* 2.21.46). The drier, solid food contributes to a continued firming as the child progresses toward maturity. For sons, that means progress toward ideal manhood—the drier, more firm-bodied of the genders. "Nurture" (*trophē*), therefore, is one of the *topoi* for praise among ancient rhetoricians since it acts as further evidence of the subject's virtue (Pseudo-Hermogenes, *Prog.* 16). Messala's maternal praise for Cornelia, Aurelia, and Atia for raising their sons on their laps and at their knees, rather than in the hands of a "silly little Greek serving maid," resonates with such a *topos*. Their special maternal care resulted in the production of "princes" (Tacitus, *Dial.* 28–29). These good mothers guided the education of their sons from birth: "The object of this rigorous system was that the natural disposition of every child, while still sound at the core and untainted, not warped as yet by any vicious tendencies, might at once lay hold with heart and soul on virtuous accomplishments" (*Dial.* 28.6 [Peterson]). Since a person takes on the characteristics of one's nurse, whether mother or not, the special qualities of an ideal man could be traced—at least in part—to the initial nurture he received.[39]

Breast Milk in Hebrews and 1 Peter

When New Testament authors use the imagery of "milk" or "nursing," therefore, they do so in conversation with a rich context—one that is replete with presuppositions concerning gender, female physiology, lactation, motherhood, and ideal character formation. As with other educational and philosophical literature from the Greco-Roman world, Hebrews and 1 Peter use this metaphor to encourage the development of their audiences into their ideal "manhood." As we will see, the "milk" consumed shapes these audiences, who are admonished to continue growing toward maturity. In

---

38. The charge of milk-dependency corresponds to characterizations of effeminacy for those eating "luxurious" diets (Seneca, *Ep.* 45.13–33).

39. Myers, "Father's Bosom," 486–87.

contrast to the larger Greco-Roman context, however, this ideal manhood and maturity is not encapsulated by philosophers and victorious emperors, but by the suffering of Jesus.

The milk metaphor of Heb 5:12–14 sits in the midst of a passage that admonishes the audience and interrupts the flow of the larger argument building in Heb 5–10. James Thompson suggests that the interruption, as well as the shaming content, in 5:11–6:12 serves to gain the audience's attention, acting as a digression challenging them to listen and understand the more difficult lesson to follow in chapters 7–10.[40] Thompson's analysis helpfully identifies various rhetorical techniques at work in the passage by offering more background on the educational language employed.[41] What Thompson and others who interpret this passage do not discuss, however, is the weight that the milk metaphor adds as a result of the cultural presuppositions surrounding breast milk. Rather than simply an accusation of childishness, the milk metaphor in Heb 5 reinforces the familial and character-forming motifs found in the larger homily, especially Heb 2, which likewise emphasizes the "perfecting" feature of Jesus' suffering.

In Heb 2 and again in 4:14–5:10, the author highlights Jesus' connection to humanity—having suffered and endured trials as other people have, but also having been perfected by them as the "pioneer of salvation" (2:10; 5:8–9). Jesus' connection to the believers is strengthened by his claim of familial affiliation in Heb 2:10–13—he calls these "sons" (*hioi*, v. 10) "brothers" (*adelphoi*, vv. 11, 12) and "the children God has given me" (*ta paidia a edōken o theos*, v. 13). In Heb 5, familial overtones again surface, but this time as an explanation for Jesus' status as the high priest "according to the order of Melchizedek" (5:5). Rather than claiming the title for himself, Jesus is granted the title in accordance with his identity as God's Son. The author of Hebrews presents Jesus as the one addressed by God's words in Ps 2: "You are my son, today I have begotten you" (5:5). Having been "begotten" in this way, Jesus has superior standing in his Father's house (3:1–6); nevertheless, resonating with Heb 2, the author claims he "learned obedience" and became mature/perfect (*teleiōtheis*) through his suffering (5:7–10). As the ideal Son, he is the ideal priest, for priests' supplications gain traction out of their sincere reverence and submission to the heavenly *paterfamilias*. Furthermore, as the ideal, Jesus is the "cause" (*aitios*) for salvation of those who now *obey him* (5:9). His familial bond with humanity and his example of

---

40. Thompson, *Hebrews*, 119. See also Attridge, *Hebrews*, 157; Koester, *Hebrews*, 224–25; and Perry, "Making Fear Personal," 120–22.

41. Thompson, *Hebrews*, 17–20, 119–37.

obedience provide believers with all they need in order to become mature/perfect as well (5:9–10).

It is here, however, that our author pauses. Just as the audience's growth has been interrupted, so too is the author's teaching. Instead of continuing on to maturity/perfection like their brother, the ideal Son of the Father, these wayward siblings are reluctant to leave the nursery. It is not that their milk has been of poor quality; rather, it has been the foundation of their learning (6:1–2), their "taste" (*guesamenous*) of the "heavenly gift," and the "goodness of the *logos* of God" (6:4–5). Indeed, the familial motif highlighted in Heb 2 and 5 reinforces the quality of this milk, since the begetting and nourishment of these followers is aligned with that of Jesus, their brother. Moreover, because of this brother's obedience, his siblings now have access to their Father and should be able to decipher his *logos* of righteousness and be bold in their approach of him (5:13; 10:19–25). The begetting and milk they received should have enabled these followers to continue onward in imitation of Jesus' model. What is wrong is that they, much like Epictetus' targets, refuse to be weaned.

Yet, in language more harsh than that of Epictetus, whose false-men continue drinking milk when they no longer need it, the author of Hebrews writes that due to their "dullness," his audience still *requires* milk for sustenance (5:11–12).[42] As infant nourishment that has sustained them for *too long*, it has made this audience weak—soft and porous—and unable to withstand the trials in which they now find themselves. For this reason, they are unable to mature through suffering; because of their weakness, the suffering penetrates and deforms their development, risking apostasy (6:4–8). Instead of leaving his charges in the nursery, however, the author of Hebrews continues on, challenging his audience with his difficult *logos* in chapters 7–10 and forcing their "manhood." Either they will come to imitate the ideal men who have come before them—Jesus and Abraham—or they will experience their Father's wrath, disowned and left outside this newly formed *familia*.

First Peter, in contrast, addresses its audience as "infants" in a positive manner, calling them to yearn for milk rather than for their weaning. The access these "newborns" have to the "uncontaminated logical milk" (*ton logikon adolon gala*) is a mark of their rebirth into the divine family rather than evidence of stunted growth.[43] Like Hebrews, however, this

---

42. On the meanings of "dullness" (*nōthroi*), see Perry, "Making Fear Personal," 103–110.

43. The translation of *ton logikon adolon gala* is notoriously difficult (Jobes, "Got Milk," 1–14). Recognizing the connection between breast milk and the *logos* considered inherent to male semen, however, clarifies the transmission of character-forming *logos*

metaphor appears again in a larger context that uses procreation language to describe the audience's relationship with God as "father" (1:13–2:3). The author describes the audience's transition from an old way of life as a "new begetting" (*anagegennēmenoi*, 1:23). No longer are they to live according to their ignorant passions and "futile ways inherited from [their] fathers" (1:14, 18). Instead, they are to be shaped to reflect their new, heavenly Father: "You shall be holy, for I am holy" (1:16). According to 1 Peter, it is their new begetting, facilitated by the "precious blood of Christ" that makes such a reformation possible. With the patterning of the "imperishable seed" (*sporas . . . aphthartou*) itself reflecting the enduring and unchanging *logos* of God, the audience can "put away all evil (*kakian*)[44] and all guile (*dolon*) and hypocrisy and envy and all slander" (2:1)—they can come to reflect God, their Father, and become "obedient children" (1:14). As "newly born babes" (*artigennēta brephē*), their longing for the best milk—*ton logikon adolon gala*—continues their initial patterning. This milk, made orderly and rational by God *him*self, persists in the transmission of his *logos* to these children, so that they may "grow up into salvation" rather than deformed by vice (2:3).

The imagery in 1 Peter is particularly vivid, resonating with the various beliefs concerning conception, generation, and breast milk described above. The *absence* of a female presence in the text is perhaps surprising. Even though many translate *anagegennēmenoi* as "born anew," the context of "seed" (*sporas*) and *logos* (1:23), along with the description of God as "Father" (*patera*, 1:17), adds elements of "new begetting" described above as well. The audience, therefore, moves from begetting to birth and nursing without explicit description of a female either providing a womb or a breast. In this way, 1 Peter's portrait is similar to the milk metaphor used in Jewish literature—either Moses' description of God as "wet nurse" in Num 11:12, the Righteous Teacher's use of the metaphor in the Qumran Thanksgiving Psalms (1QHa 15.20–21; 17.35–36), or even depictions of "Abraham's bosom" (*kolpos*) in Luke 16:22 and beyond.[45] First Peter's milk imagery also connects to the utopia of Greco-Roman desire—that of reproducing children without need for women. In such a world, a man's seed would simply foster another image of himself: a perfect reflection of his masculine virtue (Euripides, *Med.* 573–75). It is this sort of male-pregnancy and nurture that Socrates describes to his pupil Theaetetus and again to Agathon in the *Sym-*

---

described here and by the larger context of 1 Pet 1–2.

44. *Kakos*, which means "evil" or "bad," is the opposite of *aretē*, or "excellence," the Greek equivalent to the Latin *virtus*.

45. Cherian, "Moses at Qumran," 352–61; O'Kane, "Bosom of Abraham," 489–93.

posium (Plato, *Theaet.* 148e–51d; ibid., *Symp.* 201d–12c). While women are needed for physical children, Socrates proclaims, it is men who produce truly "immortal" children when they bear virtue through philosophical *eros* (*Symp.* 212a). The milk of 1 Peter, however, is superior even to that described by Socrates: it is truly masculine and perfect because it flows from the divine Father alone, without interruption through a maternal or nurse figure or even male philosopher as conduit. In this way, 1 Peter's audience tastes (*egeusasthe*) that the Lord is good and so is made ready to suffer for the sake of future glory (2:3).[46]

The milk metaphors used in Hebrews and 1 Peter *are* different—one censuring those lingering in the nurse's lap and one urging their continued presence on *his* knee. Yet, by using the same image of "milk," they both enter into a similar ideological landscape—employing certain *topoi* and assumptions while subverting and ignoring others to drive home their agendas. For Hebrews, the encouragement is to move beyond "milk," to leave behind the malleable character of an infant lazy and lolling in the nursery, and to become "mature." For 1 Peter, the encouragement is to continue relying on the divine Father as the source for the audience's character, rather than on what they have known from their earthly "fathers" before. Like Hebrews' audience, however, they too are to "grow up" as reflections of their new Father and, therefore, as imitators of his ideal Son, Jesus Christ (1 Pet 2:21–25). The shaping these audiences have received through *this* milk is superior. It is the foundation that leads to correct growth. Free from vice, the audiences are made firm and impenetrable in the face of suffering and trials. Made into "men" in this way, they can endure and look forward to future glory with their Father.

Conclusion: A Metaphor's Implications

This chapter has focused on how understanding gender constructions, particularly those around the female body, motherhood, and breast milk, can aid the interpretation of milk metaphors in Hebrews and 1 Peter. Although often overlooked, ancient physiologies and gender expectations have much to bear on the New Testament, yet they often remain implicit, assumed, or tweaked rather than argued in depth. A better understanding of the beliefs surrounding breast milk, therefore, highlights the emphasis on character formation in Heb 5–6 and 1 Pet 1–2. Moreover, it demonstrates the ways in

---

46. Suffering is a constant theme in 1 Peter. The author constantly encourages believers to remain humble, blameless, and faithful in the midst of suffering and, in so doing, to imitate the example of Christ (1 Pet 1:6–7, 2:20–25; 3:8–4:4, 12–19; 5:8–11).

which such formation resonates with familial and procreative language in their larger contexts. Philip Tite's conclusion that an awareness of ancient nursing practices and assumptions around milk quality heightens the emphasis on the "moral" implications of 1 Peter is a helpful place to begin.[47] Indeed, his findings encourage us to dig more deeply into the broader gender and physiological constructions surrounding women and breast milk that fuel the moralizing of wet nurses, mothers, and their milk in ancient literature and imagery. Both Hebrews and 1 Peter persist in the assumption of their world that masculinity is equivalent to perfection and that to be perfectly masculine is to be divine. Thus, Hebrews uses a charge of effeminacy, not simply childishness, to push his audience toward the ideal "manhood" of Jesus. First Peter omits any female presence to tie his audience more intimately with the masculinity of the heavenly Father, by whom they have been begotten and are nursed. This superior patterning results in superior children who, as in Hebrews, are to imitate Christ in obedience through suffering so that they may "grow up" into their salvation, thus becoming truly "imperishable."

In the end, then, both Hebrews and 1 Peter use milk metaphors as a part of their rhetoric of manhood—namely, that their audiences should strive to imitate the manhood of Christ. In particular, they should be made firm and endure suffering without wavering in loyalty. To be sure, such a manhood *had* to be argued in Greco-Roman settings, since Jesus' life and death had all the appearances of effeminacy: he could neither protect himself nor his followers. By reshaping the narrative to present Jesus' sufferings as "manly," therefore, the authors of Hebrews and 1 Peter repeat similar efforts made by other New Testament authors hoping to encourage and affirm believers who were part of a Greco-Roman world entrenched in "hegemonic masculinity."[48] Casting Jesus' life in this light reframes the issue of suffering in a way that leaves space for masculine honor among the believers, both in conversation with and in contrast to the expectations of their Greco-Roman culture.

In so doing, however, the milk metaphor becomes one that—at least on the surface—has surprisingly little room for mothers, or for "women" in general, for that matter. Instead, it is the Father (*Pater*) who nurses his

---

47. Tite, "Nurslings," esp. 386–95.

48. Conway, *Behold the Man*, 11. Conway explores how Jesus' masculinity interfaces with Greco-Roman constructions of masculinity in the gospels, Pauline letters, and Revelation. She notes how Jesus' masculinity is affirmed and reshaped in order to encourage various audiences. For more conversations on masculinity in the New Testament, including ways in which it is upheld and subverted, see Moore and Anderson, *New Testament Masculinities*; and Wilson, *Unmanly Men*.

young—a metaphor for immortality that tries to move beyond the frailty the ancients associated with all things feminine. Yet, at their heart, milk metaphors do not let their audiences escape from the feminine entirely. The Father is not a like the male "nurse" (*nutritor* or *nutricus*) in a household who provides care but no milk.[49] He is, instead, a *Pater Nutrix*—a "wet nurse Father"—an identity that cannot help but combine images masculinity and femininity in a single, intimate vision. Just as Jesus' graphic death exposes his vulnerability and "effeminacy" in contrast to Greco-Roman manliness, milk together with the breast it implies likewise create feminine presence in the midst of masculine preoccupation.

In order to see the shocking beauty of this feminine-masculine combination, however, it is crucial to identify and name the gender assumptions that permeate New Testament texts and their contexts, lest we unconsciously continue their repetition. The New Testament writings—1 Peter and Hebrews among them—were written in a context that assumed masculine superiority and conflated this superiority with perfection as well as divinity. Knowing this assumption enables contemporary readers to hear the ways in which New Testament authors and writings repeat, reshape, and reconstruct gender identities as a part of their proclamation concerning the seemingly impossible person and work of Jesus of Nazareth. In spite of the fact that Jesus' death would have been interpreted by many as profoundly effeminate, Jesus is adamantly pronounced as God's Christ and Son. Moreover, his status as God's Son is actually *proven by* such a death.

As marginal groups in the midst of a dominant Roman society that spared no effort in affirming its own superiority and, therefore, "masculinity," the early Jesus-believers addressed in Hebrews and 1 Peter are encouraged to pursue a new sort of masculinity by imitating Jesus. Their former patterns of life in the Roman world are cast as "effeminate" in comparison to the new masculinity of Christ, who is proven a "man" from his choice to suffer out of faithfulness to the Father. Stepping into the complex matrix of ancient Roman gender identities and constructions causes us to also step back from our own contemporary assumptions. This process also compels us to step forward into a new space that affirms faithfulness to God as the ultimate ideal, regardless of the metaphorical (gender) categories employed. In this way, we can acknowledge the goodness of a so-called "feminine" image—the nurturing breast and milk provided—without needing to excise or limit the "female." Instead, we are invited to celebrate it as one more

---

49. See n36 above and Bradley's discussion of "foster-fathers," which is the common translation for the Latin *nutritor* or *nutricus*, in Bradley's *Discovering the Roman Family*.

revelatory image as we too grow in faithfulness to God. This is the goodness of the *Pater Nutrix*.

Bibliography

Arbel, Vita Daphna. *Forming Femininity in Antiquity: Eve, Gender, and Ideology in the Greek Life of Adam and Eve*. Oxford: Oxford University Press, 2012.

Attridge, Harold W. *Hebrews*. Hermeneia. Philadelphia: Fortress, 1989.

Bonfante, Larissa. "Nursing Mothers in Classical Art." In *Naked Truths: Women, Sexuality, and Gender in Classical Art and Archaeology*, edited by Ann Olga Kolosk-Ostrow and Claire L. Lyons, 174–95. London: Routledge, 1997.

Bradley, Keith R. *Discovering the Roman Family: Studies in Roman History*. Oxford: Oxford University Press, 1991.

Conway, Colleen M. *Behold the Man: Jesus and Greco-Roman Masculinities*. Oxford: Oxford University Press, 2008.

Corbeill, Anthony. *Nature Embodied: Gesture in Ancient Rome*. Princeton: Princeton University Press, 2004.

Dean Jones, Lesley. *Women's Bodies in Classical Greek Science*. Oxford: Oxford University Press, 2001.

Demand, Nancy. *Birth, Death, and Motherhood in Classical Greece*. Baltimore: John Hopkins University Press, 1994.

Dixon, Suzanne. *The Roman Mother*. London: Croom Helm, 1988.

Flemming, Rebecca. *Medicine and the Making of Roman Women: Gender, Nature, and Authority from Celsus to Galen*. Oxford: Oxford University Press, 2000.

Gleason, Maud W. *Making Men: Sophists and Self-Presentation in Ancient Rome*. Princeton: Princeton University Press, 1995.

Hemelrijk, Emily A. *Matrona Docta: Educated Women in the Roman Élite from Cornelia to Julia Domna*. London: Routledge, 1999.

Jobes, Karen. "Got Milk? Septuagint Psalm 33 and the Interpretation of 1 Peter 2:1–3." *Westminster Theological Journal* 63 (2002) 1–14.

King, Helen. *The Disease of Virgins: Green Sickness, Chlorosis and the Problems of Puberty*. London: Routledge, 2004.

———. *Hippocrates' Woman: Reading the Female Body in Ancient Greece*. London: Routledge, 1998.

Koester, Craig R. *Hebrews*. Anchor Bible 36. New York: Doubleday, 2001.

Laskaris, Julie. "Nursing Mothers in Greek and Roman Medicine." *American Journal of Archaeology* 112 (2008) 459–64.

Leftkowitz, Mary R., and Maureen B. Fant. *Women's Life in Greece and Rome: A Sourcebook in Translation*. 2nd ed. Baltimore: Johns Hopkins University Press, 1993.

McWilliam, Janette. "The Socialization of Roman Children." In *The Oxford Handbook of Childhood and Education in the Classical World*, edited by Judith Evans Grubbs et al., 264–85. Oxford: Oxford University Press, 2013.

Myers, Alicia D. "'In the Father's Bosom': Breastfeeding and Identity Formation in John's Gospel." *Catholic Biblical Quarterly* 77 (2014) 481–97.

Perry, Peter S. "Making Fear Personal: Hebrews 5.11–6.12 and the Argument from Shame." *Journal for the Study of the New Testament* 31 (2009) 99–125.

Richlin, Amy. "Pliny's Brassiere." In *Roman Sexualities*, edited by Judith P. Hallett and Marilyn B. Skinner, 197–220. Princeton: Princeton University Press, 1997.

Solevåg, Anna Rebecca. *Birthing Salvation: Gender and Class in Early Christian Childbearing Discourse*. Biblical Interpretation Series 121. Leiden: Brill, 2013.

Temkin, Owsei, trans. *Soranus' Gynecology*. Baltimore: Johns Hopkins University Press, 1956.

Thompson, James W. *Hebrews*. Paideia Commentaries on the New Testament. Grand Rapids: Baker, 2008.

Tite, Philip L. "Nurslings, Milk and Moral Development in the Greco-Roman Context: A Reappraisal of the Paraenetic Utilization of Metaphor in 1 Peter 2.1–3." *Journal for the Study of the New Testament* 31 (2009) 371–400.

Walters, Jonathan. "Invading the Roman Body: Manliness and Impenetrability in Roman Thought." In *Roman Sexualities*, edited by Judith P. Hallett and Marilyn B. Skinner, 29–43. Princeton: Princeton University Press, 1997.

Zeitlin, Froma I. *Playing the Other: Gender and Society in Classical Greek Literature*. Women and Culture in Society. Chicago: University of Chicago Press, 1996.

7

"As Long as It's Healthy"

Responses to Infanticide and Exposure in Early Christianity

LOUISE A. GOSBELL

Introduction

At the end of 2006, I became pregnant with my third daughter. From the moment we announced we were having another child, I was inundated with questions related to the baby's gender. Were we planning on finding out the sex of the baby? Were we hoping to have a boy this time around? Would we be disappointed if we had "another" girl? I found myself incredibly frustrated with this line of questioning. First, I was irritated by the suggestion that we would be disappointed if we had "another" girl. But more than this, I was frustrated with where this conversation always seemed to end up. When I would tell people that we chose not to find out the gender of our third child, people would often respond by saying, "Well, it doesn't matter if it's a boy or a girl, so long as it's healthy." Initially, I let the comment go. I would tell myself that people had good intentions and all they meant was that my baby would be loved either way. But as this conversation continued with startling predictability, I grew less and less tolerant and I found myself responding to people by saying, "Yes, because if it's not healthy, I'm planning on sending it back." The comment shocked people. Some people would try to laugh it off. Others were embarrassed and would fumble for words, insisting they didn't mean anything by it. Perhaps I could have been more polite and simply said, "Even if it's not healthy, I will love it anyway," but I didn't. What upset me was that at the heart of the statement was the implication that if the baby wasn't healthy, somehow he or she would be less valued or less welcomed than a healthy or "normal" baby. The statement seemed to imply that I would be disappointed with any baby that didn't meet society's high expectations of infant beauty and perfection. But what if the baby *wasn't* healthy or "perfect"? There is no possibility for exchange or refund. I can't trade it in for a healthier model or throw it away and start again. This is it. This is my baby, healthy or otherwise.

In this chapter I will consider this question concerning the birth of an unhealthy or impaired newborn and the practices of infanticide and exposure in response to such a birth. While infanticide and exposure have probably existed from time immemorial and are still considered commonplace in many developing countries, in this chapter I am focusing primarily on attitudes towards infanticide and exposure in the Greco-Roman world from the Classical period (ca. the fifth century BCE) through to the early Byzantine period (ca. fifth century CE), as well as looking at the attitudes of the early church in response to these practices. Following this historical assessment, I will address the implications of these practices on the modern eugenics movement and consider the proposal given by some medical professionals that parents, in consultation with their doctors, should be allowed to choose whether a child is worth raising if it has chronic health issues or significant physical impairments.

Infanticide and Exposure in Greco-Roman Antiquity

While abortion is considered to be the deliberate termination of a fetus during the pregnancy, infanticide and exposure are methods of dealing with a neonate sometime in the early stages after delivery. While numerous writers have conflated the issues of infanticide and exposure, recent scholarship in this field has emphasized the need to differentiate clearly between the two. Judith Evans-Grubbs suggests that even though exposure "quite often . . . did result in the child's death,"[1] the "intention and means might be quite different."[2] Exposure, therefore, according to Evans-Grubbs, is "the rejection of a neonate in the first week of life, before it was accepted into the family and undergone rituals of purification and naming."[3] Regarding exposure, she suggests that "both literary and legal sources indicate that from the archaic Greek period on . . . *expositio* was considered a viable means of

1. Evans-Grubbs, "Infant Exposure and Infanticide," 83.
2. Ibid.
3. Ibid.

ridding oneself of an unwanted infant."[4] Exposing a child meant "there was always the chance that the baby would be picked up and reared by someone else and could eventually be reclaimed by its original parent. Unrealistic as this scenario appears, it did occur."[5] Infanticide, on the other hand, by which the parents make a conscious decision to kill an unwanted infant, is much more rarely attested to in the ancient world.

While scholarship is splintered over the extent to which infanticide took place in the ancient world,[6] it is apparent from our ancient sources that "[e]xposure was widespread in the ancient world, where reliable means of preventing conception were not widely used and abortion was a dangerous undertaking for the mother."[7] The prevalence of exposure is reflected in the literature of the ancient world, and exposure featured as a popular plot device in numerous plays and novels. In addition, numerous well-known mythical personages were recorded as being exposed as infants, including Oedipus, the mythical Greek king of Thebes; Asclepius, the healing god; Poseidon, the god of the sea; and Remus and Romulus, the legendary founders of the city of Rome. In all of these cases, the exposed infants were found by another who chose to raise them. While it is certain that not all exposed infants would have survived, evidence from the ancient world indicates that there were certainly infants that did. While some exposed infants were raised as adopted children,[8] numerous others were collected for the sole purpose of becoming slaves.[9] Indeed, this occurrence was so common that the Roman legal writings are replete with cases of *expositi*—exposed infants—caught in disputations regarding their legal status. Under classical law, *expositi* retained the status they had at birth. This meant that even if an infant had been left exposed and raised as a slave, they could return to their original freeborn status if their parents or another member of the community could prove their identity.

According to our ancient sources, infanticide and exposure were enacted for numerous reasons. Some sources record that these practices were carried out in response to the parents' poverty or as a means of limiting

---

4. Ibid., "Hidden in Plain Sight," 293.
5. Ibid., "Church, State and Children," 119.
6. Harris, "Theoretical Possibility," 114–16.
7. Evans-Grubbs, "Infant Exposure," 83.
8. For numerous examples, see Boswell, "*Expositio* and *Oblatio*," 15f.

9. There are numerous examples of wet nurse contracts from Roman Egypt that attest to the extensiveness of this practice, whereby a wet nurse had to be employed in order to feed a newly-found infant. For examples, see Bradley, "Wet-Nursing at Rome," 201–29.

family size;[10] other texts refer to illegitimate or questionable parentage as the reason for exposure.[11] Recent scholarship has focused on the issue of infanticide and exposure enacted upon female neonates in the ancient world;[12] however, recent scholarship reveals an increasing interest in infanticide and exposure of infants born with obvious congenital malformations.[13]

While there are numerous references to infanticide and exposure in extant literature from the ancient world, the number of texts that specifically mention the infanticide or exposure of impaired or ill infants is rather limited. However, as Eleanor Scott notes, the way we interpret these texts has a direct impact on the arguments used by modern eugenicists who advocate for the right to kill a deformed infant even after birth.[14] One of the arguments made by ethicist Peter Singer in favor of the termination of "defective" infants after birth is that the practice was thought morally acceptable by our Greek and Roman predecessors, especially those considered superior moral thinkers, such as the Roman philosopher Seneca.[15] These great thinkers of the ancient world, he suggests, were unshackled by the dogma of the monotheistic faiths that presented a belief in the sanctity of human life.[16]

Many modern scholars writing on the issue of infanticide or exposure of infants often assume that all infants born with visible impairments in the ancient world would have been killed, or at the very least exposed, shortly after birth.[17] However, recently scholars like Martha L. Rose have questioned the extent to which these practices took place in Greco-Roman antiquity.[18] It is therefore worthwhile to briefly address some of the key Greek and Roman texts that refer specifically to either the infanticide or exposure of defective newborns.

10. E.g., Musonius Rufus, 15.

11. Augustus forbade his granddaughter Julia from raising her illegitimate child (Suetonius, *Aug.* 65.4).

12. Cf. Scott, "Unpicking a Myth."

13. Amundsen, "Medicine and the Birth," 50–69; Edwards, "Cultural Context of Deformity," 79–92; Scott, "Unpicking a Myth," 143–51.

14. Scott, "Unpicking a Myth," 146.

15. Singer, *Practical Ethics*, 153, refers to Seneca, *On Anger*, 1.15.2: "Mad dogs we knock on the head; the fierce and savage ox we slay; sickly sheep we put to the knife to keep them from infecting the flock; unnatural progeny we destroy; we drown even children who at birth are weakly and abnormal" (Lasore, LCL).

16. Singer, *Practical Ethics*, 154.

17. For example, Dixon states, "Exposure was the usual fate of deformed children and was taken for granted as a general means of family limitation" (Dixon, *Roman Family*, 122).

18. Rose, *Staff of Oedipus*, 35. Cf. Garland, *Eye of the Beholder*, 13–16.

Probably the most well known text referring to infanticide in the Greco-Roman world is Plutarch's *Lives*, in which he describes the Spartan practice of infanticide of deformed infants. According to Plutarch, those infants who were ill-born (that is, of low birth) and those who were deformed (*amorphon*) were allegedly thrown into a chasm at the foot of Mount Taygetus. However, while this text is often used as evidence for the widespread nature of infanticide in the ancient world,[19] archaeological evidence from the site does not support Plutarch's claims.[20] While archaeologists found numerous remains at the chasm, they "failed to establish the presence of infant or child bones."[21] This evidence suggests that while the site may have been used to deposit skeletal remains, they were not unwanted neonates but rather the remains of Spartan traitors and "those convicted of serious crimes."[22]

As with Plutarch's claims regarding Sparta, Dionysius of Halicarnassus (writing in the second century BCE) also speaks of a legal responsibility to dispose of the defective infant. However, in this case, the text speaks specifically of exposure (*ektithenai*) rather than infanticide. Dionysius attributes a law to Romulus—the founder of Rome who was himself a victim of exposure[23]—requiring all citizens to raise all their male children and the first-born of the female children, explaining that Romulus "forbade them to destroy any children under three years of age unless they were maimed (*anapēron*) or monstrous (*teras*) from their very birth."[24] While scholars doubt the historical accuracy of this law,[25] in the very least the text probably does still reflect "contemporary (Augustan) concerns about child-rearing and perhaps also social practices."[26]

Dionysius' description of infants as monstrous (*teras*) is significant. While a "maimed" infant might refer to a neonate with any number of physical anomalies,[27] the language of *terata*, or monstrous births, focuses

---

19. Brennan, for example, refers to Plutarch's text as "conclusive" evidence for infanticide in Sparta (Brennan, "Evidence of Infanticide and Exposure," 100).

20. Pitsios, "Ancient Sparta," 15.

21. Ibid.

22. Ibid.

23. Livy, *History of Rome*, 1.4.

24. Ibid., 2.15.2. Cf. Cicero, *Laws*, 3.8.19: "Quickly kill . . . a dreadfully deformed child."

25. Evans-Grubbs, "Infant Exposure and Infanticide," 90. Cf. Allély "Les Enfants Malformés," 128.

26. Evans-Grubbs, "Infant Exposure and Infanticide," 90.

27. Aristotle uses the same word to describe a baby being born with the head of a monkey (Aristotle, *Gen. an.* 769b) as he does in describing "the deformity of baldness"

Dionysius' discussion on births of a portentous significance. *Terata* were considered to be harbingers of evil, especially in the Roman world, and thus it was considered necessary for such monstrous births to be expiated for the sake of the community. Livy, in his extensive list of portentous signs, describes not only those infants born with physical deformities but also those born with any unusual characteristics. Examples include the birth of an infant with teeth,[28] the birth of an infant "as large as a four-year-old,"[29] those born of indeterminate sex[30] as well as the birth of twins or other multiple births.[31] In this sense, the need to "destroy" the infant was less about whether the child would be an economic burden on its family or whether it would be unable to contribute to the greater good, and more about keeping the city safe from the gods' impending wrath.[32]

A number of other texts are often used to confirm the practices of killing or exposing defective newborns in the Greco-Roman world. Plato, for example, in his *Republic*, states that the "offspring of the inferior" and those who are "born defective (*anapēron*), they will properly dispose of them in secret, so that no one will know what has become of them."[33] While many argue that Plato's reference to disposing of infants in secret is a euphemism for infanticide,[34] this interpretation seems less likely when the text is read in connection with Plato's additional comments on this topic in *Timaeus*.[35] Here, Plato summaries his previous argument on limiting the breeding of the inferior and adds that the offspring of the bad (*kakōn*) should be "secretly dispersed among the inferior citizens."[36] He goes on to say that as the children grow, they should be re-examined to ascertain their abilities with the possibility they might be brought back again. When these texts are read together, Plato does not seem to be endorsing the killing of defective newborns but rather recommending some form of abandonment or exposure whereby a defective newborn is raised away from the general populace.

(ibid., 784A). Cf. Rose, *Staff of Oedipus*, 33.

28. Livy, *History of Rome*, 41.21.12.
29. Ibid., 27.37.5.
30. Ibid., 39.22.5. For more on this, see Brisson, *Sexual Ambivalence*.
31. Obsequens, *De Prodigiis*, 14. For more on multiple births, see Dasen, "Multiple Births."
32. Allély, "Les Enfants Malformés," 128.
33. Plato, *Resp.* 460c (Shorey, LCL).
34. Delcourt, *Stérilités mystérieuses*, 42–43.
35. Cf. Patterson, "Not Worth the Rearing," 106.
36. Plato, *Timaeus*, 19a (Jowett, LCL).

However, the difficulty with interpreting Plato's proposal, along with a similar recommendation made by Aristotle,[37] is the suggestion that these texts are not actually reflective of current practice but rather are part of the authors' vision of a future utopia. In this sense, Plato and Aristotle are only discussing a hypothetical "highly-regulated utopian state."[38] Indeed, Robert Garland suggests that "[t]he fact that Aristotle found it necessary to recommend that there should be a law 'to prevent the rearing of deformed children' . . . demonstrates that some parents were inclined . . . to rear them."[39]

Indeed, in her monograph on disability in ancient Greece, Martha L. Rose suggests that the only text that appears to have instructions meant for "practical application" is that of the second-century medical writer Soranus.[40] In a section entitled "How to Tell the Newborn That Is Worth Rearing," Soranus writes:

> the infant which is suited by nature for rearing will be distinguished by the fact that . . . when put on the earth it immediately cries with proper vigour; for one that lives for some time without crying, or cries but weakly, is suspected of behaving so on account of some unfavourable condition. Also by the fact that it is perfect in all its parts, members and senses . . . that the natural functions of every [member] are neither sluggish nor weak . . . by conditions contrary to those mentioned, the infant not worth rearing is recognised.[41]

In regards to all of these texts and others referring to the infanticide or exposure of defective newborns, we are left with a number of uncertainties. First, in each of these examples, the vocabulary used in relation to the actual "deformity" of the infants is "frustratingly imprecise."[42] This makes it difficult to ascertain the extent to which a baby would have needed to be visibly deformed to be considered not worth rearing. Indeed, while in the modern world we have complicated medical systems for measuring the physical responsiveness of a newborn such as the Apgar test,[43] in antiquity there would only have been a very small number of conditions that would have been

---

37. Aristotle, *Pol.* 1335b 19–21.

38. Rose, *Staff of Oedipus*, 34; cf. Huys, "Spartan Practice," 47.

39 Garland, *Eye of the Beholder*, 15; Evans-Grubbs, "Infant Exposure and Infanticide," 88; Huys, "Spartan Practice," 62; Scott, "Unpicking a Myth," 147.

40. Rose, *Staff of Oedipus*, 34.

41. Soranus, *Gyn.* 2.10 (Temkin).

42. Amundsen, "Medicine and the Birth," 11.

43. The Apgar test is "used to assess the physical condition of newborns" (Slee et al., *Child, Adolescent and Family Development*, 130).

detectable within the first week of life. As a result, it would only have been in the most obvious cases of deformity that such a condition would have been noticed early and called into question.

In addition to the ambiguity of the language used, the texts are also unclear about who, if anyone, enforced such directives. While many secondary sources indicate that infanticide and exposure were enacted at the directive of the *paterfamilias*, or male head of the household, the ancient sources themselves seem to also place an emphasis on the role of the midwife. Indeed, Evans Grubbs suggests that the "midwife would be the likely person to dispose of the body of an infant who had died at or shortly after birth and might also be the one to take an unwanted infant and expose it or hand it over to someone who wanted a child."[44] In either case, Cynthia Patterson suggests that "[j]ust how carefully a newborn child was examined and with what care the decision as to its physical viability was made would surely have depended in part on just how much the child was wanted."[45]

Finally, paleopathological studies of skeletons from the ancient world indicate that despite the recommendations for the disposal of infants with congenital deformities, some parents chose to raise their children anyway. Numerous adult skeletons have been unearthed that display the effects of substantial congenital conditions that would have been noticeable at birth, such as various types of spinal deformation.[46] In addition, the medical writings of the Hippocratic school indicate methods of treatment existed for infants and adults who had congenital dislocations of the hip, ankle, and wrist, all of which would have been apparent at birth.[47] This signals that at least some parents chose to raise their infants with congenital anomalies regardless of the prevailing belief of Greco-Roman philosophers that deformed infants should be disposed of.

Despite the fact that there is less clarity in these texts than modern writers have allowed for, what we do know is that exposure—and to a far lesser extent infanticide—did take place throughout Greco-Roman antiquity. While there is no way to determine the extent to which these practices took place, we can be certain there were numerous factors involved in a family's decision to kill or expose their infant(s). We certainly cannot assume this was an easy decision for any parent, with many probably opting to keep their deformed child rather than kill or expose it.

---

44. Evans-Grubbs, "Infant Exposure and Infanticide," 85.
45. Ibid.
46. See Grmek, *Diseases in the Ancient Greek World*, 69–70.
47. Hippocrates, *Joints*, 55.

The Response of Early Christianity

The writings of the early church were certainly not the first to condemn the practices of infanticide and exposure in the Greco-Roman world. Tacitus recalls that the Jews were known throughout the Empire because, unlike their pagan neighbors, they did not participate in infanticide and exposure.[48] Jewish writers such as Josephus and Philo of Alexandria openly expressed abhorrence at the practices of infanticide and exposure as well as abortion, condemning them all as barbarous acts.[49] For Philo, it was not only infanticide but also exposure that resulted in the gruesomeness of such infant deaths: "For all the beasts that feed on human flesh visit the spot [where the child has been exposed] and feast unhindered on the infants."[50] In addition to this, even some Stoic philosophers, such as Musonius Rufus in the first century CE, spoke out against the practices, condemning those who expose their "later-born offspring in order that those born earlier may inherit greater wealth."[51]

While the New Testament is silent on the issues of infanticide and exposure,[52] the writings of the early church are replete with condemnations of Greco-Roman practices that they felt stood in contradistinction to the values of the early Christians. These included gladiatorial battles, public executions, and abortion, as well as infanticide and exposure.[53] Indeed, their opposition was so vehement that they labeled not only infanticide but also exposure and even abortion as "parricide."[54] Parricide was a term that was known and used in the Greco-Roman world to refer to the killing of a close relative, but it was not a term usually used in connection with the death of an infant.[55] The early Christians, however, considered "conception, gestation, birth, and nurture as a continuous process"[56] and therefore considered the termination of life at any point through this process as an act of murder. As a result, many of the early Christian texts openly condemned infanticide, exposure, and abortion. The *Didache*, for example, which is a

---

48. Tacitus, *Hist.* 5.5.3.

49. Philo, *Spec.* 3.110–119; Josephus, *Ag. Ap.* 1.60, 2.202; *Sibylline Oracles*, 2.280–282.

50. Philo, *Spec. Leg.* 3.115; Pseudo-Phocylides, *Sentences*, 184–85.

51. Cf. Scott, "Unpicking a Myth."

52. For the possibility that Acts 15:20 is a reference to infanticide, see Instone-Brewer, "Infanticide and the Apostolic Decree of Acts 15."

53. E.g., Athenagoras, *Legatio*, 35.1.

54. Ferngren, "Status of the Defective Newborn," 49.

55. Ibid.

56. Ibid.

Christian treatise dated from the late first to the early second century, states, "There are two ways—the way of life and the way of death, and the difference between these two ways is great. Therefore, do not murder a child by abortion or kill a newborn infant."[57] Other texts, such as the Apocalypse of Peter[58] and the *Ecologae Propheticae* of Clement of Alexandria,[59] make mention of the eternal punishment for those who kill their children through abortion, infanticide, or exposure.

A number of the Christian apologists from the second century onwards also refer to the practices of infanticide and exposure. Lactantius, for example, who wrote in the late third to early fourth century CE and served as advisor to Emperor Constantine, spoke specifically about the plight of exposed infants by stating, "Can those persons be considered innocent who expose their offspring as prey for dogs? As far as their participation is concerned, they have killed them in a more cruel manner than if they had strangled them."[60] Lactantius' description here expresses a view common amongst the Christian apologists: either an *expositi* would die, perhaps as fodder for dogs as Lactantius states, or they would become slaves, possibly prostitutes, for the rest of their days.[61]

Throughout the texts of the early church, no specific mention is made of the health of the infant in regards to infanticide or exposure until the work of Augustine. In his early fifth-century treatise *City of God*, Augustine states that every human being, regardless of any "peculiar . . . power, part, or quality of his nature," is part of God's good and diverse creation.[62] In other works, Augustine states that God ordains the life of all infants who are born so that all life, "irrespective of the circumstances of their conception or their physical or mental condition," should be preserved and protected.[63] Augustine likewise suggests that while people might be offended by the "deformity" of an individual human being, they are still a vital component of God's creation and part of his "design."[64] As Nicole Kelley suggests, "By arguing that even seemingly imperfect bodies reveal their Creator's benevolence and infallibility, Augustine invites his Christian readers to view deformed

---

57. *Didache* 2.2.
58. *Apocalypse of Peter* 8.10.
59. Clement of Alexandria, *Ecologae Propheticae*, 41, 48–49.
60. Lactantius, *Divine Inst.* 7.187; cf. Tertullian, *Apol.* 1.15.
61. Lacanius, *Divine Inst.* 6.20; Clement of Alexandria, *Paed.* 3.3–4; Justin Martyr, *First Apology*, 27.
62. Augustine, *City of God*, 16.8.
63. Ferngren, "Status of Defective Newborns," 52.
64. Augustine, *City of God*, 16.8.

individuals, including deformed children, as intentional and valuable parts of God's creation."[65]

However, Augustine is unique in his presentation of the inherent value of deformed infants, as we have no evidence for other discussions regarding this issue within the first five centuries of the Common Era. Despite this, "concern for the welfare [of deformed infants] may be surmised" from a number of factors.[66] First, as already discussed, the early church openly condemned the practices of infanticide and exposure, despite the fact it was a socially acceptable practice throughout the Greco-Roman world. While they did not specifically address the plight of infants with physical deformities, they did vehemently oppose the general practices of infanticide and exposure based on the belief that God created all people in his image, and thus each human is imbued with an inherent value. In comparison to the Greco-Roman world, which generally considered one's worth to be based on the value of the contribution one could make to the greater community, the early Christians promoted the idea of inherent value that came from being created in the image of God.[67] Thus, as Gary B. Ferngren notes, "In their blanket condemnation of exposure the Christians implicitly affirmed the right of even the defective to live."[68]

Secondly, the church responded to the practices of infanticide and exposure through their care of exposed infants. From the earliest days of the Christian church, Christians collected funds for distribution to the poor and sick. As part of their concern for the vulnerable members in their community, the early Christians acted to protect exposed infants. This was done through the development of hospitals with designated sections for foundlings and through the later development of orphanages that would house and care for foundlings as well as for infants whose parents had died. Indeed, the Christian church gained such a reputation for their care of exposed infants that churches became the established site for abandoning infants.[69] In addition, numerous individuals within the early church are also remembered by the church fathers for personally adopting exposed infants.[70]

Finally, the response of the early church can also be seen from a political and legal perspective: "Imperial law before Constantine neither

---

65. Kelley, "Deformed Child," 207–208.
66. Ferngren, "Status of Defective Newborns," 53.
67. Amundsen, "Medicine and the Birth," 54.
68. Ferngren, "Status of Defective Newborns," 53.
69. Cf. Corbier, "Child Exposure," 64.
70. Augustine, *Epistles*, 98.6.

penalized nor promoted the abandonment of newborn infants."[71] In 331 CE, the Christian Roman emperor Constantine revoked the ruling that allowed exposed infants to be reclaimed by their parents as a means of deterring those who were exposing their infants and reclaiming them at a later stage. However, exposure continued to be an issue throughout the empire and in 374 CE. Constantine's successor, Valentinian I, passed down the first law requiring parents to rear their children. Valentinian I also decreed that the killing of an infant was a capital offence.[72] Eventually, in 529 CE, another Christian Roman emperor, Justinian I, "overturned all previous regulations on the status of *expositi*. Henceforth, all abandoned infants, whatever their status at birth, were to be considered freeborn"[73] and could no longer be kept as slaves.

Conclusion

Through this brief historical analysis, it has been noted that infanticide—and to a greater degree, exposure—were common practices throughout the Greco-Roman world. While there were numerous reasons a parent might have chosen to kill or expose an infant, at least one reason may have been as a response to the health status of the infant. As a means of countering the wide-scale impact of infanticide and exposure on the community, the early church responded by openly condemning the practices as well as by acting with benevolence towards the victims. In a major change of political and legal policy, Christian Roman emperors also altered the legislation regarding infanticide and exposure. No longer were the practices sanctioned by the state. Instead, they were discouraged and eventually outlawed. The basis of these actions was a belief that all life possessed inherent value because it is representative of the image of God; this view stood in opposition to the Greco-Roman belief that one's potential for worth was based on personal utility and ability to contribute to society.

Some modern eugenicists see merit in the Greco-Roman system for assessing neonates in terms of their potentiality. These modern eugenicists have proposed that there should be an interim period after birth prior to declaring the neonate an actual "person," similar to the view expressed in the Greco-Roman literature. This delay would allow time to assess the infant's "genetic endowments" so that "if it fails [this assessment] then it forfeits its

---

71. Evans-Grubbs, "Church, State and Children," 120.
72. *Cod. Theod.* 9.14.1.
73. Evans-Grubbs, "Church, State, Children," 129.

right to live."[74] Medical professionals, in consultation with parents, could thus choose to let the infant die, "sav[ing] a lot of misery and suffering."[75] Advocates of this view state that strictly speaking this should not even be classified as infanticide but as "after-birth abortion,"[76] because it is only taking away a life that is "comparable to that of a fetus," not someone with the "moral status" of an actual child.[77]

Peter Singer suggests the merit of the Greco-Roman ideal is that under that system, "deformed or weak infants" were killed in order to avoid "all the problems [such an infant] might bring."[78] However, as Eleanor Scott has noted, "Peter Singer's ideas are predicated on a fundamental misunderstanding of the role of infanticide in the past."[79] She suggests that infanticide primarily served as a means of contraception in a world where abortion was potentially dangerous.[80] In this sense, Scott sees the primary motivating factor behind infanticide and exposure in the ancient world as an issue of access to contraception rather than a desire to improve the human stock. However, even in those texts that do express eugenic aims, such as the utopic ideals of Plato and Aristotle, it is by no means apparent that either author is advocating infanticide. Aristotle speaks specifically of exposing the deformed infant, not killing it, while Plato recommends that deformed infants should be "secreted away" but later reassessed in terms of their own individual merit and potential contribution to the community. In relation to the small number of texts that do address infanticide more specifically, not only are there issues regarding historical accuracy, but also the fundamental motivation is based not on eugenics but rather on a belief that "monstrous" births were portentous. The motivation to kill was not focused on the infant being a burden to its family or the greater community—which is Singer's assumption—but rather on protecting the people from divine displeasure.

In addition to this, there is a general issue with terminology used throughout our ancient sources. The language surrounding deformity is vague at best and gives us no real indication of what kind of conditions the ancients considered to be severe enough to contemplate infanticide or exposure. Indeed, in the texts that do refer more specifically to the disposal

---

74. Dr. Francis Crick, co-discoverer of the structure of DNA, as cited in Mackellar and Bechtel, *Ethics of the New Eugenics*, 229.

75. Dr. James D. Watson, co-discoverer of the structure of DNA, as cited in Mackellar and Bechtel, *Ethics of the New Eugenics*, 229.

76. Giubilini et al., "After-birth Abortion," 1.

77. Ibid., 2.

78. Singer, *Practical Ethics*, 75.

79. Scott, "Unpicking a Myth," 149.

80. Ibid.

of "monstrous" infants, the conditions described are as diverse as babies born with teeth to multiple births, neither of which would likely be deemed "monstrous" by modern standards. The fundamental flaw in Singer's reasoning is that what is considered "monstrous" or "deformed" shifts from culture to culture and age to age; there is no fixed ideal of beauty or "deformity" that allows us to directly compare modern motivations and ideals to those of the ancient Greco-Roman community.

The one commonality between the views of the early church and that of the modern-day eugenics movement is the belief that the moral value of the fetus in utero and the delivered neonate are identical. Advocates of the "after-birth abortion" suggest it is not "plausible to think that there is any moral change that occurs during the journey down the birth canal,"[81] and therefore to advocate for "after-birth abortion" should be no different from advocating abortion.[82] The point of departure between the early church and these members of the eugenics movement is, of course, what value should be ascribed to this life. Some bioethicists suggest that neither during the pregnancy nor in the early stages of life outside the womb can a fetus be considered a "person" and further that the potential for future "personhood" is not enough to consider the life of a fetus or neonate as inviolable. As they see it, "[m]erely being human is not in itself a reason for ascribing someone a right to life."[83]

The view of the early church was likewise that the status of a fetus and neonate are identical. Second-century Christian apologist Athenagoras wrote that "the same man cannot regard that which is in the womb as a living being and for that reason an object of God's concern and then murder it when it comes into light."[84] For the writers of the early church, abortion and infanticide were equally repugnant because at each stage of development, the fetus or infant is more than just a potential for personhood and, in fact, already possesses intrinsic value as a unique and valuable member of humanity. The belief that God had created all people in his image meant that each infant, irrespective of his or her physical or intellectual capabilities, constituted a life that should be preserved and protected.

In the introduction to this chapter, I recalled my experiences of my pregnancy with my third daughter. In declaring I would "return" an imperfect baby, I was, of course, being ironic. It was my intention to express that irrespective of chronic health issues or physical impairments, my child

---

81. John Harris, cited in Glover, "Human Life and Twisted Logic," n.p.
82. Giubilini et al., "After-birth Abortion."
83. Ibid., 2.
84. Athenagoras, *Leg.* 35.6.

was wanted, loved, and valuable. However, while people were shocked at my comments that I would "send back" an infant that didn't meet societal expectations, the reality is—with increasing technological advances and a growing movement of medical professionals who consider "after-birth" abortion a viable option for genetically "deformed" infants—it is possible that in the not-too-distant future such an option may indeed be available. Indeed, pressure on parents, especially mothers, is mounting, with increasing expectations that the power to give birth to a "normal" child rests primarily with the mother. Women are encouraged to take folic acid supplements even prior to becoming pregnant to decrease the risk of giving birth to a child with spinal bifida. Increasingly, pregnant women have been directed to avoid smoking and alcohol during pregnancy as well as to limit caffeine intake and the consumption of soft cheeses and other foods with the potential to cause bacterial infections that could drastically impact the health of the fetus. As the pregnancy continues, the expectant mother is pressured to also agree to various scans and possibly other procedures in order to ascertain the health and viability of the fetus. Such tests are deemed especially important for expectant mothers over the age of thirty-five.

This pressure on mothers to birth only "normal," healthy neonates often comes from medical professionals, with growing numbers of obstetricians pushing for mothers to become financially liable for their infants' health needs, forfeiting any government subsidies toward the child's health costs if they knowingly give birth to an infant with some form of disability. However, this pressure on mothers is also growing in the general populace. I met a woman recently who has a five-year-old daughter with Down Syndrome. I was stunned to hear how many times she has found herself being abused in the streets by strangers with comments such as "There are tests available so children *like that* don't have to be born." In this perspective, it is the responsibility of the mother to ensure they bear only infants who will not become a "burden" on our society. If, however, such an infant is born, it is occasionally deemed the responsibility of medical professionals, but most often the blame resides wholly with the mother.

Ultimately, it has been the aim of this chapter to address the outcomes for those infants born with "defects" or disability. While the issues raised in this chapter occasionally dovetail with those on abortion, I have deliberately chosen to address only the issues of exposure, infanticide, and "after-birth" abortion" here. In our assessment of the ancient world we considered that while the prevailing view of philosophers and medical professionals may have been that "defective" infants were not worth rearing, the response of contemporary Jewish and Christian faith communities was to uphold the sanctity of all human life on the basis of the *imago Dei*. Thus, in response to the various ethical issues raised by the possibility of "after-birth abortions" in the modern world, we might well ask what response modern faith communities might have. Will it be to continue to advocate for the value of all human life in the belief that all people are made in the image of God? Or will faith communities become susceptible to prevailing medical views that suggest life has no inherent value but is only worthwhile in terms of an infant's measurable potential for physical ability, resistance to health issues, autonomy, or ability to contribute to society? How much do statements such as "It doesn't matter if it is a boy or a girl, so long as it's healthy" from those within faith communities reveal the pervasiveness of the belief that human value is something to be achieved through physical and intellectual potential rather than something that is imbued? How much will pressures from medical professionals impact a mother's right to choose to *keep* rather than to *terminate* the life of a "defective" neonate? While these things will inevitably be revealed with time, hopefully, as we ponder the consequences of these medical advancements, we will continue to assess the role faith communities already play in the lives of those born with disability and the mothers and families who support them. While theological interest in the area of disability is certainly growing, many faith communities are still sorely behind the secular world in their inclusion of people with disability. Many older church buildings simply cannot be accessed by wheelchairs. Others with disability cannot read the small type on our Powerpoint slides or are unable to hear the sermons because there is no hearing loop for people with hearing aides. If we take seriously our belief that all life is valuable because we are each made in God's image, then we must also take seriously our commitment to shaping our faith communities as places of belonging for all people.

Bibliography

Alléry, A. "Les Enfants malformés et considérés comme prodigia à Rome et en Italie sous la République." *Revue des Études Anciennes* 105 (2003) 127–56.

Amundsen, D. W. "Medicine and the Birth of Defective Children: Approaches of the Ancient World." In *Euthanasia and the Newborn: Conflicts Regarding Saving Lives*, edited by R. C. McMillan et al., 50–69. Dordrecht, the Netherlands: Reidel, 1987.

Boswell, J. "*Expositio* and *Oblatio*: The Abandonment of Children and the Ancient and Medieval Family." *American History Review* 89 (1984) 10–33.

Brennan, K. "Evidence of Infanticide and Exposure in Antiquity: Tolerated Social Practice, Uncontrolled Phenomenon or Regulated Custom?" *University College Dublin Law Review* 2 (2002) 92–119.

Brisson, L. *Sexual Ambivalence: Androgyny and Hermaphroditism in Graeco-Roman Antiquity*. Translated by J. Lloyd. Berkeley: University of California Press, 2002.

Corbier, M. "Child Exposure and Abandonment." In *Childhood, Class and Kin in the Roman World*, edited by S. Dixon, 52–73. London: Routledge, 2001.

Dasen, V. "Multiple Births in Graeco-Roman Antiquity." *Oxford Journal of Archaeology* 16 (1997) 49–63.

Delcourt, M. *Stérilités Mystérieuses et Naissances Maléfiques dans l'Antiquité Classique*. Bibliothèque de la Faculté de Philosophie et Lettres de L'université de Liège 83. Paris: Librairie Droz, 1938.

Dixon, S. *The Roman Family*. Baltimore: Johns Hopkins University Press, 1992.

Evans Grubbs, J. "Church, State and Children: Christian and Imperial Attitudes toward Infant Exposure in Late Antiquity." In *The Power of Religion in Late Antiquity*, edited by A. Cain et al., 119–31. Surrey, UK: Ashgate, 2009.

———. "Hidden in Plain Sight: *Expositi* in the Community." In *Children, Memory, and Family Identity in Roman Culture*, edited by V. Dasen et al., 293–310. Oxford: Oxford University Press, 2010.

———. "Infant Exposure and Infanticide." In *The Oxford Handbook of Childhood and Education in the Classical World*, edited by J. Evans-Grubbs et al., 62–82. Oxford: Oxford University Press, 2013.

Ferngren, G. B. "The *Imago Dei* and the Sanctity of Life: The Origins of an Idea." In *Euthanasia and the Newborn: Conflicts Regarding Saving Lives*, edited by R. C. McMillan et al., 23–45. Dordrecht, the Netherlands: Reidel, 1987.

———. "The Status of Defective Newborns from Late Antiquity to the Reformation." In *Euthanasia and the Newborn: Conflicts Regarding Saving Lives*, edited by R. C. McMillanet al., 47–64. Dordrecht, the Netherlands: Reidel, 1987.

Garland, R. *The Eye of the Beholder: Deformity and Disability in the Graeco-Roman World*. 2nd ed. London: Duckworth, 2010.

Glover, Stephen. "Human Life and Twisted Logic." *Daily Mail*. April 29, 2004. Accessed June 20, 2014. http://www.dailymail.co.uk/columnists/article-228985/Human-life-twisted-logic.html.

Grmek, M. D. *Diseases in the Ancient Greek World*. Translated by M. Muellner and L. Muellner. Baltimore: Johns Hopkins University Press, 1989.

Giubilini, A., and F. Minerva. "After-birth Abortion: Why Should the Baby Live?" *Journal of Medical Ethics* (2012) doi:10.1136/medethics-2011-100411.

Harris, W.V. "The Theoretical Possibility of Extensive Infanticide in the Graeco-Roman World," *The Classical Quarterly* 32 (1982) 114–16.

Huys, M. "The Spartan Practice of Selective Infanticide and its Parallels in Ancient Utopian Tradition." *Ancient Society* 27 (1996) 47–74.

Kelley, N. "The Deformed Child in Ancient Christianity." In *Children in Ancient Christianity*, edited by C. B. Horn et al., 199–225. Tübingen: Mohr Siebeck, 2009.

Mackellar, C., and C. Betchel. *Ethics of the New Eugenics*. Oxford: Berghahn, 2014.

Patterson, C. "'Not Worth the Rearing': The Causes of Infant Exposure in Ancient Greece." *Transactions of the American Philological Association* 115 (1985) 103–123.

Pitsios, T. K. "Ancient Sparta–Research Program of Keadas Cavern." *Bulletin der Schweizerischen Gesellschaft für Anthropologie* 16 (2010) 13–22.

Rose, M. L. *The Staff of Oedipus: Transforming Disability in Ancient Greece*. Ann Arbor: University of Michigan Press, 2003.

Scott, E. "Unpicking a Myth: The Infanticide of Female and Disabled Infants in Antiquity." In *TRAC 2000: Proceedings of the Tenth Annual Theoretical Roman*

Archaeology Conference, London 2000, edited by G. Davies et al., 143–51. Oxford: Oxbow, 2001.

Singer, P. *Practical Ethics*. 3rd ed. Cambridge: Cambridge University Press, 2011.

Slee, P. T., M. Campbell, and B. Spears. *Child, Adolescent and Family Development*. 3rd ed. New York: Cambridge University Press, 2012.

Part III

Christian Theology and Spirituality and Motherhood

8

Matrescence and the Paschal Mystery

A Rahnerian Reflection on the Death and Rebirth Experiences of Mothering Infants

CRISTINA LLEDO GOMEZ

The birth of a child can be an experience of death as well as an invitation into new life for a first-time mother. Contemporary western lifestyles and expectations often leave women unprepared for the dramatic changes motherhood brings, particularly for those women who choose to stay at home as full-time mothers. Often, sacrifices such as putting one's career and social life on hold, along with the experiences of monotony, exhaustion, social invisibility, and isolation have never been contemplated, let alone prepared for. Furthermore, the difficulties of the first few months of a baby's life and the required redefinition of a mother's self-identity create a series of crises for her. These crises are ongoing as a mother continues to redefine herself at different stages of her child's life.

This chapter explores the idea that motherhood is an invitation to engage with the paschal mystery and can thus be a salvific experience in the lives of women. This is of even greater significance for a Christian mother who can explicitly name the experience as her own sharing in the paschal event of Jesus. This chapter will focus on crisis moments of motherhood in a contemporary western context, exploring particularly the issues raised upon first becoming a mother and in the initial years of mothering.

The paschal mystery is at the heart of the Christian faith. It is celebrated in every liturgical gathering of the people of God. It is highlighted every year during the Easter Triduum. It underpins all the sacraments, feasts, and seasons of the church's year. From Baptism to the Anointing of the Sick, from the Annunciation to the Triumph of the Cross, from Advent to Lent, it is the paschal mystery that is being celebrated. Yet while it is at the heart of Christianity, for some Christians, the paschal mystery can seem distant and unconnected to their daily lives. This can be true, moreover, for mothers who consider the paschal mystery as an idealistic notion in contrast to dealing with the practical realities and difficulties of the everyday.

The Catechism of the Catholic Church suggests otherwise.[1] The Catholic Church says that while one encounters the paschal mystery explicitly in the liturgy, this mystery can also be encountered implicitly in daily life.[2] Karl Rahner's theology of grace develops this further by saying that people do the will of God whenever they pursue the truth and show commitment and love in their daily duties, even without having an explicit faith assent to Jesus.[3] In this, they are saved.[4]

Employing Rahner's theology of grace, which explains that in the midst of human experience God's grace and salvation may be found, this chapter begins with the naming of the joys (the resurrection moments) and sorrows (crosses and deaths) of early motherhood. Rahner's thoughts on

---

1. Catechism of the Catholic Church, §1260.

2. Paul VI, *Gaudium et Spes*, §22.

3. See Karl Rahner's "Anonymous Christians." While I am a Christian mother reflecting on the Christian concept of the paschal mystery, I am strongly conscious of the salvific effect motherhood can have in the lives of non-Christian mothers too. This is why I propose that the saving grace offered through the experience of the paschal mystery via motherhood can be available to all mothers, whether they are Christian or not. Following on from Rahner's theology of grace, one can conclude that all mothers are invited to undertake a lived experience of the paschal mystery—whether it is explicitly acknowledged or not—whenever they undergo the difficulties of motherhood and rise from these difficulties to become more mature, compassionate, life-affirming, life-giving, other-centered, and forgiving people, as exemplified by Jesus in the journey through his passion and death to the resurrection.

4. I do not intend to suggest that a mother who undergoes an experience of the paschal mystery will ultimately present us with an idealized picture of motherhood. Such a portrait of idealized motherhood has already been developed in the cult of the Virgin Mary. Ironically, this high Mariology effectively removes from the mother of Jesus her human nature, making her a model impossible to live up to. Mary is imagined as a paragon of womanly virtue, a sinless virgin-yet-mother who never gets angry, loses her patience, or gets tired and doubts herself. Rather, she is all-giving and devotes herself completely and wholeheartedly to her son. Such unattainable perfection is far from the reality of what is experienced as a mother in twenty-first-century Western culture. While women experience rebirth and renewal by engaging with the paschal mystery through motherhood, they still remain imperfect human beings who can sometimes be impatient, insecure, unforgiving, and so on.

Christ's cross, death, and resurrection are then used to start theologizing on early motherhood. Throughout this chapter I will be asking: How is motherhood a lived experience of the paschal mystery of Jesus (and therefore a potentially salvific experience for a mother)?[5]

Motherhood and the Paschal Experience

The Human Struggles in Daily Living: Cross Experiences in Motherhood

When a woman becomes pregnant for the first time, there seems to be a great emphasis on preparing for the difficulties of birth and the baby's physical needs. According to western culture, one prepares for a baby by becoming medically well informed and acquiring the requisite baby paraphernalia. However, preparation for the emotional and spiritual upheavals that may follow after the birth is generally lacking. Although labor and birthing as physical experiences are incredibly painful, life after birth—especially in terms of dealing with motherhood emotionally—can be far more difficult.[6]

In *Of Woman Born: Motherhood as Experience and Institution*, Adrienne Rich speaks of the cross of responsibility for her children, her feelings of inadequacy, and her frustrating realization of and confrontations with her own limitations, but she also writes of her great enjoyment of the beauty of her children, their love for her, and her love for them.[7] Some expectant women may anticipate difficulties in early motherhood. Others may

---

5. This is really an advanced question from the simple questioning of a mother that says, "Is there salvation in the midst of the exhaustion and unrecognized work?" or "Where is God in the chaos of early motherhood?" I would like to clarify that this chapter does not imply that motherhood is the ultimate goal of true womanhood or that only in motherhood can a woman truly be saved. This chapter does not imply either that full-time, "stay-at-home" mothering is the only proper way to mother a child, or that by contrast, working mothers are better mothers. Although motherhood is a universal experience, the experiences spoken of in this article are not to be taken as encompassing the experience of mothers for all times and cultures. This chapter also does not seek to promote motherhood above fatherhood. In fact, many of the experiences discussed can apply equally to fathers. Finally, this chapter is written with acknowledgement of the loving support fathers can provide mothers, thereby assisting them in undergoing the paschal mystery in motherhood.

6. Yet there are women who have transitioned into their new role as mothers with relative ease due to a combination of factors such as their exposure to babies or the presence of many helping hands.

7. Rich, *Of Woman Born*, 21–22. While this book was published nearly twenty years ago, Rich's experience still speaks aptly of the experiences of joys and sorrows in motherhood.

imagine just the love and pure enjoyment of their children. Either way, new mothers can be highly unprepared for the difficulties new motherhood may reveal—their own dark sides, including the selfishness, resentment, despair, and rage Rich discusses in her book. Yet it is through these difficulties—the cross experiences in motherhood—that women are forced to face the truth about themselves, their own strengths and weaknesses: it is by the presence of these difficulties—the crosses—that mothers are able to experience extreme joys, such as the love and enjoyment of their children.

One particular example of a cross experience in motherhood that contributes greatly to the frustrations of new motherhood is the cross of monotony.[8] Reference to "the cross" generally conjures up images of physical torture. But the mind-numbing, isolating, and repetitive work of caring for a baby can be both a source of suffering and self-emptying experience for mothers. The work of caring for an infant is a never-ending cycle of feeding, cleaning, and settling. The monotony of childcare provides no sense of permanent or recognizable achievement. There is no public recognition for the work accomplished. There is no creativity required. There is just the menial and tedious repetition of unrewarded and seemingly endless physical labors—the punishment of Sisyphus.[9]

Giving Up the Old Self: Death Experiences in Motherhood

Facing the crosses of motherhood inevitably leads to crucial moments of decision in a mother's life. A woman may decide to accept the necessary deaths in motherhood, moving from the old person she once was to become the new. Or she may decide to ignore these deaths, attempting to cling to her old self. Sheila Kitzinger makes the point that motherhood can either completely change a woman such that she is everything to a child and nothing to herself. Or a woman can hire someone else to mother and care for her child's needs to the point that having a child makes a minimal disruption on her life.[10]

---

8. For a table outlining "The Cross, Death and Resurrection Experiences in Motherhood," see Gomez, "Early Motherhood and the Paschal Mystery," 131–50 It contains other possible crosses of motherhood—each of which calls for further exploration in its own right.

9. In Greek mythology, Sisyphus was punished by the gods with having to roll a boulder up a steep hill, but before he could reach the top of the hill, it would always tumble back down again, forcing him to begin again
(Homer, *Od.* XI 593, 141.

10. Kitzinger, *Ourselves as Mothers*, 194–95.

When a mother insists that a child would not impose on her lifestyle and choices for the future, maintaining that motherhood would not force her to make personal sacrifices, she refuses to face the death of her old identity as a non-mother. This shows that having a child can be the onset of an identity crisis for a woman, for while physically she has become a mother, psychologicallt a woman can refuse to integrate her new identity as "mother" into her old self.

Ideologies of motherhood still exist within western culture that do not assist in the formation of a woman's new identity as mother. One example of such ideology is that "motherhood and womanhood are intermeshed; to be considered a mature, balanced, fulfilled adult a woman should be a mother."[11] The impositions such ideologies make on a woman can contribute to her confusion over the formation of her new identity. They impose particular values on her and appear to threaten the annihilation of her old self. Because such ideologies exist, a woman may be made to feel that she has but two extreme choices: to become a mother whose individuality is completely absorbed into motherhood or to become a mother only in a physical sense with a mostly unchanged spiritual and emotional sense of self.

While a child may seem alien to a mother when he or she is first born, the time spent together and the mother's growing love for this child eventually moves a mother to respond in love and wonderment to this growing being who is of her own flesh and blood. The battle between mothering and being mothered is resolved only when the new mother is able to see that the two states of being can coexist within her. She can mother herself by attending to her own need for affirmation and self-actualization. She can, at the same time, respond to her own child's needs and eventually to the community around her. The decision to recognize the death of the old self and the resurrection of the new self is not a single moment in a mother's life. Rather, it is the ongoing growth in loving relationship with the child. By entering into the authentic death of her old self, a mother opens herself up to the resurrection moments of her new self and also to basic enjoyment of the rewards of motherhood.

Salvific and Life-Changing Moments: Resurrection Experiences in Motherhood

Resurrection experiences in motherhood are the life-giving and salvific moments in a mother's life. They are salvific in the sense that following these

11. Wearing, *Ideology of Motherhood*, 72.

struggles—the kenotic (self-emptying) but also revelatory (self-revealing) experiences—the resurrection moments are the fulfilling (refilling) and positively transformative experiences of a woman's new life (renewed life).

A possible resurrection experience in motherhood is giving birth to new life.[12] Birthing can transform a woman's intense suffering in labor into extreme joy over the creation of a new life and her participation in it. The pain of birthing itself is so great that the screams and groans of women in labor may be their only relief. Bodies may shake involuntarily and violently from the intense pain. Stress levels are at full capacity as women attempt to undertake an almost impossible and yet natural process of life. Death may even seem a desired reprieve at the time.

The salvific moments are not only found in the peak experiences of life, but also in the everyday quotidian moments that more commonly present themselves. One such experience is the constant giving required of a mother. It hurts to give, especially when a mother feels she would rather curl up in bed and pretend she is not a mother for just five minutes. But it is in this giving that love grows. The child learns through the mother's response that does hear its cries and can be counted on to respond, demonstrating to the child that he or she is ultimately loved.

But it is not only the mother who loves unconditionally—the child feels the same love for his or her mother. This too is the resurrection experience. In a world where love seems to be given with condition (you are acceptable only if you look the part, have the right qualifications and experience, or possess the right social etiquette or moral characteristics), a child loves his or her mother with complete acceptance, forgiveness, and loyalty.[13]

Women who mother have the opportunity to learn about themselves, transform into better selves, and grow into appreciation of themselves and others. Resurrection experiences indicate the positive transformations of

12. The experience of childbirth is paradoxical, as it can be both the most excruciating and exhilarating experience of one's life encompassed in a single event. In one sense, Christ's cross, death, and resurrection experience resonates strongly with this particular experience. To explore this idea in this chapter would not give justice to its depth and possibilities. The scope of this chapter only allows for the exploration of a few examples of resurrection experiences. I am conscious too of the possibility that birth can be anything but a resurrection experience. For various reasons, some mothers would consider birthing as just a cross and death experience.

13. The resurrection experiences in motherhood are numerous, but they may be categorized in (but not limited to) three areas as shown in *Engendering Motherhood*. They are (1) personal growth and development, (2) transcendent change, and (3) practical changes in lifestyle and the use of their time (McMahon, *Engendering Motherhood*, 147). See also Penelope Washbourne, *Becoming Woman*, 128. She articulates that the positive transformational effect that motherhood can offer women as "an occasion for growth that involves moments of renewal" (ibid.).

women who have grown to be more honest, more true to themselves, more loving of their children and others, and ultimately more human.

Towards a Theology of Motherhood

The question being answered in this chapter is "How is motherhood a lived experience of the paschal mystery?" The previous section named the struggles of daily living, the death of the old self, and positive self-transformations in motherhood as implicit life experiences of the cross, death, and resurrection for mothers. This section now focuses on the paschal mystery as an explicitly Christian theological concept and explores how this mystery is truly present in the life of a mother. Therefore, this section shows how the experiences of daily struggles, dying, and resurrection moments are a means of "taking up the cross of Christ," "dying with Christ," and "resurrecting with Christ."[14]

Taking Up the Cross of Christ

The phrase "taking up the cross" can be a dangerous phrase to use in today's western culture. It can reinforce the caricature image of Christians as a group of people attracted to self-imposed guilt and unnecessary, meaningless suffering. Yet it is the very phrase Rahner uses himself when theologizing about the cross of Christ.[15] This phrase may be better understood in opposition to the avoidance of suffering so prevalent in current western popular culture. "Taking up the cross" is not taking on suffering wherever it may be found or a mere end in itself. Instead, it is facing and undertaking the difficulties of life that come with one's commitment to another person: especially when that person is a dependent and fragile other. It is an easier option to avoid the suffering one must undergo to fulfill one's commitment.

Rahner says there are two ways of living:[16] either taking up one's own cross (facing the task ahead even if it includes suffering) or avoiding this cross (pretending one's task can be accomplished by avoiding any possible suffering involved). Avoiding the cross keeps one in a state of anxiety or frustration, while taking up that cross transforms that anxiety into something that is truly life-giving rather than simply appearing to be.

---

14. On "taking up the cross of Christ," see Matt 16:24, Mark 8:34, and Luke 9:23. On "dying" and "rising" with Christ, see 2 Cor 4:7–10 and Rom 6:1–11.

15. Rahner, "Self Realisation," 253–57.

16. Ibid., 256–57.

Yet what relevance does taking up the cross signify for mothers in abusive situations? These mothers can be given the "Christian message" to remain victims: to take on their suffering passively, as Jesus supposedly did.[17] Elisabeth Schüssler Fiorenza says the basic experience of women is inferiority and "otherness" in a patriarchal society and religion, adding that women "internalise that their experience of alienation and anger is just our personal problem, that something must be wrong with *us* and that we have to accept and adapt to things as they are."[18]

Rahner's advocacy for taking up one's own cross is not to be understood in the sense of accepting resignation in the face of abuse.[19] Rahner says that taking up one's cross implies an acceptance of death and of the suffering that is inevitably involved with this death as a part of living.[20] Taking up one's cross means to be called away from a shallow life wherein "happiness" is experienced without any struggle or expectation of death. A mother—who, as Rahner would say, accepts the abiding fear of death—accepts the frustration and darkness of undergoing the monotony, exhaustion, doubt, isolation, and other forms of suffering in mothering.[21]

Rahner believes that taking up one's own cross in daily life is synonymous with taking up the cross of Christ, whether it is acknowledged openly as such or not.[22] For a mother, then, to take up the cross of Christ is to take up her own crosses in motherhood. The converse is also true: to take up the crosses in motherhood is to take up the cross of Christ.

And yet facing the difficulties—accepting them as part of reality—is more likely to occur from within the loving support of a community. Mothers may have the support of family and friends, but it is in sharing the difficulties and joys with other mothers—immersed in their own happiness and struggles too—that a mother is more able to face her crosses.

Dying with Christ

Facing death as Christ did must involve more than a personal character transformation wherein one accepts the abiding fear of death. Since the Christian God is a God involved from the beginning of the world and constantly present in the Holy Spirit, dying as Christ died cannot simply

17. See Reid, *Taking Up the Cross*; Daly, *Beyond God the Father*, 77.
18. Fiorenza, "Breaking the Silence–Becoming Visible," 169.
19. Rahner, "Self Realisation," 257.
20. Ibid.
21. Ibid.
22. Ibid.

be about following the example of the historical Jesus. It has to be about Christ's death also incorporating humanity into his death. It has to be that even before we choose to follow the example of the historical Jesus—in his taking up the cross, in his way of dying, and in his courageous conviction in God's power as stronger than death or any power on earth—we must have already died with Christ. The possibility of our following Jesus in his dying can only result from Jesus having already incorporated humanity's state of constant struggle and death into his own death.

For Rahner, Christ's death is to be understood as the ongoing presence of death in life. This is what he calls "Christian realism."[23] While taking up the cross of Christ can be about facing the difficulties in one's own life, dying with Christ requires first realizing that to live is to also be at death's door. This reality cannot be ignored. Yet, as discussed in the previous section, the reality of death's constant presence is ignored in popular western culture in preference to the pursuit of instant gratification. Tantalus from Greek mythology exemplifies this human tendency towards pleasure and its fruitless promise of the everlasting. For Tantalus, food and drink are forever just out of reach. Thus, life for him becomes a desperate pursuit of a lasting happiness that will always remain elusive.[24]

For a new mother, the acceptance of death's constant presence is the acceptance that new motherhood, like any other stage in life, entails experiences of dying. Rather than being surprised by the death required of her old self—that it is happening at the expense of her previously somewhat ordered life—a mother who realizes death's constant presence also realizes that it is a normal part of any human experience. She realizes that what is happening to her as a new mother is the constant call of the death of her old self.

For Rahner, death is that point at which we do not have anything, not even ourselves, to save us from the "apparently empty infinity."[25] This "apparently empty infinity" is what Rahner calls the absurdity or contradictory nature of death.[26] It is, as he says, a place where one cannot even console oneself,[27] for "In the last resort what happens in death is the same for all:

---

23. See Egan, "Karl Rahner," 175.

24. In Greek mythology, Tantalus' punishment for stealing from the gods was to be condemned to an eternity of hunger and thirst in Hades. He was made to stand in a pool of water beneath a fruit tree with low branches. Whenever he reached to pluck the fruit, the branches receded from his grasp. Whenever he bent down to get a drink, the water drained before he could get any (Homer, *Od.* XI 583, 141).

25. Rahner, "Ideas for a Theology of Death," 182.

26. Ibid.

27. Ibid.

we are deprived of everything, even of ourselves; we all fall, each of us alone, into the dark abyss where there are no further ways."[28] New motherhood can often reach moments of "apparently empty infinity" and "dark abysses." The change of identity from non-mother who "wants to be mothered," to a mother who must "enact the mothering she longs for her own self" is one example. The points of "apparently empty infinity" for a new mother may come at times when her difficulties seem to overwhelm her, bringing her to a stage where she does not know herself anymore or if she will ever find herself again.

Yet to die with Christ does not mean we must remain in this nothingness or absurd circumstance. For Rahner, there are two ways to respond to death:

> Either the subject in the last resort culpably refuses to accept any freely bestowed love from another person . . . or it accepts with resignation and hope this eclipse of all particular realities as the dawn and approach of that silent infinity into which each particular act of freedom has hitherto always risen above its individual object.[29]

A mother can refuse the love of God as shown through her child, or she can accept with resignation and hope the formation of a new identity, integrated into her old self, that is her formation into a more human, loving, and godly being. The love of a child, representing God's complete love, can be easily rejected by a mother when she becomes caught up in the hurts of her own childhood or in her own needs. The alternative is that even as a mother carries her unmourned past, she chooses to stay in the present moment.[30] When she does this, a mother acts on the belief that attending to the quotidian—the seemingly ordinary, nitty-gritty, difficulties of motherhood—is not an end in itself but is instead the necessary work of love for a child. More often it is a thankless job, but sometimes the child rewards with a smile, a look, or a hug of complete love and gratitude, and the absurdity of the difficulties of a mother's life seem to be transformed. Moreover, when a mother sees her child thrive, it can be a life-giving and salvific experience for her.

---

28. Ibid., "Following the Crucified," 166.

29. Ibid., 164.

30. See Richo, *How to Be an Adult*, 14. Richo explains that adults can carry hurts from childhood, which in turn affects the way they relate both with others and their parents in the present moment.

This is not to say that a mother must completely surrender herself to motherhood such that her own identity is found only in her work as a mother. Surrendering, according to Rahner, is:

> the abandoning of oneself in the hope of finding the inconceivable fullness—[it] takes place in the ultimately inaccessible depths of one's freedom when this freedom calmly "lets go," i.e., lets the particular die, believing in hope that in this way (and ultimately *only* in this way), the whole, the fullness, "God" will be received.[31]

Jesus is the perfect example of complete surrender to God and is thus seen as the perfect model of human living. Rahner says Jesus took on the fate of human beings, namely death, but he also made death his own act.[32] This he did by his complete surrender to God, which contrasts the idea that death was something that happened to Christ without his consent. According to Rahner, in making death his own act, Jesus himself assumed "that which is beyond all human conception and control, and himself enacts what has to be suffered."[33]

But Jesus is also "the other," the incarnation of the incomprehensible love of God in the history of humanity. We can now answer the question posed previously: How does Jesus incorporate humanity into his death? Jesus does this by embodying death as it should be (exemplifying for us the death we must embrace) and embodying God's reconciliation with humanity through this death (God gives Godself to us in Jesus first, before we can give of ourselves to God in death). For a mother then, dying with Christ not only entails following Jesus' example of complete surrender to God in death, it also involves living in the reality that it is God who first reached out to her (through Jesus) to save her in her death.

In his death, Jesus completely surrendered himself to God. God in turn accepted this complete surrender and raised Jesus from the dead. This is what is meant by the resurrection of Christ. In motherhood, does this mean that when a mother completely surrenders herself to life—and thus to God—God raises her from her death? How so? We know that accepting God's offer of love is to accept the resurrection, one's own salvation. But what does the resurrection of a mother look like?

---

31. Rahner, "Self Realisation," 255.
32. Ibid.
33. Ibid., "Theological Considerations," 320.

Living in Christ's Resurrection

To Rahner, the first principle of the resurrection is "the definitive redeemed state of the person and the history of a human being with God; it does not mean a return to our spatial-temporal biological life."[34] The resurrection is not to be seen as a resuscitation of Jesus' body and therefore of our own bodies. Rather, it is God's saving act in a person's life. This saving act is seen as part of a history in which both God and the human person have reached out to one another: God's presence is seen in the processes and people of life and in the human person transcending herself as she is transformed by her suffering and death experiences. Resurrection in a mother's life is seen in her ongoing transformations through crisis moments she thought she would not survive. Resurrection comes as she grows in trust that she will not be overcome by her cross and death experiences. Rather, she will become stronger, more resilient, wise, and strategic.

In this transformation, she experiences the resurrection. Birth can exemplify this resurrection experience. In labor, a mother's pain can be overwhelming, Yet after the birth of her child, she is in the position to realize her own strength, resilience, and wisdom.

The second principle of the resurrection, according to Rahner, is that "man can gain such an experience of a unique character only when and insofar as he brings to it his own hope for *himself* that his own existence will be definitively revealed."[35] That is, one can only believe in Jesus' resurrection if one also believes in his or her own resurrection—his or her own salvation from nothingness and despair. Rahner explains that one believes in his or her own resurrection "wherever there is real hoping and loving . . . even when a person with this hope and love lacks the ability or courage to verbally thematicize and objectify the hope of resurrection implicit in the mere continuance of his existence."[36]

For a mother, as demonstrated above, this hope appears as a trust that motherhood is not swallowed up by its own crosses and deaths. A mother's trust in God is a surrender to God—the acceptance of the bigger reality and the complete love of God, which she can experience in the immediate sense through her children. By accepting her children as they are as she spends time with them, teaches them, cares for them, and even fights with them, she loves them completely. In conjunction, in her children's complete acceptance of her (even in their rebellion and assertion of their own

---

34. See ibid., "What Does It Mean?" 151.
35. Ibid.
36. Ibid., 152.

individuality), a mother receives the complete love of God. For as Rahner believes, love of oneself through the complete acceptance of oneself and love of one's neighbor (by true loving and commitment) is the true encounter with God.[37]

The third principle, according to Rahner, is that "this hope of ours of our own resurrection and the encounter with the claim that Jesus' fate makes on us then encounter the disciples' message of his resurrection and the faith of two thousand years of the history of hope of Christendom."[38] Our faith in Christ's resurrection, and thus in our own resurrection, is not based on idealism but instead on the witnesses of the first disciples. As Rahner says, Jesus' resurrection was "perceived and attested to by men plunged into despair by the sight of the disaster of Jesus' life and in no way inclined to believe anything of this kind."[39] The hopes of the Christian community over two thousand years attest to this faith in the resurrection. A mother can look at mothers from the past—her own ancestors as well as other mothers in general—who have survived, hoped, believed, and lived through birthing, the first year, "terrible twos," the unpredictable teenage years, and so forth; if they survived, hoped, loved, and believed throughout motherhood, she can too. Again, the mother's community plays a vital role in this hoping and believing.

Rahner's fourth principle is:

> if our own transcendence to God's immediacy in freedom is alive in what we describe as grace, if it is realized and becomes explicit in history and in the encounter with history, if with our questing Christology we encounter Jesus of Nazareth, then we certainly have the opportunity for our own experience of the Risen One, even though that experience is not entirely independent of the testimony of the first disciples.[40]

By our constant searching for truth in life, and in our human orientation towards the transcendent—whether it is acknowledged as God, or Jesus, or complete love, or the absolute, and experienced in our lives as such—we can thus believe that our own resurrection is possible.

---

37. The idea that loving one's neighbor is hope in the face of death is from Rahner, "Ideas for a Theology," 186. The implication here is that God and the individual can be made partners in death, resurrection, and ultimately the individual's salvation.

38. Rahner, "What Does It Mean?" 152.

39. Ibid.

40. Ibid., 153.

Conclusion

This chapter has attempted to answer the question: How is the paschal mystery a lived experience in motherhood? In response, it has explored how motherhood can be a locus for the saving actions of God. It has shown that both Christian and non-Christian mothers experience the paschal mystery implicitly through motherhood's daily difficulties, its call for the death of the old self, and its many joys and positive transformations. Rahner's insights into the practical application of the paschal mystery in one's life have made possible a theological reflection on the experiences of motherhood. In such a light, Christ's cross, death, and resurrection are not just statements for a Christian mother's belief, separate from daily life. Rather, they can state God's intimate concern for her as an individual, but also for mothers all over the world.

Motherhood is an invitation to participate in the reality of living—the undeniable crosses, the constant presence of death, and the hope of the resurrection (that does come into fruition) that always comes *with* the crosses and deaths. The paschal mystery in motherhood is experienced inasmuch as a mother "takes up the cross of Christ" (does not run away from difficulties), dies with Christ (lets go of her old sense of self to incorporate a new self fostered by a new relationship), and lives in Christ's resurrection (living in the hope beyond the attractive pull of despair brought about by Christ's resurrection). Even if a mother does not explicitly believe in Christ, by her actions—in loving her children as well as herself and in learning to love and be loved by others—she lives her true self, In these acts of motherhood, she implicitly believes in the paschal mystery and is therefore saved by it.

For a Christian mother who seeks God in the midst of her motherhood, the memorial acclamation she proclaims in the liturgy "Christ has died, Christ is risen, Christ will come again" can become a deeply meaningful statement. Insofar as she takes up the cross of Christ, dies with him, and lives in hope of his resurrection, she lives this paschal mystery in the struggles, deaths, transformations, and joys of motherhood. By the work and the very being of her own body, a mother is invited to carry the mystery of the cross, death, and resurrection of Jesus.

Bibliography

Catholic Church. *Catechism of the Catholic Church*. Vatican City: Libreria Editrice Vaticana, 1993. http://www.vatican.va/archive/ENG0015/__P3M.HTM.

Daly, Mary. *Beyond God the Father*. Boston: Beacon, 1973.

Egan, Harvey D. *Karl Rahner: Mystic of Everyday Life*. New York: Crossroad, 1998.

Fiorenza, Elisabeth Schüssler. "Breaking the Silence—Becoming Visible." In *The Power of Naming: A Conciliuim Reader in Feminist Liberation Theology*, edited by Elisabeth Schüssler Fiorenza, 161–74. Manila: St. Pauls, 2004.

Gomez, Cristina. "Early Motherhood and the Paschal Mystery: A Rahnerian Reflection on the Death and Rebirth Experiences of New Mothers." *Australasian Catholic Record* 88 (2011) 131–50.

Homer. *The Odyssey*. Translated by Walter Shewring. Oxford: Oxford University Press, 1980.

Kitzinger, Sheila. *Ourselves as Mothers: The Universal Experience of Motherhood*. London: Doubleday, 1992.

McMahon, Martha. *Engendering Motherhood: Identity and Self-Transformation in Women's Lives*. New York: Guildford, 1995.

Paul VI, Pope. *Gaudium et Spes* [Pastoral Constitution on the Church in the Modern World]. Second Vatican Council. December 7, 1965. http://www.vatican.va/archive/hist_councils/ii_vatican_council/documents/vat-ii_const_19651207_gaudium-et-spes_en.html.

Rahner, Karl. "Anonymous Christians." In *A Rahner Reader*, edited by G. McCool, 211–14. New York: Seabury, 1975.

———. "Following the Crucified." In *Theological Investigations* 18:157–70. London: Darton, Longman & Todd, 1978.

———. "Ideas for a Theology of Death." In *Theological Investigations* 13. London: Darton, Longman & Todd, 1975.

———. "Self Realisation and Taking up One's Cross." In *Theological Investigations* 9:253–57. London: Darton, Longman & Todd, 1972.

———. "Theological Considerations on Moment of Death." In *Theological Investigations* 11. London: Darton, Longman & Todd 1974.

———. "What Does It Mean Today to Believe in Jesus Christ?" In *Theological Investigations* 18. London: Darton, Longman & Todd, 1978.

Reid, Barbara E. *Taking Up the Cross: New Testament Interpretations through Latina and Feminist Eyes*. Minneapolis: Fortress, 2007.

Rich, Adrienne Cecile. *Of Woman Born: Motherhood as Experience and Institution*. New York: Norton, 1995.

Richo, David. *How to Be An Adult: A Handbook on Psychological and Spiritual Integration*. New York/ Mahwah: Paulist, 1991.

Washbourne, Penelope. *Becoming Woman*. London: Harper & Row, 1977.

Wearing, Betsy. *The Ideology of Motherhood*. Sydney: Allen & Unwin, 1984.

9

Reverend Mother

Conversations in Motherhood and Ministry

REBECCA LINDSAY

Thread One: A Conversation Partner

Who Am I?

I am a young(ish) woman newly ordained within the Uniting Church in Australia (UCA). I love the church, and my life is enmeshed within it. My sense of call has been developing within me for half my life. When I was sixteen and assisting a crèche at a mission conference, I experienced God's voice drawing my life towards work within the church. From conference to ordinand, the journey has not been a straightforward one. Within a denomination that denied my call according to my sex, I learned not to tell my story. Now, within a community that affirms my identity and confirms my call, I have found my own authentic voice. I know who I am; I know who God asks me to become. I am called to be a minister of the Word, proclaiming God's good news and presiding at God's generous table.

Alongside of this, in many ways a surprise to myself, I find myself married. When I first dreamed of my ministry, it was always alone. Perhaps I doubted I would meet someone who would want to share life with me as a partner, as an equal, as someone called to ordination. Finding a journey companion has been a great blessing. But it has also complicated things. Stepping into my role as partner, I have begun to wonder what place family and children might play within my priestly calling. Can I be both minister and mother?

In belonging to a "post-feminist" generation, I have imbibed the rhetoric of equality. Growing up in an all-girl's school, there was never any question that we were not as capable, as intelligent, and as worthy as our male counterparts. Careers beckoned—whichever and whatever we might desire. On the cusp of Generations X and Y, I have seen tension between a culture promoting everlasting youth and the fertility problems that can accompany childbearing later in life. I wonder why it is that the busy racing between work, children, and home to "have it all" is such a dream? Yet those who choose a path without children are labeled "selfish," "barren," and often have their worth questioned.[1] With competing priorities pulling at my peers, the "choice" of whether to have children becomes a weighty one.[2]

For myself, the question centers around how I resolve the tension between my (strongly experienced and affirmed) call to live out the vocation of an ordained minister and the place children might find within that life. What will it mean for my own life to inhabit multiple vocations? While I acknowledge that I already inhabit multiple roles, the difficulty emerges when these roles appear—to myself or others—to be exclusive. There appears to be little difficulty in combining the roles of husband, father, and minister. Indeed, this combination is often encouraged. But something different inhabits the space of ministry and motherhood.

This chapter explores the complex questions of ministry and mothering. Noting the lack of resources in this area, it draws into dialogue four feminist theologians who inhabit diverse traditions: Bonnie Miller-McLemore, Sarah Coakley, Janet Martin Soskice, and Anita Monro. This folded conversation opens space for a multiplicity of identities and the transgression of fixed boundaries as encountered in Christ. In doing so, it provides resources for understanding the ordained ministry of word, sacrament, and pastoral care. The issues explored within this chapter are deeply theological in terms of understanding human vocation, identity, and ministry. They are also practically grounded in the lived and messy experience of women who seek to find ways of becoming both mothers and ordained ministers.

---

1. Carey et al., "Discourse, Power and Exclusion," 128.

2. See, for example, Leslie Cannold's *What, No Baby?* Cannold questions the notion of "choice" for women (particularly professional women) who desire to both work and bear children, given external societal factors that do not support this combination.

A Gap Appears

The messy coexistence of ministry and mothering is attested in the dearth of resources exploring this topic. When I realized my own uncertainty about the complex relationship between ministry and mothering, I approached it as I would any other theological quandary. I sought something to read and people to talk with. I found very little. Most of the women I knew in ministry were mothers *before* they were ordained. Anecdotally, it seemed that many of their children were teenagers or well into primary school before these mothers entered formation. The literature was also fairly silent. Emerging volumes such as Marcia Bunge's *The Child in Christian Thought* and *The Child in the Bible* reveal how little attention is paid to children within the Scriptures and the tradition that developed from them. Christian reflection has often silenced women and children. The ways in which the lives of women and children are enmeshed together from conception to mothering has been largely neglected.

Furthermore, even within my own denomination, which affirms the ordination of women as "a fundamental implication of the Gospel of God's love in Christ for all human beings, without distinction,"[3] there has historically been a double standard at play. Discussion at an early Gathering Conference for women in the UCA noted that ordained women were often asked questions about how they would combine a pastoral role with that of good wife and mother.[4] The number of women ministers in UCA Presbytery, Synod, and Assembly leadership positions continues to be significantly fewer than their male counterparts.[5] Women are underrepresented on the committees that make decisions about the life of the church. How is it that even within a church tradition that believes there is a theological imperative to ordain women, so little energy has been spent reflecting on the practical implications of such a stance?

Thread Two: Entering Conversation

The key issue surrounds the ways in which we attribute and understand identity. Ordained ministry and motherhood appear to be mutually exclusive vocations—an opposing binary pair. How, then, might these issues be

---

3. Uniting Church Assembly, "Why the Uniting Church," 614.

4. Wood, "Participating with Purpose," 106.

5. For example, since union in 1977 there has only been one female president of the UCA Assembly. Within the NSW/ACT Synod, there have been five female moderators (out of twenty-eight) and no female general-secretary of the Synod (out of seven).

brought into dialogue? I open up these questions by bringing four feminist theologians into conversation with each other. They represent different places within the Christian tradition and academic theology ranging from philosophy of religion to systematic and pastoral theology. They have lived, worked, taught, presided, mothered, and studied in Australia, the United States, and the United Kingdom. At times their ideas converge, and at times they conflict. At first glance, Bonnie Miller-McLemore, Sarah Coakley, Janet Martin Soskice, and Anita Monro do not appear to be easy conversation partners on the issue of motherhood and ministry. Three are ordained ministers; three are biological mothers. Miller-McLemore and Soskice write directly of biological mothering experiences; Monro writes of Eucharistic presidency as mothering; Coakley does not speak of motherhood at all, yet her feminist theology is valuable to this conversation all the same. Each of their voices has been fruitful for me in my own struggle to name issues and formulate questions around motherhood and ministry.

Bonnie Miller-McLemore

Bonnie Miller-McLemore is the most obvious partner for a conversation around Christian theology, ministry, and motherhood. An American pastoral theologian, she is at the forefront of theology that reflects upon children. Over twenty years, her research has been her own response to the vacuum she discovered as a feminist academic, minister, theologian, and mother. She names the "silence" she discovered in the conflict between work and family commitments as "caught up in a much larger cultural debate about the nature of faith, contemplation, chaos, and children."[6]

Miller-McLemore points to the key question of how women combine their multiple vocational roles, particularly work and child-rearing. "On the one hand, must women who have children give up their lives and aspirations beyond their children? On the other hand, must the birthing and upbringing of children be something that women hide or simply do on the side?"[7] This is a tension that men do not seem to face, even those who seek to share involvement with their children's care: "Few men seem to feel the strain of value-laden questions about marriage and children. I did not hear many of them asking, How will I combine work and family, and which is more important now?"[8]

---

6. Miller-McLemore, *In the Midst of Chaos*, 12.
7. Ibid., *Also a Mother*, 88.
8. Ibid., 115.

Economic and psychological ideologies that problematize parenting underpin cultural norms. Christian tradition and Scripture have been used to cement ideologies of gender that claim male generativity as normal and simultaneously limit women's generative potential. Yet Miller-McLemore suggests that "women's embodiment, specifically the bodily and still painful experience of birth, as well as pregnancy and lactation, represents a distinct perspective and may evoke particular ways of perceiving and thinking."[9]

Miller-McLemore explores the concept of parenting as a facet of discipleship. It is a spiritual practice whose aim is mutual love. Children are not commodities. They are gifts who shine "light on life, love and work."[10] Yet the relationship between parents and their children includes a "fundamental non-reciprocity."[11] Even within mutual human relationships, people dip in and out of greater need and giving. Indeed, "Self-giving love never rests on its own, alone, unaided and uninterrupted. It must be alleviated and countered by contrasting moments of self-gratification, within the broader network of dependency that makes up human community."[12] Relationships of mutual love require a balance between giving and receiving.

Miller-McLemore asks how it is possible to maintain a "spiritual life" within the midst of chaotic family life, highlighting the disconnection between a pattern of faith born in contemplation and the daily activities of many Christians.[13] She describes her own moment of movement away from stillness as the heart of faith, as she read Henri Nouwen on the desert fathers while watching her young children in the bath. Discontent with silence as a motif for experiencing God, she recognized the importance of "words with holy potential."[14] This is not to discount the profound experience of God found within silence and solitude but instead to "widen the circle" so that parents and children may find inclusion within the heart of faith. Miller-McLemore names simple, everyday activities shared by parents and children through which God might be invoked and experienced, including practices such as playing, reading, and taking children seriously.[15]

---

9. Ibid., 135.
10. Ibid., 156.
11. Ibid., "Feminism, Children and Mothering," 24.
12. Ibid., *Also a Mother*, 167.
13. Ibid., *In the Midst of Chaos*, 5.
14. Ibid., 9.
15. Ibid., 20.

Sarah Coakley

Unlike Miller-McLemore, Sarah Coakley's writing never directly addresses motherhood. However, her *"theologie totale"* offers resources for naming and re-framing ideas surrounding gender. Coakley is one of the foremost feminist contemporary systematic theologians. She is an English academic, mother, and Anglican priest. In her "unsystematic systematics," Coakley places gender studies firmly within theological orthodoxy's center.[16]

In *Powers and Submission*, Coakley points out the gendered assumptions brought to theology. Rather than accepting the particular feminist critique that *kenosis* is always dangerous for women, she suggests that all human beings fall somewhere between power and vulnerability.[17] While acknowledging the danger of accepting all forms of vulnerability, Coakley suggests there is a greater danger for Christians when vulnerability is repressed. Through the practice of contemplative prayer, the self is willingly ceded in response to God. In the discipline of contemplation, "we 'make space' for God to be God," for healing and transformation through the non-abusive power of God.[18]

Coakley is careful to note the elitist framing that contemplation has received within western Christian tradition. She seeks to define the practice of contemplation more broadly: "such prayer may be use of a repeated phrase to ward off distractions, or be wholly silent; it may be simple Quaker attentiveness, or take a charismatic expression."[19] Here, contemplation is at the heart of theology, for it recognizes and embodies the radical dependence of all creatures upon God:

> The very act of contemplation—repeated, lived, embodied, suffered—is an act that, by grace, and over time, precisely inculcates mental patterns of un-mastery, welcomes the dark realm of the unconscious, opens up radical attention to the other, and instigates an acute awareness of the messy entanglement of sexual desires and desire for God.[20]

Patience, waiting, and acknowledging the gap between Christ's cross and resurrection bear witness to the struggle of a new self being birthed.[21]

---

16. Coakley, "Is There a Future?" 9.
17. Ibid., *Powers and Submission*, 22.
18. Ibid., 34.
19. Ibid., 35.
20. Coakley, "Is There a Future?" 5.
21. Ibid., *Powers and Submission*, 39.

For Coakley, it is precisely through contemplative prayer that God's triunity is experienced. In the incarnation, the ontological boundary between God and not-God is transgressed and transformed by Christ, infusing creation with God's life. Similarly, gender transformation occurs through participation in the life of the Triune God:

> Just as in the Spirit he crosses that ontological twoness transformatively, but without obliteration of otherness, so the interruptive work of the trinitarian God does not obliterate the twoness of human gender, either, but precisely renders it subject to the labile transformations of divine desire. Whatever this redeemed twoness is . . . it cannot be the stuck, fixed twoness of the fallen gender binary.[22]

The mutuality of desire between God and a person in contemplative prayer provides an example that allows for both difference and equality.

Triune subversion of binary gender is also found within the drama of the Eucharist. Coakley sees the presiding priest occupying a liminal space between Christ and Church, bride and bridegroom, male and female.[23] Her playfulness does not seek to find an androgynous space whereby gender is ignored or negated. Rather, the differentiation between human creatures in gender mirrors that between creature and God.

Janet Martin Soskice

Janet Martin Soskice shares a passion for exploring gender and theology with Coakley and Miller-McLemore. She writes richly of metaphor, language, identity, and friendship. She is a philosopher of religion who converted to Catholicism from a nominal Anglican background. Her theological framework is based in the belief that love of God and love of neighbor belong together. Her writing on "women's problems" developed while teaching at an Anglican training college. Noticing the double standards applied to male and female students, Soskice came to the deep realization that "God *loves* women!"[24]

In advocating for women, Soskice draws attention to the reality of sexism: "Sexism is not something that hurts women's feelings, sexism kills millions and millions and millions of girls and women each year."[25] The

---

22. Ibid., "Is There a Future?" 10.
23. Ibid., "Woman at the Altar," 76.
24. Soskice, "Women's Problems," 50.
25. Ibid., "Just Women's Problems?" 55.

church has often been complicit within a patriarchal system, historically rendering women silent and disenfranchising them from decision-making. There is a "double-think about women" that states, "women are *equal* to men insofar as they do not have different insights or visions to bring to the Church, or spiritual needs to be met, but they are *different* in ways that make them unable to contribute fully to the Church's ministerial, theological and evangelical life."[26]

Soskice sees the belief that contemplation is closest-to-God as particularly disenfranchising to women, partly because such a framework cannot include children. One compelling anecdote sees her comparing a (bachelor) colleague's peaceful, monastic vacation spent re-reading Augustine's *City of God* in Latin to her own messy "holiday" with her children. She wonders, "Is the busy new mother a sort of Christian on 'idle'?"[27] To this question Soskice brings the divine activity in Jesus, where the chaotic activities of life take center stage: "The body, no less than the soul, is the place where God acts."[28]

From the experience of God's incarnation, Soskice criticizes the division within Christian tradition between the sacred and the secular, between the *polis* and domestic life. Might not domestic or everyday tasks be more than duties in service of God but spiritual practices in themselves, within which God can be experienced and known? Women, who have often spent much time attending to repetitive, "ordinary" tasks, "realize there is something inchoately graced about these dealings."[29] Soskice here develops the idea of attention. Being *fully* human, she suggests, requires attending to the other with love. The experience of pregnancy and caring for an infant provides an example of how rational and bodily love and attention combine in response. As they receive attention, children grow into a sense of identity. As they offer attention, parents also experience change. In disciplined humility, over time, parents are "unselved" as they make space for the child.[30] In the same way, God's loving attention is directed towards creation, to each thing in its own particularity.

---

26. Ibid., "Women's Problems," 53.
27. Ibid., *Kindness of God*, 14.
28. Ibid., 23.
29. Ibid., 24.
30. Ibid., 31.

Anita Monro

Like Miller-McLemore, Coakley, and Soskice, Anita Monro is a feminist theologian who explores the issues of gender and identity. An ordained minister of the Word in the UCA, her writings acknowledge the paradox between the contemporary applause of plurality, on the one hand, and the presentation of a single and dominant solution on the other. Monro names "unity in diversity" as a common catchphrase of identity for her denomination. Yet when diverse opinion exists around issues of theology and practice, unity is not easily maintained: "How does Christian theology both maintain its identity and manage diversity within that identity?"[31] Or, "who is the 'other' when she is sitting beside you and identified as part of you in a collective situation?"[32] Monro develops "erotic transgressive resurrection" as a theological methodology able to hold together the tensions of shared identity and the diversity within identity. This approach is termed "erotic" in its desire for meaning-making, termed "transgressive" as it crosses boundaries, and termed "resurrection" because it believes in a constant process of meaning-making and remaking.[33]

Monro situates her approach within poststructuralism's defiance of the binary structures that have been used to maintain women as secondary to men. She seeks to move beyond duality by making use of the concept of "alterity" to step outside binding dichotomies. The ambiguous identity of Christ—identified within the Christian tradition as fully God and fully human—reveals the possibility of multiple identity.[34] Here she draws upon Derrida's challenge to the notions of absolutes within western philosophy in *différance* and Kristeva's development of Lacan's concept of *jouissance*.[35]

As Monro explains:

> *Différance*, as the moment and space preceding the construction of meaning, is entirely elusive to full description and entirely necessary in the construction process. Yet, its exposure exposes the arbitrary and fragile nature of the structures of meaning by uncovering the non-existent base upon which they are understood to stand.[36]

---

31. Monro, *Resurrecting Erotic Transgression*, 1.
32. Ibid., 44.
33. Ibid., 13.
34. Ibid., 18.
35. For more on *jouissance*, see Kristeva, *Desire in language*. For more on *différeance*, see Derrida, *Writing and Difference*.
36. Monro, *Resurrecting Erotic Transgression*, 95.

Jouissance is "the painful enjoyment of the movement beyond duality and singular, unitary identity."[37] In other words, Monro's approach attends to ambiguity and multiplicity of meaning and identity. This attending to "otherness" shatters the possibility of a fixed, singular subjectivity. Monro offers "poetic reading" as a playful and imaginative textual hermeneutic leaning towards *jouissance*. Poetic reading celebrates multiplicity of meaning in language and identity.[38]

Monro's project is risky: in order to transgress dualities and allow for the emergence of new and multiple identities, loss of previously gained identity will occur. Yet any fixed subjectivity is elusive. Taking the central Christian symbol of Eucharist, Monro notes the ambiguity of Christ's feeding of his people from his own body as a mother feeds her children.[39] When the presider is male, he acts to incorporate the (feminine, heterogeneous) church into the singular male identity as the body of Christ: "The female body of Christ, the church, achieves completion through this identification with the masculine."[40] When a woman presides at the Eucharist, she confronts the "stark and messy reality of the drama of the incarnation."[41] Ambiguity is embodied as "the body of the presider slides into the body of Christ (the Eucharist) and the body of Christ (the Church). The feminine body (Church) is fed by the feminine body (Eucharist) by the feminine body (Presider) . . . Christ feeds her people with her very self at her own hand."[42]

Thread Three: The Conversation Folds Together

Points of Dissonance, Agreement, Ambiguity, Tension . . .

Pamela Cooper-White suggests that women are complicated. She sees women as a "folding together" (*complicato*) of multiple roles, identities, and relationships.[43] She recognizes a sense of fluidity, flexibility, and complexity that resonates with women's experiences. Here, wholeness is found not in the simple cohesion of multiples, but rather is "constituted *by* the multiplicity of the folds."[44] Having heard the individual voices of Miller-McLemore,

---

37. Ibid., 109.
38. Ibid., 136.
39. Monro, "And Ain't I a Woman," 123.
40. Ibid., 128.
41. Ibid., 124.
42. Ibid., 128.
43. Cooper-White, "Complicated Woman," 9.
44. Ibid., 19.

Coakley, Soskice, and Monro, conversation emerges. Ideas fold together, unfold, and re-fold.

Contemplation and Chaos

In addressing the role of motherhood in ministry, a question arises: Where to begin? In seeking identity—that of our selves or that of God—where do we start? Does theology begin in the preciously passed on resources of Scripture and tradition, or do we find it in the vibrant messiness of lived experience? While each of these theologians recognizes the negative impact of patriarchy (for women, children, *and* men) upon the content and interpretation of experience, tradition, and Scripture, they seek to address this problem from differing vantage points.

For Miller-McLemore, "A Feminist maternal theology . . . begins with a thick description of human experience that gives privileged voice to the underside, the oppressed, the outcast, who often struggle to hear their own voices . . . In this case, it is mothers and children who have been silenced and need to be heard."[45] She does not claim a universal experience as her beginning point, but she has come to recognize that her own stories of interwoven relationships and vocation have directed her academic questions and motifs. While rich in Scriptural resonance, her theology grows primarily from experience.

The starting point for Soskice and Monro is more ambiguous. Soskice seems to begin with her profound realization of God's love for women, embedding Scriptural stories within her exploration. Monro acknowledges "the primary theological sources of scripture and tradition as well as the tapestry of Christian community," noting that for Protestant communities, Scripture tends to take priority.[46] She brings her hermeneutic to Scriptural interpretation, but also equally to her lived experience of a Gathering Conference for women in the UCA.

Coakley seeks to begin her theology from the Christian theological tradition, claiming that "*only* systematic theology (of a particular sort) can adequately and effectively respond to the rightful critiques that gender studies and political and liberation theologies have laid at its door."[47] In describing the place the practice of contemplation takes within her work, she comments,

---

45. Miller-McLemore, *Also a Mother*, 104.
46. Monro, *Resurrecting Erotic Transgression*, 5.
47. Coakley, "Is There a Future?" 2.

> It is important, first, to underscore that I am not here appealing to 'experience' in a naively empiricist way, as if some particular 'experience' could offset deficiencies in what is otherwise provided by Scripture or tradition or 'reason.' Rather, the regular undertaking of an intentional form of what I term 'dispossession' underwrites and progressively transforms all that one goes on receiving from those other sources.[48]

Yet Coakley does draw upon embodied experience in expounding

> . . . a methodology that seeks to attend not only to 'high' academic discourse but also to lived experiences of the liturgical, pastoral, aesthetic, cultural and incidental. In this manner, ordinary bodily negotiations must also come to bear on the systematic enterprise— moves that gather up previously neglected fragments and ensure that the process is truly 'systematic.'[49]

It seems significant that even Coakley, whose frame of inquiry is systematic theology, seeks to integrate the depth of life experience. This is a subversive approach within a discipline criticized for discounting the realities of everyday life. However, I cannot help but wonder if there is not more honesty in Miller-McLemore's acknowledgement of the role personal relationships have played in her research projects. Is there not an element of this influence within all theology? Our very questions are framed by the themes or areas that drive the problems we wrestle with in our own experiences. Or, as in the case of Soskice, in the experiences of those we see around us. Even this chapter emerges from my own inability to easily find a way to hold together competing vocational desires.

The diverse genesis of their theological reflection underpins the deep tension between contemplation and chaos found within the work of Coakley and Miller-McLemore. I find myself drawn first to one, then the other, bouncing between them in appreciation for and dissatisfaction with their reflection.

For Coakley, the stillness of silent, contemplative prayer to God is essential to her theological program. She acknowledges that this is not easy but claims it is essential nonetheless. I hear the wisdom of Ps 46: "Be still and know that I am God." I sense there is something to Coakley's claims that in our intentional inactivity of contemplative prayer, we make space for the Spirit to be active, to crack open the human heart for a new future. I admire the ways in which she draws together Scripture, patristics, orthodoxy, and

---

48. Ibid., "Fresh Paths in Systematic Theology," 71.
49. Rees, "Sarah Coakley," 28.

particular practices of faith so that desire and sexuality cannot be ignored by the theological academy. This is indeed a systematic theology, but it is a fleshy one.

Yet I see the inadequacy of contemplation for those whose lives are structured in ways that cannot hold silent contemplative prayer, including mothers. As noted by Soskice, the faithful discipleship of these women cannot merely be "on hold." I resonate with the noisiness of God's creativity in John 1: "In the beginning was the Word, and the Word was with God, and the Word was God." I admire Miller-McLemore's realism in addressing this issue, in adamantly claiming that God is just as present with those who live messy, busy, loud lives as those who live in the calm. Issues of justice and the full recognition of each person's humanity are at stake.

I return to Monro's work destabilizing duality: Do chaos and contemplation, and the broader frameworks they represent, need to be experienced as polarity? Must one be privileged over the other? Sarah Bachelard writes of Christian vocation, "The fundamental practice of spiritual growth is to bring our *actual* life before God."[50] Will this not mean silence and noise, contemplation and chaos? I wonder what the church has lost in richness of faith by marginalizing noise in favor of silence, losing the opportunity to attend to the voices of those such as mothers and their children. Through the history of the church, contemplative voices have been highly prized. Thinkers such as Miller-McLemore and Soskice help us to recognize that the church has often marginalized noisy voices arising from the midst of chaos. Ought we follow a liberationist claim by daring to suggest that God is *more* present in the midst of such noise?

Attention and Self:

Importantly, each of these four theologian picks up on the element of self-giving within the Christian tradition, a concept that has been criticized by feminist theologians as harmful to women. In their own way they see incarnation, selflessness, and self-giving as integral to Christian life alongside mothering, for "Whether we wish it or not, at the heart of the Eucharist is sacrifice."[51] Coakley speaks of the "unmastery" inherent in contemplative prayer.[52] Miller-McLemore notes the "moments of self-diminishment" experienced through parenting.[53] Soskice writes of "unselving" through in-

50. Bachelard, "Spiritual Maturity," 137.
51. Monro, "And Ain't I a Woman," 125.
52. Coakley, "Is There a Future?" 5.
53. Miller-McLemore, *Also a Mother*, 163.

tentional attention offered in love.[54] Monro speaks of the "loss of identity" that occurs in making space for multiple identities.[55]

Ministry requires unmastery, unselving, and what will, at times, be the loss of self-identity in stepping into a role representing Christ. Does not then parenting—with the demands it makes of patience, humility, and its moments of self-diminishment—offer insight into what it is to be a minister of Christ? As Soskice states:

> To attend to the child properly is also to employ the proper passivity of 'letting the other be.' The love of the parent, at the best of times, holds the child up without holding them back, for they must grow, and the parents must in gradual but continual steps 'let go' without ceasing to love unstintingly.[56]

Does this not describe the love of God for a creation sustained in freedom? Does this not mirror the role of clergy, who care for and tend a community of faith, holding them up, and seeking their growth and maturity? The risk of such self-sacrifice is the oppression it can bring in place of the mutuality it intends. Through history, women have borne many of the human consequences of that risk. Does this mean that the experience of mothers offers insight into God's very inner life—the conflicting emotions of joy and pain found in the freedom of creation?

In exploring poetic reading through planning and participation at the Gathering Conference for women in the UCA, Monro relates the difficulty women who already had a firm sense of themselves have in letting that stable sense of self go in order for new identities to emerge.[57] This raises questions for women who are called to exercise priesthood and motherhood as they locate themselves within multiple identities:

- What might be lost, as something new emerges?
- Is it difficult to lose the previous understanding of the identity 'priest' to make space for 'mother'?
- Is it difficult to lose the previous understanding of the identity 'mother' to make space for 'priest'?
- How does one inhabit roles of Mother, Priest, Mother and Priest, Priestly Mother, Motherly Priest?

---

54. Soskice, *Kindness of God*, 31.
55. Monro, *Resurrecting Erotic Transgression*, 56.
56. Soskice, *Kindness of God*, 31.
57. Monro, *Resurrecting Erotic Transgression*, 54.

(The) Ministry of Word, Sacrament, and Pastoral Care

Unconsciously, but perhaps unsurprisingly, I find the conversation between these four women drawing me back to the heart of ministry: worship, witness, and service. Miller-McLemore, Coakley, Soskice, and Monro each explore sacramentality and what it means to experience the grace-filled presence of God. They raise questions about how an ordained representative minister might embody this sacramental presence in his or her role as a minister of Christ. How do the threefold tasks of the ordained office—preaching the good news, presiding at the sacraments, and pastoral care with a focus on enabling all members of the church to participate in God's mission in the world—sit with the endless activities of the ministry of all believers? What happens when they seem to conflict?

An expansive notion of sacramentality is useful here. Coakley and Monro explicitly invoke the sacramental moment of Eucharistic presidency. At the table is a dangerous, disturbing, transforming experience of God, "where the miracle of divine enfleshment challenges and undercuts the rigid orderings of the world."[58] There is a radical and generous hospitality at play, wherein "Christ feeds her people with her very self at her own hand."[59] Miller-McLemore and Soskice highlight the presence of this same radical, disturbing, generous, transformative, dangerous grace even in a place where it has often been ignored or denied: the mundane, beautiful, ordinary, monstrous, inchoately graced task of caring for children. Ann Loades seeks to expand understandings of sacramentality in a similar way. She writes, "If we see children as gifts to the human community and not simply to their genetic or 'social' parents, parenting arguably brings human beings close to a sense of divine grace and generosity."[60] This raises an important question: Can Christ's table be disconnected from the nourishment and care of small, vulnerable ones who also bear God's image?

Each of these theologians explores the word of God's good gospel news for women and children. Coakley reminds us of God's presence in the silence of contemplative prayer that opens space for God's Spirit to be at work. Monro reminds us that the Scriptures are open to new and liberative interpretations that affirm the experiences of women. Soskice and Miller-McLemore remind us that silence is not always the prerequisite for encountering the gospel, for the Spirit hovers in the chaos. The gospel can be known as much through the care of children as from a pulpit.

---

58. Coakley, "Woman at the Altar," 92.
59. Monro, "And Ain't I a Woman," 128.
60. Loades, "Sacramentality and Christian Spirituality," 259.

The re-framing of word and sacrament offered through the tension and dialogue between these women's writing also serves to unsettle and expand the traditional "shepherd" image of Christian pastoral care. Images of mothering are lifted up as images of Christ's ministry. These images place women and children within the center of Christian faith rather than on its fringe. What would it mean for the church to take this gift on board? What might it mean for a person ordained into Christ's ministry of word, sacrament, and care to allow this role to embody chaos (Miller-McLemore), fleshy systematics (Coakley), inchoate grace (Soskice), and ambiguity (Monro)? Is there a particularly "feminist" way of being a minister of the Word that can take these concepts on board? In other words, can we as a church make space within ordained ministry for the multiplicity of identities and the transgression of fixed categories we encounter in the Christ?

Motherhood and Fatherhood amidst Priestly Calling

Towards the end of my ministry formation, two male, ordained members of the faculty of the college where I studied were sharing aspects of their journey to ordination and beyond. Both are fathers, ministers of the Word, and academics. Unsure whether this would be too personal, I asked them to comment on the way their families and children have shaped their ministry. There was a pause as they looked at each other, intuiting who might answer first. Momentarily, one responded, "To be honest, I didn't do that very well." I have a sense that further reflection upon the place of mothers in ordained ministry will not only enable women such as myself to think about how I will engage two roles with deep demands, it will also allow us to give voice to the tensions male clergy also experience in their vocations as fathers and priests.

Bibliography

Bachelard, Sarah. "Spiritual Maturity and Ministerial Obligation." In *Called to Minister: Vocational Discernment and Contemporary Church*, edited by Tom Frame, 127–42. Canberra, Australia: Barton, 2009.
Bunge, Marcia J., ed. *The Child in the Bible*. Grand Rapids: Eerdmans, 2008.
———. *The Child in Christian Thought*. Grand Rapids: Eerdmans, 2001.
Cannold, Leslie. *What, No Baby?* Fremantle, Australia: Curtin University, 2005.
Carey, Gemma, et al. "Discourse, Power and Exclusion: The Experiences of Childless Women." In *Theorising Social Exclusion*, edited by Ann Taket, 127–33. Oxford: Routledge, 2009.

Coakley, Sarah. "Fresh Paths in Systematic Theology." In *God's Advocates: Christian Thinkers in Conversation*, edited by Rupert Shortt, 67–85. Grand Rapids: Eerdmans, 2005.

———. "Is There a Future for Gender and Theology? On Gender, Contemplation, and the Systematic Task." *Criterion* 47 (2009) 2–11.

———. *Powers and Submission: Spirituality, Philosophy and Gender*. Oxford: Blackwell, 2002.

———. *Religion and the Body*. Cambridge: Cambridge University Press, 1997.

———. "The Woman at the Altar: Cosmological Disturbance or Gender Subversion." *Anglican Theological Review* 86 (2004) 75–93.

Cooper-White, Pamela. "Complicated Woman: Multiplicity and Relationality across Gender, Race and Culture." In *Women out of Order: Risking Change and Creating Care in a Multicultural World*, edited by Jeanne Stevenson Moessner and Teresa Snorton, 7–21. Minneapolis: Fortress, 2010.

Loades, Ann. "Sacramentality and Christian Spirituality." In *The Blackwell Companion to Christian Spirituality*, edited by Arthur Holder, 254–68. London: Wiley, 2010.

Miller-McLemore, Bonnie. *Also a Mother: Work and Family as Theological Dilemma*. Nashville: Abingdon, 1994.

———. "Feminism, Children and Mothering. Three Books and Three Children Later." *Journal of Childhood and Religion* 2 (2011) 1–32.

———. *In the Midst of Chaos: Caring for Children as Spiritual Practice*. San Francisco: Jossey Bass, 2007.

Monro, Anita. "'And Ain't I a Woman': The Phronetic Dramaturgy of Feeding the Family." In *Presiding Like a Woman*, edited by Nicola Slee and Stephen Burns, 123–32. London: SPCK, 2010.

———. *Resurrecting Erotic Transgression: Subjecting Ambiguity in Theology*. London: Equinox, 2006.

Rees, Janice. "Sarah Coakley: Systematic Theology and the Future of Feminism." Master's thesis, Charles Sturt University, 2009.

Shortt, Rupert. *God's Advocates: Christian Thinkers in Conversation*. Grand Rapids: Eerdmans, 2005.

Soskice, Janet Martin. "Just Women's Problems?" In *Spiritual Classics from the Late Twentieth Century*, edited by Ann Loades, 55–58. London: National Society & Church House, 1995.

———. *The Kindness of God: Metaphor, Gender and Religious Language*. Oxford: Oxford University Press, 2007.

———. "Women's Problems." In *Spiritual Classics from the Late Twentieth Century*, edited by Ann Loades, 47–54. London: National Society & Church House, 1995.

Uniting Church in Australia. "Why the Uniting Church in Australia Ordains Women to the Ministry of the Word?" In *Theology for Pilgrims*, edited by Rob Bos and Geoff Thompson, 562–615. Sydney: Uniting Church, 2008.

Williams, Dolores S. *Sisters in the Wilderness: The Challenge of Womanist God-talk*. Maryknoll, NY: Orbis, 1993.

Wood, Janet. "Participating with Purpose: Reflection on the Report *Women in the Uniting Church in Australia*." In *The Church Made Whole. National Conference on Women in the Uniting Church in Australia 1990*, edited by Elizabeth Wood Ellem, 27–35. Melbourne: Lovell, 1990.

10

Motherhood as a Metaphor for Contemporary Latina Theology and Spirituality

Pregnant Mary (Maria) on a Pilgrimage

CLAUDIA H. HERRERA

"And Mary kept all these things, reflecting on them in her heart."
—Luke 2:19[1]

This chapter will examine motherhood, particularly the journey of Mary, as a metaphor for Latina spirituality using *lo cotidiano*, a Spanish notion for the everyday life, as a practical theological source in the construction of Latina theology and spirituality. *Lo cotidiano* has become a source of theology revamped within the work of US contemporary Latino/a theology. It calls for transformation in theological discourse through an examination of the lived experiences of individuals and their social contexts. Latino/a theologians "are not merely attempting to bring forth the particular religious reality and practices of Hispanics; they are also seeking to transform the very discourse of theology."[2] This transformation happens uniquely. The thinking, knowledge, and spirituality about God become embodied, shaped, incarnated, and constructed from the heart of its people in everyday

---

1. Unless otherwise noted, the biblical verses used in this chapter are taken from the New American Bible (NAB) translation.
2. Michelle Gonzalez, *Sor Juana*, 15.

life,³ and it becomes transformative as it emerges from our practices and encounters with the people. *Lo cotidiano* "is a way of approaching theology as a space where God encounters those who are oppressed at the very place of their suffering,"⁴ and it brings a new message of salvation.

In the first section of this chapter, I will enter into conversation with the journey of the pregnant Mary. Mary's journey embodies *lo cotidiano* in its encounter with the sacred amidst her journey of hope and suffering. *Lo cotidiano* is built, then, not just upon daily stories, but rather within the lived experiences of the people. Even in the most unexpected conditions, God is born in unexpected places and through unexpected people. Mary's yes to God is reflected in the practice of the faithful disciple that moves to action and participates in the history of salvation. Empowered by the Holy Spirit, Mary walks with her people and for her people in the mission of hope and evangelization.

This chapter begins with narratives of the motherhood of Mary as metaphor for Latina theology and spirituality—including Mary's yes to God, episodes of her pregnancy, and when she gave birth to Jesus—it concludes the conversation where it begins: by inviting the reader to move to new places and announce the good news. Readers are invited to listen, explore, and reflect on the lived experiences of the people. In this way, critical questions and new knowledge will arise. This section presents a practical theological example of the lived experiences of young-generation Latinas. Here, we will recognize the value of our daily practices by living in the world and consider how theology is transformed, embodied, and shaped by our cultural context, experience, and tradition, where deep and authentic truth is waiting to be born.

The Pilgrimage of Mary in lo cotidiano⁵

Through the lenses of Latina/o eyes, imagery of Mary and thinking about God are built upon reflections of *lo cotidiano*—our everyday experiences or daily life. The Spanish term has strongly and naturally bloomed out of the hopes and struggles of Latinas/os living in the borderlands of the context of the United States.⁶ Everyday life is where new metaphors and imageries be-

---

3. Espín and Diaz, *From the Heart of Our People.*
4. Conde-Frazier, "Participatory Action Research," 235.
5. For the purpose of this chapter, *lo cotidiano* ("the everyday") is interpreted as the lived experiences of Mary in her journey as a pregnant Virgin: "*Lo cotidiano* is not a static category, but rather transformative" (Herrera, *Understanding Contemporary*, 11).
6. Maria Pilar Aquino explains *lo cotidiano* as *dynamis* dimension that "seek for a

come essential to our spirituality. The core of our everyday, lived experiences is where God reveals to Latinas and Latinas reveal to God their true selves. In this space of encounter between God and the people, there is no longer language, skin color, immigration status, economic level, or gender.

In the process of motherhood and labor, there is struggling hope, faithful pain, beautiful messiness of the uncertain, and a risen joy for salvation. Ivone Gebara defines daily life as "the fight to live today; our personal stories, the way we feel about events, our reactions as we read the papers or watch television; in short, our responses to reality. Into this milieu we are born, suffer, love and die."[7] The everyday becomes flesh when the heart and the body experience different forms of hope and suffering. Moreover, in the midst of our pilgrimage, our domestic life is not separated from the public life[8] or "the great challenges of culture."[9] It shapes the conditions of how we live and experience the world.

Imagine Mary and Joseph looking for shelter as foreign visitors in Judea. Their struggling journey as they looked for a place to stay only to find the only option would be giving birth in a humble manger became the main scene of a family trying to participate in an enrollment.[10] Mary's pilgrimage from town to town becomes a metaphor for Latina spirituality and theology in the way that it is incarnational. Mary travels as a pilgrim, embodies the conditions of the people, meets their needs, and identifies with them: "As mother of all, she is a sign of hope for peoples suffering the birth pangs of justice. She is the missionary who draws near to us and accompanies us throughout life, opening our hearts to faith by her maternal love. As a true mother, she walks at our side, she shares our struggles and she constantly surrounds us with God's love."[11]

---

better quality of life, including the right to friendship, bread, employment, and beauty" (Aquino, "Theological Method," 38).

7. Gebara, *Out of Depths*, 77.

8. Ada María Isasi-Díaz notes that "*lo cotidiano* makes social location explicit, for it is the context of the person in relation to physical space, ethnic space, social space" (Isasi-Díaz, *Mujerista Theology*, 71).

9. Gebara, *Out of Depths*, 77.

10. "In those days a decree went out from Caesar Augustus that the whole world should be enrolled. This was the first enrollment, when Quirinius was governor of Syria. So all went to be enrolled, each to his own town. And Joseph too went up from Galilee from the town of Nazareth to Judea, to the city of David that is called Bethlehem, because he was of the house and family of David, to be enrolled with Mary, his betrothed, who was with child. While they were there, the time came for her to have her child, and she gave birth to her firstborn son" (Luke 2: 1–7).

11. Francis, *Evangelii Gaudium*, §286.

In the midst of the routines and the unexpected conditions of daily life or *lo cotidiano*, Mary becomes not only a companion of the people, she also embodies and understands her people through her own human journey. Filled with the Holy Spirit, she participates in the dynamics of the everyday. Elizabeth Conde-Frazier reflects on the "internalization of the *presencia* ["presence"] of the Spirit. The Spirit works in us a oneness with God that awakens the fullness of who we are."[12] We who are women remember who we are when we are allowed to become "active participants" of our own journey and the journeys of the people who are part of our communities. In our daily living, this active *presencia*, who lives in us, allows the Spirit to move, transform, and enfold our true selves and who we are called to become in the pilgrimage of life. Ada María Isasi-Díaz refers to daily survival as "more than barely living. Survival in the day-to-day life has to do with the struggle *to be* fully."[13] It freely allows us to flourish and to *freely, faithfully say yes* to the divine call of service as active disciples!

Mary's Yes to God

In honoring each *pueblo*, or community, for its religious devotions, experiences, and interpretations of Mary, the pregnant Mary is of particular interest, and her relationship with motherhood becomes a metaphor for Latina spirituality. Her faithful, tender, yet courageous spirit moved her to respond as an active participant and "a prominent actor in her own right."[14] Mary's yes to God is more than just the social imaginaries of humility and self-giving stereotyped as weaknesses. Mary's yes to God is interpreted as the revolutionary response of a beloved disciple who is moved by the Spirit to follow Christ. As Pope Francis encourages in his apostolic exhortation *Evangelii Gaudium*, "whenever we look to Mary, we come to believe once again in the revolutionary nature of love and tenderness. In her we see that humility and tenderness are not virtues of the weak but of the strong who need not treat others poorly in order to feel important themselves."[15] Mary responds and acts as the "Spirit-filled evangelizer, fearlessly open to the working of the Holy Spirit."[16]

Mary's path of saying yes to God involved listening, reflecting, questioning, and acting. In Luke's Gospel, the evangelist describes Mary as

---

12. Conde-Frazier, *Latina Evangelicas*, 22.
13. Isasi-Díaz and Tarango, *Hispanic Women*, 4.
14. Gaventa and Rigby, *Blessed One*, 9.
15. Francis, *Evangelii Gaudium*, §288.
16. Francis, *Evangelii Guadium*, §259.

an active participant and "called by name"[17] as an active disciple. Mary is troubled, and she brings questions, asking, "How can this be?" (Luke 1:34). Mary speaks up, anticipates, and gives feedback to the angel, saying, "May it be done" (Luke 1:38). Mary acts as faithful disciple in *lo cotidiano*: "during those days Mary set out and traveled to the hill country in haste" (Luke 1:39). Mary proclaims: "My spirit rejoices in God my savior" (Luke 1:47) and "Mary kept all these things in her heart" (Luke 2:19). Within Catholic tradition, Pope Francis' exhortation *Evangelii Gaudium* describes Mary as "the mother of the living Gospel"[18] and therefore as "mother of evangelization"[19] by bringing Jesus' gift to the people.

Con-vivencia: When "the time came for her to have her child"[20]

In this section, I will interpret Mary's experience of pregnancy during her pilgrimage to Judea through the lenses available to me as a Latina theologian, particularly through my social location as Latina, Catholic, mother, wife, lay campus minister, and scholar living in the United States, specifically in South Florida. These theological lenses help me to retrieve and re-interpret the journey of the pregnant *Maria* as the faithful journey of a disciple who brings hope to her people along with a call for justice, even in the midst of her own struggles. Mary's journey to Judea was troubled by the pains of labor—she was about to give birth and there was no room at the inn. She moved from place to place until she found room for her son's birth in the most unexpected place. She faithfully responded to the divine call in the midst of ordinary life. Beginning with the incarnation of the divine mystery of Christ, God firmly reveals this to the people: "Her exceptional pilgrimage of faith represents a constant point of reference for the Church. Mary let herself be guided by the Holy Spirit on a journey of faith towards a destiny of service and fruitfulness."[21] Mary and Joseph experience the episode of two parents who are about to give birth without a shelter in a

17. Joel B. Green describes Mary's role in Luke's narrative. He notes that "Mary is a prominent actor in her own right. Indeed, in Luke 2:5 Joseph is introduced in relation to Mary; in 2:16 she is named before Joseph; in 2:33–34 Simeon, having blessed 'them' both, addressed himself to Mary; and in 2:48 Mary speaks for herself and her husband. Throughout his narrative, Luke mentions Mary by name thirteen times and refers to her directly" (Gaventa and Rigby, *Blessed One*, 9).

18. Francis, *Evangelii Guadium*, §287.

19. Ibid., 287–88.

20. Luke 2:6.

21. Francis, *Evangelii Gaudium*, §287.

foreign town. In her role as one who is called by God to be the mother of Jesus, Mary experiences what it is to be human in the faithful journey of motherhood.

Pope Francis points to what we already see in Luke's Gospel: Mary's faithfulness is demonstrated in her active openness to serve and love her people as an active disciple in *lo cotidiano*: "Mary was able to turn a stable into a home for Jesus, with poor swaddling clothes and an abundance of love."[22] With the birth of Jesus, this pilgrimage moves from the private to the public dimension because Mary's journey was not walked in isolation but rather in *convivencia* with the people. *Convivencia* is interpreted in this case as *con-vivencia*, where *con* signifies "to live with" and *vivencia* signifies "the lived experiences of the people." Putting these two terms together, *convivencia* signifies, therefore, *con la vivencia del otro*—to live with the lived experiences of the other. It reflects the practice of journeying together and walking with the lived experiences of one another. Carmen Nanko-Fernandez refers to the goal of *convivencia* as "living together as community that is predicated upon the analysis of the complexity of that living with the hopes of living together justly as well."[23] *Convivencia* is lived in the midst of beauty, messiness, and the hopes of reality—of deeply engaging, participating, listening, and articulating the lived expressions, movements, and *sentimientos* ("aesthetics").[24] Oscar Garcia Johnson includes *sentimientos* in *lo cotidiano*, which in the Latino/a sense is a form of "aesthetic reasoning" as it is "merged with action and ideals."[25] Mary's *lucha* ("battle") of giving birth in the most precarious conditions brought *sentimientos* of hope and beauty to the world with the gift of Jesus.

This Latino/a perspective of *convivencia* is also emphasized in the Gospel of Luke when the evangelist refers to the shepherds as participants and benefactors of the good news of the birth of Jesus: "Do not be afraid; for behold, I proclaim to you good news of great joy that will be for all the

22. Ibid.

23. Nanko-Fernandez, *Theologizing en Espanglish*, xviii.

24. For the purpose of this work, I am introducing the term "aesthetics" provided by Oscar Garcia-Johnson in order to translate the Spanish term *sentimiento*. Garcia-Johnson makes reference to "the grace of God and the power of the Spirit *with* me and *within* me" when he refers to *sentimiento* (Garcia-Johnson, *Mestizo/a Community of the Spirit*, xvii). Moreover, I would like to connect the interpretation of the term *sentimiento* with the perspective provided by Alejandro Garcia-Rivera on theological aesthetics. Alejandro Garcia-Rivera notes that "theological aesthetics recognizes in the experience of the truly beautiful a religious dimension" (Garcia-Rivera, *Community of the Beautiful*, 9). *Sentimiento* as beauty is incarnational and it is interpreted as "the human dynamism of the human spirit" in the encounter with the sacred (ibid.).

25. García-Johnson, *Mestizo/a Community of the Spirit*, 18.

people. For today in the city of David a savior has been born for you who is Messiah and Lord." (Luke 2:10–11). It is important to note that these shepherds were unprivileged individuals in the society of their times. However, "the great news of joy" as a message of salvation was transmitted in *convivencia*: a message of hope "that will be for all people," as Scripture tells us.

Sentimientos also makes reference to the core of *la lucha*[26] *cotidiana* ("the everyday struggles") of Latinas in order to survive. It represents hope amidst the daily routines and it plays a fundamental role because it invites people to move forward with faith. Ada María Isasi-Díaz refers to Hispanic women's struggle for "salvation" as "the struggle to become fully human as God intends them to be."[27] This goal becomes a methodological framework for Latinas doing theology, as "it requires a clear identification of the day-to-day life of those engaged in doing this theology, their needs and their struggles."[28] This perspective invites us to go deeper and listen to the lived experiences of the people—their practices and different encounters with God.

Acompañamiento: "When they saw this, "they made known the message" that had been told them about this child"[29]

Another theological term from Latina theology and spirituality—one that enters into a deep relationship with the pilgrimage of Mary as she gives birth to Jesus—is the practice of *acompañamiento* ("accompaniment"). *Acompañamiento* is a critical dynamic within the methodological framework of Hispanic or Latino/a theology in the construction of the good news or and the task of making "known the message" in solidarity with a large community.

Roberto Goizueta analyzes accompaniment as a theological category within the framework of Hispanic or Latino/a theology. This notion places the individual in relationship with the public sphere. It recognizes "the intrinsically relational or communal character of human persons and human action."[30] This relational character of the individual calls Latino/a

26. Ada María Isasi-Díaz introduces the notion of being in *la lucha* ("in the struggle") as a theological framework in Hispanic Women's Liberation Theology. See Isasi-Díaz, *En la Lucha*.

27. Isasi-Díaz and Tarango, *Hispanic Women*, 2.

28. Ibid.

29. Luke 2:17.

30. Goizueta, *Caminemos con Jesus*, 178.

theologians to opt for the needs and the lived experiences of the poor, the voiceless, the marginalized, the other, and those who are coming after.

Convivencia correlates with the notion of accompaniment. Accompaniment happens in *convivencia*, and it is lived out *en la comunidad* ("within the community"). Within US Latino/a theology, the thinking, knowledge, and reflections on God have been constructed in *comunidad* rather than in isolation. By witnessing the practices, needs, and lived experiences of the people, the communal construction of the good news creates a legacy for the upcoming generations: "*La comunidad* ["the community"] is the immediate reality within which Hispanics find their personal identities and function."[31] María Pilar Aquino and Roberto Goizueta refer to the "*praxis of accompaniment*—a theology that arises from our experiences being part of the life of our communities."[32] This circular dynamic of giving and receiving happens in mutual relationship between Latinas and their communities. Latinas' lived experiences shape their communities even as their community shapes them. In the goal of salvation, Latinas pursue "bringing a new reality."[33] It is a matter of actively participating in the construction of hope, joy, peace, justice, and reconciliation in our communities. In the words of Ada María Isasi-Díaz, "Hispanic Women believe they have a distinct and valuable contribution to make."[34] This gift to the world is unique, for it embodies lived experiences.

This notion of accompaniment is found throughout the story of Mary's life. In the Gospel of Luke, God accompanied Mary from the moment she was called to fulfill God's plan as she accompanies her people in the journey of motherhood and discipleship. As a faithful disciple and mother of God, Mary carries Jesus in her womb (Luke 1:26–46; Luke 2:1–5), embodies his birth (Luke 2: 6–20), and accompanies his life (Luke 2:22–52; John 2:1–12) before her heart is pierced by his passion (Luke 2:34–35, 51), death (John 19:25–27) and resurrection (Acts 1:14–10:41; Matt 28:10). From the beginning, when she was called, "Mary kept all these things in her heart" (Luke 2:19, 51).

Within the framework of *la comunidad* ("the community"), *la familia* ("family") becomes the public sphere where faith is not merely passed to children and grandchildren as a gift, it is also constructed and made known to the extended community. Within *la familia*, religious identity

---

31. Isasi-Díaz and Tarango, *Hispanic Women*, 6.

32. Aquino, "Theological Method," 27; Goizueta, "U.S. Hispanic Mestizaje," 22; cited in Martell-Otero, "Introduction: *Abuelita* Theologies," 5.

33. Isasi-Díaz and Tarango, *Hispanic Women*, 4.

34. Ibid.

and practices are transformative as they become part of the dynamics of everyday life. Within the dynamic of accompaniment, *las abuelas* ("grandmothers") become a source for theology: "The stories of our mothers and grandmothers are remembered and lived in our spiritual lives. This is why Latina scholars include the voices of everyday, grassroots Latinas."[35] Those mothers and grandmothers who helped shape self-identity and spirituality pass down the love for God.

In a humble manger, motherhood was underestimated by the world, and yet the community of believers lifted up motherhood and the message of salvation. Similarly, Loida Martell-Otero argues that "our traditions have too easily been dismissed."[36] It is in the traditions of families where the dynamics and the construction of evangelization and catechesis of Latinos/as in the United States begin. Our *abuelas* ("grandmothers") become the carriers of God's message. Our *abuelas* are the shepherds and the prophets who "made known the message that had been told them" about God (Luke 2:17). Latinas' hearts are "amazed by what had been told them by the shepherds" (Luke 2:18) as they listen to the traditions passed down from their *abuelas* and construct new religious identities. Like these *abuelas*, Mary presented Jesus to the world similarly to how Latinas/os pass their faith from generation to generation. In my own research on emerging adult Latinas, I have found the presence of *abuelas* and mothers hold great importance in their faith formation and spirituality. Spanish language is at the core of spirituality, for it is the language that has been used to pray and live in the routines of the everyday life.

Latina Spirituality and Religious Identity of the Young Generation of Latinas

In practical theology, one learns to listen to the lived experiences of the people and enter into their context, experience, and tradition. The categories of God, *familia*, relationships, church, devotional practices, and language are shaped by our grassroots as we imagine Mary and God. There is a strong faith carried within Latinas' lived experiences. Religious practices, devotions, traditions, and beliefs are reshaped between the dynamic of those who share "common experiences of bilingualism, multiculturalism, popular religious faith, marginality, poverty, colonization, migration, and cultural alienation."[37] Particularly in a generation born and raised as Catholic Lati-

35. Gonzalez, *Embracing Latina Spirituality*, 7.
36. Martell-Otero, "Introduction: *Abuelita* Theologies," 3.
37. Ibid., 4.

nas, new religious identities are emerging out of the practices and devotions constructed within the family. In my own research with college-age Latinas,

> I utilize participatory action research in order to articulate the lived experiences and religious practices, devotions and beliefs of these young women. Listening to this group, I have encountered a generation that, besides overcoming the transitions of young adulthood such as searching for meaning and purpose, they have to negotiate life between two worlds; the world of their home which is the same their parents once lived behind in Latin-America, and the context of the United States in which they were born, grew up, and live.[38]

In fact, "Preliminary results show that Latinas' hopes and struggles are still hidden in the tension between two worlds in which they have to negotiate values, morals, and virtues."[39] My initial findings suggest there is a gap between the faith that is taught at home and young Latinas' knowledge of tradition and church teachings. *La familia*, therefore, is interpreted as a metaphor of motherhood for Latina spirituality in the sense that it becomes the *iglesia domestica* ("domestic church") and a key community in the construction of the public sphere. It is where practices such giving birth, struggling, hoping, journeying, suffering, praying, and breaking bread take place. *La familia* becomes the place where God reveals God's self in *lo cotidiano*, even journeying with the metaphorical narratives and daily stories of Mary's yes to God and her journey as a pregnant mother. It is customary to find *altarcitos* ("little altars") and images of Mary in her various personifications in the homes of fervent immigrant Latino/a homes in the United States. These expressions of faith and spirituality are not simply decorations. Rather, for some Latinas/os, they represent accompaniment. These sacred places, like our home altars, our prayers, and *novenas*—such as the *novenas* prayed nine days before Christmas—the medals (*medallitas*) around our necks, and even the native language we use to communicate directly with God are symbols that represent our expressions of faith and represent the manger through which God is revealed to the people.

Mary's Pilgrimage to Calvary: A Path Yet to Be Discovered

In the process of interpreting motherhood through the lenses of Latina spirituality and the lived experiences of Latinas, there is a hidden path yet to

---

38. Herrera, "Understanding Contemporary . . . ," 6.
39. Ibid., "Rethinking Lo Cotidiano?" 11.

be discovered. There are lived stories to be heard, told, and articulated that are not written in the text. It is important to reimagine and reinterpret new metaphors by listening to *lo cotidiano* ("the everyday experiences") of the people. Mary walked to Judea with Jesus in her womb, just as she walked with him in his passion to Calvary—except she took that second path in painful silence as she wept and wept. Mary's invisible path to Calvary opens the door to reimagine the invisible path of Latinas in twenty-first century United States. Mary's journey to Calvary becomes a shared pilgrimage with Latinas who weep, struggle, and experience faith, hope, love, passion, and strength. This is the path of those who pray in silence and question; it is the journey of those who experience uncertainty, guilt, shame, fear, joy, redemption, and other *sentimientos* that are hidden in *la lucha* ("the struggle") of being Latinas. Mary shows us in her example of motherhood a faithful journey of prayer, reflection, and action. Just as "Mary kept all these things, reflecting on them in her heart" (Luke 2:19) as she was called to be the mother of Jesus, Mary continues to provide a means for such reflection today in her role as mother to all.

In words of Pope Francis' prayer to Mary, "we advance confidently towards the fulfilment of this promise, and to her we pray":

> Mary, Virgin and Mother,
> you who, moved by the Holy Spirit,
> welcomed the word of life
> in the depths of your humble faith:
> as you gave yourself completely to the Eternal One,
> help us to say our own "yes"
> to the urgent call, as pressing as ever,
> to proclaim the good news of Jesus.
>
> Filled with Christ's presence,
> you brought joy to John the Baptist,
> making him exult in the womb of his mother.
> Brimming over with joy,
> you sang of the great things done by God.
> Standing at the foot of the cross
> with unyielding faith,
> you received the joyful comfort of the resurrection,
> and joined the disciples in awaiting the Spirit
> so that the evangelizing Church might be born.[40]

---

40. Francis, *Evangelii Gaudium*, §288.

Bibliography

Aquino, María Pilar. "Theological Method in U.S. Latino/a Theology: Toward an Intercultural Theology for the Third Millennium." In *From the Heart of Our People: Latino/a Explorations in Catholic Systematic Theology*, edited by Orlando O. Espín and Miguel H. Díaz, 6–48. Maryknoll, NY: Orbis, 1993.

Conde-Frazier, Elizabeth. "Participatory Action Research." In *The Wiley-Blackwell Companion to Practical Theology*, edited by Bonnie J. Miller-McLemore, 234–43. Malden, MA: Wiley-Blackwell, 2011.

Espín, Orlando O., and Miguel Diaz. *From the Heart of Our People: Latino/a Explorations in Catholic Systematic Theology*. Maryknoll, NY: Orbis, 1999.

Francis, Pope. *Evangelii Gaudium* [The Joy of the Gospel: On the Proclamation of the Gospel in Today's World]. Rome: Vatican Press, 2013.

García-Johnson, Oscar. *The Mestizo/a Community of the Spirit: A Postmodern Latino/a Ecclesiology*. Eugene, OR: Pickwick, 2009.

Garcia-Rivera, Alejandro. *The Community of the Beautiful: A Theological Aesthetics*. Collegeville, MN: Liturgical, 1999.

Gaventa, Beverly Roberts, and Cynthia L. Rigby, eds. *Blessed One: Protestant Perspectives on Mary*. Louisville: Westminster John Knox, 2002.

Gebara, Ivone. *Out of Depths: Women's Experience of Evil and Salvation*. Minneapolis: Fortress, 2002.

Goizueta, Roberto S. *Caminemos con Jesús: Toward a Hispanic/Latino Theology of Accompaniment*. Maryknoll, NY: Orbis, 1995.

———. "U.S. Hispanic Mestizaje and Theological Method." In *Migrants and Refugees*, edited by Dietmar Mieth and Lisa Sowle Cahill, 22–30. New York: Orbis, 1993.

Gonzalez, Michelle A. *Embracing Latina Spirituality, A Woman's Perspective*. Cincinnati: Messenger, 2009.

———. *Sor Juana: Beauty and Justice in the Americas*. Maryknoll, NY: Orbis, 2003.

Herrera, Claudia H. "Rethinking Lo Cotidiano through the Lenses of Catholic Latinas in Their 20s: A New Marianismo?" Paper presented at the Academy of Catholic Hispanic Theologians of the United States Colloquium, San Diego, CA, June 1–4, 2014.

———. "Understanding Contemporary Latino/a Theology through the Lenses of Latinas in Their 20s." PhD diss., St. Thomas University, in progress.

Isasi-Diaz, Ada Maria. *En La Lucha/In the Struggle: Elaborating a Mujerista Theology*. Minneapolis: Fortress, 1994.

———. *Mujerista Theology: A Theology for the Twenty First Century*. Maryknoll, NY: Orbis, 1996.

Isasi-Díaz, Ada María, and Yolanda Tarango. *Hispanic Women: Prophetic Voice in the Church—Toward a Hispanic Woman's Liberation Theology*. New York: Harper & Row, 1988.

Martell-Otero, Loida I. "Introduction: *Abuelita* Theologies." In *Latina Evangélicas: A Theological Survey from the Margins*, edited by Loida I. Martell-Otero, Zaida Maldonado Pérez, and Elizabeth Conde-Frazier, 1–13. Eugene, OR: Cascade, 2013.

Martell-Otero, Loida I., Zaida Maldonado Pérez, and Elizabeth Conde-Frazier. *Latina Evangélicas: A Theological Survey from the Margins*. Eugene, OR: Cascade, 2013.

Nanko-Fernandez, Carmen. *Theologizing en Espanglish*. Maryknoll, NY: Orbis, 2010.

11

Matrescence and Spiritual Transformation
Finding God in the Disorientation of New Motherhood

SARAH FOLEY MASSA

Introduction

We live " . . . in a history where we are dying and rising, and in a history where God is at work, ending our lives and making gracious new beginnings."

—Walter Brueggemann[1]

Matrescence, or the process of becoming a mother, contains the often-untapped potential for spiritual transformation.[2] A sense of loss of self, being drained of physical and emotional energy, and feelings of isolation are challenging experiences common to mothers, as revealed in contemporary midwife studies. Lesley Barclay and Francis Rogan have identified and analyzed these experiences of new motherhood in a series of studies in the Australian context.[3] This chapter proposes that a Christian engagement with the challenges of motherhood enables recognition of the divine in the

---

1. Brueggemann, *Praying the Psalms*, 15.
2. Thomas, "Becoming a Mother," 89.
3. Barclay, "Becoming a Mother"; Rogan, "'Becoming a Mother."

ordinary—an acknowledgment of God in all things—that opens a mother to the possibility of spiritual transformation. Reflecting on the psalms, Walter Brueggemann has developed a way of speaking about a life of faith as "moving" with God through repeating stages of secure orientation, painful disorientation, and surprising reorientation.[4] This chapter will explore the challenges and processes of change experienced in early motherhood in conversation with Brueggemann's scheme. The function of painful disorientation is to drive us from complacency to seek the "Holy One."[5] New motherhood entails a sense of disorientation that can confront a mother with a choice between despair and hope. Disorientation is an opportunity for mothers to re-evaluate their deepest values and their relationship with God. Attending to the present moment and to different prayer practices can be ways for mothers to consciously engage with this transformative process. Surprising reorientation becomes an opportunity and a gift from God—one that does not return us to the old but instead becomes an entry into "all things new."[6]

1: Context and Methodology

Context

In this chapter, we will explore the context of motherhood discussed in Barclay's contemporary midwife study: first-time middle class Australian mothers of infants up to twenty-six weeks old.[7] Barclay's paper presents the results of a qualitative study into fifty-five women's experiences of new motherhood. Rogan's paper is an extension of Barclay's findings and presents a "framework" with which to understand the difficulties associated with new motherhood.[8] These studies highlight that contemporary mothers in the western world are experiencing increasing challenges when entering motherhood: "'Becoming a mother' for most women caused them to feel isolated, alone, and depleted rather than nurtured and supported."[9]

First-time mothers face increasing challenges in the contemporary world as a result of a variety of factors. We will explore four of these factors: (1) the changing role of women, (2) the silences surrounding motherhood's

---

4. Brueggemann, *Praying the Psalms*, 16.
5. Ibid., 19.
6. Ibid., 22.
7. Barclay, "Becoming a Mother," 719.
8. Rogan, "Becoming a Mother," 884.
9. Barclay, "Becoming a Mother," 727.

challenges, (3) secularism, and (4) the frenetic pace of life. All these factors can shape a mother's sense of self.

On the changing role of women, a contemporary western middle class context offers a multitude of choices and opportunities regarding self-development. Opportunities exist for an Australian mother to be involved in professional work while also being a primary caregiver. Gone are the days when a woman's role was solely household duties and child-rearing. Porter uses the contemporary term "motherwork" to describe the entirety of house- and child-related duties a mother performs.[10] Part of the complexity of motherhood today is juggling paid work with this "motherwork."

In terms of the silences on motherhood, one contemporary clinical nursing study showed that a "conspiracy of silence existed" for mothers.[11] The study found that mothers felt unprepared for the enormity of mothering and wished they had better preparation. Indeed, "nothing in their life had prepared them for the realities of motherhood and infant care."[12] Thomas identifies a "mask of motherhood," describing society's silence surrounding the "chaos and complexity" of motherhood. This mask of silence "prevents our society from realistically preparing prospective mothers."[13] Contemporary mothers need ways of listening and speaking about motherhood's challenges.

Brueggemann also expresses the importance of "speaking" one's truth in his interpretation of Jeremiah's prophetic voice: "Despite all our talk about 'freedom of speech,' serious human discourse has, in reality, all but disappeared among us. Issues are not much joined. Serious hope is scarcely practiced. Deep hurt is largely unacknowledged."[14] Brueggemann suggests the need to counter this destructive silence by "utterance, unafraid speech that brings holiness back into history . . . that owns suffering . . . that voices hope in the midst of despair."[15] In using Brueggemann's schema of orientation/disorientation/re-orientation, a mother must first own her disorientation so that she can then make the journey toward transformation.

The complex and evolving reality of secularism is another factor affecting mothers in the contemporary Australian context. Secularism can be identified with modernity insofar as to be modern is "to assert that human reason is the ultimate authority" with an accompanying tendency to

10. Porter, "Focus on Mothering."
11. McVeigh, "Motherhood Experiences," 341.
12. Ibid., 346.
13. Thomas, *Spirituality in the Mother Zone*, 36.
14. Brueggemann, *Like Fire in the Bones*, 83.
15. Ibid.

ignore or deny the "principles of supernatural religion."[16] This is important to note because it can mean that in this secular context, a mother may not be encouraged to reflect on her relationship with God. Living in a secular society, it can be easy to identify less with Christian values and more with cultural values. On the challenge of being a Christian in a secular world, Rolheiser notes, "We must recognize that we ourselves are part of this world . . . and are inextricably bound up in our culture." He asserts the importance of avoiding falling into "any kind of oversimplistic duality" within which Christians see themselves as good and the world as evil.[17]

The frenetic pace of life in contemporary times also has a significant role in shaping a mother's sense of self. Rolheiser elaborates on the loss of interiority in contemporary times as a result of increased busyness and restlessness.[18] People seek identity and meaning through doing rather than being. Productivity and performance are considered the determinants of personhood. A busy, rushed lifestyle does not encourage the internal reflection through which one meets with one's own deepest values. This impacts how new mothers perceive their change in roles in relation to their sense of self.

Methodology

In *Praying the Psalms*, Brueggemann develops a scheme of spiritual development that focuses on the fact that there are certain events in life "which drive us to the edge of humanness and make us peculiarly open to the Holy One."[19] This chapter explores how matrescence is a powerful liminal experience that can be an invitation to such a transformation. Brueggemann's scheme provides a way of understanding the experience of disorientation in motherhood. In using this scheme, this essay will show how mothers can reframe their experience of motherhood such that they choose hope over despair.

Brueggemann's scheme consists of a "life of faith" that "consists in moving with God in terms of (a) being securely oriented, (b) being painfully disoriented, and (c) being surprisingly reoriented."[20] He uses this scheme in conversation with praying the psalms, whereby the psalms reflect and express the extremities of human experience. These three states are examined

16. Rolheiser, *Secularity and the Gospel*, 39.
17. Ibid., 45.
18. Rolheiser, *Shattered Lantern*, 49.
19. Brueggemann, *Praying the Psalms*, 17.
20. Ibid., 16.

with the underlying understanding that in reality the move from phase to phase is not concrete or immediate, but is often a gradual process involving a back-and-forth movement between states.[21] Brueggemann expands upon this scheme in his book *Hopeful Imagination*, in which he highlights the movements from exile to freedom in Jeremiah, Ezekiel, and Isaiah. The process is painful, but hope and restoration have the last say.[22] Brueggemann suggests this scheme is applicable to examinations of any facet of life: "It can permit us to speak of 'passages,' the life-cycle, stages of growth, and identity crises."[23]

In Brueggemann's scheme, "moving with God" has two aspects. First, "with God" anchors the three phases of orientation firmly in the Christian context of a relationship between God and the individual. Second, "moving with" indicates that this ongoing relationship is not static but is instead a journey that involves growth and transformation through various phases. Movement between phases requires openness on the part of the one journeying to stay "with" God and "move" with God when it is time. Brueggemann's scheme highlights that life entails movement and growth, providing an opportunity for spiritual transformation into "all things new."

2: Brueggemann in Conversation with New Motherhood Experiences

Being Securely Oriented

Trust in the Lord, and do good;
So you will live in the land,
And enjoy security.

—Ps 37:3

According to Brueggemann, the first phase of being "securely oriented" is a "state of equilibrium" where "one is well-settled, knowing that life makes sense."[24] It is a security many long for. Contemporary society fosters the belief that life is about personal comfort and we should avoid any sort of pain or disruption. Brueggemann comments,

---

21. Ibid.
22. Ibid., *Hopeful Imagination*.
23. Ibid., *Praying the Psalms*, 16.
24. Ibid., 17.

> For the normal, conventional functioning of public life, the raw edges of disorientation and reorientation must be denied or suppressed for purposes of public equilibrium . . . And mostly the Holy One is not addressed, not because we dare not, but because God is far away and hardly seems important. This means that the agenda and intention of the Psalms is considerably at odds with the normal speech of a stable, functioning, self-deceptive culture in which everything must be kept running young and smooth.[25]

Contemporary society, then, contributes to this desire to remain in a state of equilibrium and secure orientation.

The Experience of Secure Orientation in Pre-Motherhood

In relation to motherhood, the state of secure orientation may be experienced before having a baby. Prior to motherhood, a woman may have experienced life feeling securely oriented in relation to her sense of self and daily circumstances. This may be a time of spiritual complacency when life seemed to have some sort of order and control. Concerning people whose life is one of uninterrupted continuity and equilibrium, Brueggeman states that "few of us live that kind of life. Most of us who think our lives are that way have been numbed, desensitized, and suppressed so that we are cut off from what is in fact going on in our lives."[26] Following childbirth, there is little chance of maintaining a false state of equilibrium. Motherhood can be an opportunity to connect more deeply with life in all its messy reality.

Painfully Disoriented

> O Lord, God of my salvation,
> When, at night, I cry out in your presence,
> Let my prayer come before you;
> Incline your ear to my cry.
> For my soul is full of troubles,
> And my life draws near to Sheol.
> I am counted among those who go down to the Pit.
>
> —Ps 87:1–4

---

25. Ibid., 19.
26. Ibid., 23.

The second movement in Brueggemann's scheme—being "painfully disoriented"—occurs in situations of extremity "for which conventional equilibrium offers no base."[27] Brueggemann believes times of painful disorientation—those experiences of life that lie beyond our "conventional copings"—"drive us to speak to the Holy One."[28] Thus, times of disorientation can become opportunities to engage with God. This chapter will now turn to an exploration of the challenges evident in Barclay's study in conversation with Brueggemann's scheme.

The Experience of Painful Disorientation in Motherhood

The experience of disorientation is common in the lives of new mothers. Contemporary writers on new motherhood use this term "disorientation" in a similar sense to Brueggemann's understanding of disorientation. For example, in her reflections on responses from ninety-three mothers, Trudelle Thomas comments that "running through many accounts of birth and matrescence is the sense of disorientation."[29]

Contemporary midwife studies reveal the magnitude of change first-time mothers experience during the overwhelming process of becoming a mother.[30] In a study exploring the perceptions and emotions of first-time mothers, Barclay identifies six sub-categories that help define the core category of "becoming a mother." The six sub-categories are "realizing, readiness, drained, aloneness, loss, and working it out."[31] These categories help us name the challenges of new motherhood. The first five of these sub-categories can be grouped within Brueggemann's scheme as times of disorientation. The sixth sub-category, "working it out," and the core category of "becoming mother" can be viewed as a "moving" into times of reorientation.

REALIZING AND UNREADY

> I felt like I was walking into, say, someone else's life, that's what it felt like . . . I was saying to myself this isn't my life anymore—it's someone else's and I'm watching a film, it's not really mine . . . it

---

27. Ibid., 18.
28. Ibid.
29. Thomas, "Becoming a Mother," 91.
30. Rogan, "Becoming a Mother," 877.
31. Barclay, "Becoming a Mother," 721.

took me at least a week and a half to realise . . . that it was actually mine and that it was my life that was changing.

—Lesley Barclay[32]

In Barclay's study, "realizing" describes "facing the overwhelming process of becoming a mother and the consequences this has on one's life. The impact of this realization was huge for many women."[33] "Realizing" included a growing awareness of how the consequences of motherhood impact a woman's lifestyle, body, and relationships. It involved learning something "totally new," and the learning was continual.[34] "Realizing" also entailed a realization that early motherhood was different from new mothers' expectations. One mother commented, "'Cause I hadn't realized how much work went into it actually doing things . . . they all said to me 'Oh it's so easy' . . . and then all of a sudden I realized it wasn't quite that easy."[35] "Realizing" was also closely related to Barclay's second category: "unready." The more "unready" a woman felt when faced with the "realization" of everything motherhood was to entail, the more overwhelmed she became.[36] A mother's level of preparation had direct bearing on her feeling "unready." Together these processes of "realizing" and being "unready" contributed to feelings of upheaval and a "disturbed" sense of self.[37] Other studies also observed the "process" of becoming a mother: "the women talk about conflicting attitudes they experienced and a disorientation and constant reflection on self-concept."[38] The process of becoming a mother involves a re-definition of a woman's sense of self.

Drained, Aloneness, and Loss

I find it's a mental tired too, you don't know what's going on, you're learning as each day goes by anyway and you're constantly watching people and what they do and you're wondering if that doesn't

---

32. Ibid.
33. Ibid.
34. Ibid., 722.
35. Ibid.
36. Rogan, "Becoming a Mother," 881.
37. Ibid.
38. Atkinson, "Gaining Motherhood, Losing Identity?" 172.

work. Plus you've got everybody else telling you how you should do things. I think that becomes tiring too.

—Lesley Barclay[39]

Drained, aloneness, and loss were the three categories used in Barclay's study to further describe the feelings of upheaval experienced in new motherhood. The term "drained" expressed physical, emotional, and mental tiredness. The physical tiredness of new motherhood connects to sleep deprivation and to the physical demands required by young infant care. The physical and emotional fatigue associated with new motherhood has been widely documented. In a study exploring the early motherhood experiences of seventy-nine first-time mothers, McVeigh identifies fatigue as a "great stress factor during the post-partum period."[40] Other research points to the sleep loss during pregnancy escalating during the first few weeks postpartum and having "tangible" effects in terms of fatigue, irritability, and loss of concentration.[41] In McVeigh's study, one mother observes, "the utter relentlessness of infant care is overwhelming . . . I'm quite taken back by how tired I am."[42]

Mental tiredness also contributed to being drained. Barclay comments, "the women said that the mental tiredness was associated with uncertainty and the process of constantly learning."[43] Uncertainty and the process of learning were impacted by the mothers' perception of outsiders "monitoring their inadequate mothering skills."[44]

The category "aloneness" reflected the isolation some of the new mothers experienced. The contemporary social context for mothers can contribute to their feelings of isolation because "the nuclear household reduces women's contact with the real world in the early post-partum weeks, resulting in disorientation, depression, and despair."[45]

Barclay's third category describing the upheaval in a new mother's life was "loss." "Loss" was experienced in a variety of ways, from loss of time and

---

39. Barclay, "Becoming a Mother," 723.
40. McVeigh, "Motherhood Experiences," 336.
41. Ibid.
42. Ibid., 343.
43. Barclay, "Becoming a Mother," 723.
44. Ibid.
45. Rogan, "Becoming a Mother," 883.

freedom to loss in relationships and loss of a sense of self.[46] One mother commented,

> Well, none of your time is your own. It's you know, like sort of having a lifestyle where you can actually have a lot of freedom and enjoy your life . . . now you've got this tiny little thing that runs your whole life 24 hours a day. It just doesn't stop.[47]

This comment reflects the losses in lifestyle mothers experience and the struggle of adapting to the new routines life with a baby brings. A new mother's immersion into the constant day-to-day duties of care can impact her emotional state. Paramount to a mother's inner contentment or frustration will be how she sees these repetitive day-to-day tasks. It is difficult to place a value on household tasks in a contemporary society that values external success and efficiency. McVeigh observes the huge degree of necessary adjustment to daily routine: "no-one had told them how hard being a mother could be. They had not realized how much work was involved in infant care and how boring and repetitive it could become."[48] Adjustment to the daily demands required during the early baby phase can pose a challenge to any new mother's sense of identity and contribute to her sense of loss.

In Barclay's study, many women experienced a loss of a sense of self as "loss of confidence, self-esteem, and a negative perception of themselves as mothers."[49] The expectations contemporary mothers bring to mothering deeply impact this loss of a sense of self. Mothers' expectations are shaped by the society in which they live. Research by Adrienne Rich reveals the origins of the "should" in motherhood and the false expectations around what a "good mother" should be. Rich describes motherhood as an "invisible institution" that has shaped society's expectations of mothers.[50] In contemporary times, the model of motherhood is one of "intensive mothering"—a model researchers agree is unattainable.[51] Ellyn Sanna comments, "We're so busy trying to be everything—both professionals and mothers, good housekeepers and intelligent career women—that our spiritual vision is clouded by exhaustion and frustration. Finding the balance between our roles is hard, perfection is impossible, and the load of guilt we pull onto

---

46. Barclay, "Becoming a Mother," 724.
47. Ibid.
48. McVeigh, "Motherhood Experiences," 341.
49. Barclay, "Becoming a Mother," 724.
50. Rich, *Of Women Born*, 276.
51. Porter, "Focus on Mothering," 13.

our shoulders sometimes takes all our energy to carry."[52] Unexamined, false expectations can contribute greatly to a mother's confusion regarding the loss of her sense of self and the accompanying disorientation she may experience.

Understanding a mother's disorientation in the light of Brueggemann's scheme requires a reminder of the scheme's "God" context—that is life consisting of a "moving with God." This places the experience of disorientation in a context of meaning that can remind a new mother that her sense of self is based on the reality that she is loved by God, always and in all things. A mother may experience overwhelming feelings when "realizing" all that having a baby entails: the huge process of learning, feeling unready, experiencing fatigue and loss, being drained, and feeling isolated at times. Yet in Brueggemann's scheme, even deeper than these experiences lies an awareness that God is present in all of life's happenings. This interpretation offers hope because the experience of a mother's disorientation—rather than being an isolated event—is only one of a "series" of movements, all of which take place within the presence of a loving God.

According to Brueggemann, the function of disorientation is to drive one to speak to God. In experiencing the disorientation of new motherhood, a mother is driven beyond her limits. In her experience of upheaval and disorientation, a mother has the opportunity to enter deeply into her life and question her challenging experiences. At this time, she needs a way of being able to think about her life—a way of understanding. Viewing her life through Brueggemann's scheme shows her that disorientation need not be faced alone, but in God. It is an invitation to engage with God through her despair and find the hope she needs. Disorientation in motherhood becomes an opportunity to know God afresh—to encounter the God who understands the troubles of this world: "In the world you will have hardship. But take courage; I have overcome the world" (John 16:33).

Surprisingly Reoriented

Bless the Lord, O my soul,
And all that is within me . . .
Who redeems your life from the Pit,
Who crowns you with steadfast love and mercy,
Who satisfies you with good as long as you live

---

52. Sanna, *Motherhood*, 2.

So that your youth is renewed like the eagles

—Ps 103: 1,4–5

Brueggemann describes the third movement in his scheme as "being surprisingly reoriented." This involves the "surprising move from disorientation to a new orientation which is quite unlike the old status quo."[53] Brueggemann states that reorientation is "not an automatic movement which can be presumed upon or predicted. Nor is it a return to the old form . . . It is rather 'all things new.'"[54] The term "surprisingly" indicates that ultimately we are not in control over the unfoldings of life or the timing or way of reorientation. "It is the recognition of the disoriented person that a new orientation must come as a gift."[55] This "gift" of surprising reorientation involves a "new joyous orientation" that invites thanksgiving.[56]

The Experience of Surprising Reorientation in Motherhood.

In Barclay's study, the sub-category of "working it out" and the core category of "becoming a mother" provide opportunities for a new "orientation" in motherhood.

Working It Out: Becoming a Mother

So, bit by bit, and all the ideas, things sort of worked out . . .

—Lesley Barclay[57]

In the stage of "working it out," the new mothers developed skills and gained confidence in being mothers and caring for their babies.[58] Barclay's study demonstrated that "becoming a mother" in an emotional and personal sense was a process that took time but that ultimately led to an experience of reorientation and, with it, a greater enjoyment of motherhood. The women described themselves as "being in tune with their baby . . . developing a

---

53. Brueggemann, *Praying the Psalms*, 22.
54. Ibid.
55. Ibid., 45.
56. Ibid., 23.
57. Barclay, "Becoming a Mother," 724.
58. Ibid.

sense of synchronicity with the baby and a sense of self as mother."[59] Other contemporary researchers have also observed a "settling in process" as mothers began to feel competent and to develop confidence with their infant: "The psychosocial development of a mother was a continuous process . . . as mothers oriented themselves toward a 'new normal.'"[60]

In the light of Brueggemann's scheme, reorientation in motherhood—where things "sort of worked out bit by bit"—reflects the element of "surprise" or mystery.[61] Consequently, mothers are invited to reflect upon the source behind this surprising reorientation. Reorientation, then, has the potential for a deeper engagement with the divine. Reflection on the experience of reorientation enables a mother to recognize God's active presence in her life with "all things working together for good" (Rom 8:28). It is in this recognition of God's good, active presence that deep thankfulness is born.

3: Motherhood's Potential for Transformation: Getting Stuck in the Disorientation or Entering into Hope

As noted earlier, Brueggemann discusses the movement from disorientation to reorientation not as a return to the "old status quo," but as a movement into "all things new." Contemporary research also touches on this "transformative" process within motherhood. Atkinson finds that becoming a mother involves moving into a "new reality."[62] Ramona Mercer discusses the initial transformation and continued growth of the mother identity.[63] Transformation in social science literature, then, is concerned with the growth of the mother's identity revolving around success in "becoming a mother." That is, a mother's sense of self is based around understanding herself as "mother."

Transformation within a Christian context, however, points to a mother's sense of self, first and foremost, as one who is loved by God. Richard Byrne comments: "the first relationship we have is to our own self, constituted and called into being as a unique image in God."[64] A woman may be a mother, a sister, a friend, but primarily she is one who is loved by God. "Becoming a mother" in a Christian context recognizes God's hand in all things. Faricy quotes Teilhard in describing this notion: "nothing should

59. Rogan, "Becoming a Mother," 882.
60. Mercer, "Becoming a Mother," 230.
61. Barclay, "Becoming a Mother," 724.
62. Atkinson, "Gaining Motherhood, Losing Identity?" 174.
63. Mercer, "Becoming a Mother," 231.
64. Byrne, "Journey," 576.

at any moment be able to shake us from the true communion that God gives us in his action on us through everything, everyone, every event."[65] In relation to motherhood, the process of "becoming a mother" begins and continues when a mother remembers what is of utmost value: she has been created by love and is called more deeply into love in the concrete immediacy of mothering.

Getting Stuck

Each day in the life of a mother is an opportunity for entering into and moving within the "movements" life brings, be it secure orientation, painful disorientation, or surprising reorientation. Painful disorientation is obviously the most difficult of life's movements. Brueggemann maintains that our natural tendency in times of disorientation is to deny it, "yearning to hold on to the old orientation that is in reality dead."[66] In McVeigh's study, one mother reflects a similar experience, saying, "sometimes I just wish I could go back to the way it used to be. It has been so hard looking after the baby 24 hours a day."[67] Atkinson discusses a possible link between identity loss and postpartum depression.[68] In motherhood, it is possible to become "stuck" in times of disorientation, to remain in denial, and to yearn for the old orientation of life before baby. Many mothers experience this sense of being "stuck" as part of postpartum depression.

Entering into Hope

Painful disorientation is an invitation for a mother to remember the presence of a loving God within herself and the events around her. God is revealing Godself continually, through the beauty of the day—possibly through the unexpected help of a neighbor—and through inner resources waiting to be tapped into. A mother may experience this only in retrospect after she has moved naturally out of disorientation, when she can look back and see the hand of God present all along. For example, a breastfeeding mother may despair when her baby, rather than feeding every four hours, requires twice-hourly feeding for some days and nights to accommodate a growth spurt. Once the mother's milk reestablishes itself and feeding becomes less

65. Teilhard, qtd. in Faricy, "Heart of Christ," 175.
66. Brueggemann, *Praying the Psalms*, 31.
67. McVeigh, "Motherhood Experiences," 341.
68. Atkinson, "Gaining Motherhood, Losing Identity?" 173.

demanding, a mother can look back and see meaning in the prior chaos. Perhaps in the next mini-cycle of disorientation, the mother might remember this previous time and live with more hope in her present discomfort, knowing there is a loving presence sustaining her. On moving from the pit of disorientation towarrd hope and reorientation, Brueggemann comments, "When one is in the 'pit' one cannot believe or imagine that good can come again. For that reason, the Psalmist finally focuses not on the pit but on the One who rules there and everywhere. It is the reality of God which makes clear that the pit is not the place 'where you ought to be.'"[69]

On daily struggles and decisions on how to live, Joan Chittister states, "The essence of struggle is neither endurance nor denial . . . it is the decision to become new rather than simply to become older . . . it is the gift of beginning again."[70] "Beginning again" is the journey toward transformation that mothers are called to—each present moment is an opportunity for reorienting oneself. In a Christian context, it is Christ who provides the orientation, "choosing Christ as the goal that orients, illumines, and guides . . . it is not a single choice . . . rather it is a habitual direction."[71] For a mother to constantly turn to her Creator is a choice to habitually direct her situation towards God. In this way, she participates in her own transformation.

Regarding the transformative process, Mercer suggests strategies to help adapt to the new reality of motherhood. One of these strategies includes "seeking information for the construction of a new self-definition."[72] A mother can participate in her own "reconstruction" of self in the process of becoming a mother. Brueggemann's scheme is one way a mother can think about the events in her life in direct communication with God as her "transcendent center." The disorientation experienced in new motherhood can be viewed as an opportunity for mothers to respond to questions of meaning surrounding the nature of being a mother and where God may be found in the experience of motherhood. In this way, a mother can actively grow in her spiritual journey as she enters consciously into the "shaping" and "construction" of her life of faith. Mothers have choices in times of disorientation. As Brueggemann explains,

> in the deep dislocation where God has now placed us, we must do some new deciding. While the deciding we face is complex and demanding, in the end it comes down to a few large choices

69. Brueggemann, *Praying the Psalms*, 2nd ed., 36–37.

70. Chittister, *Scarred by Struggle*, 23.

71. Theological-Historical Commission for the Great Jubilee of the Year 2000, *Jesus Christ*, 129.

72. Mercer, "Becoming a Mother," 226.

> . . . a choice of fearful self-preoccupation that invites a shriveled human spirit or a fresh embrace of this buoyant alternative that subverts fearful preoccupation and calls to a large re-entry into the pain of the world (denial) and into the possibility of God's newness (despair).[73]

Deliberately attending to God in her life and incorporating prayer into her day are ways a mother can construct her life around God.

Practical Suggestions for Entering and Living in the Disorientation-Reorientation Cycle

A mother's conscious engagement with the transformative process can be facilitated through mindfully attending to the present moment, which can be supported and supplemented through various forms of prayer.

Attending and Being Present

Entry into the spiritual journey requires a seeing and "attending." David Ranson elaborates on the term "spiritual moments" and observes, "to the extent that this 'moment' . . . is attended to, the person discovers himself or herself on a deepening and widening journey of consciousness."[74] "Attending," then, is a tool that can be practiced by a mother on the road to spiritual transformation.

Attending involves discerning one's own internal world of self-concept and beliefs in an active participation with God. In the words of Thomas Merton, "our vocation . . . is to work together with God in the creation of our own life, our own identity . . . It demands close attention to reality at every moment, and great fidelity to God as He reveals Himself, obscurely, in the mystery of each new situation."[75]

Seeing and attending in the life of a new mother involves simply being present to each moment, whatever it entails. One moment could be an attending to the beauty and miracle of the wonderful new little being as a mother nourishes and cuddles her baby. Elizabeth Gandolfo insightfully reflects on breastfeeding as contemplative practice and a source for theology.[76] Truly attending to the wonder of her baby and lingering a little

---

73. Brueggemann, *Deep Memory, Exuberant Hope*, 68.
74. Ranson, *Across the Great Divide*, 22–23.
75. Merton, *New Seeds of Contemplation*, 32.
76. Gandolfo, "Mary Kept These Things," 163–86.

longer in this attending can lead to awe, thanks, and recognition of God as the giver of life. Attending could also involve the acceptance of fatigue and frustration as a mother gets up for the sixth time in one night. Being present to these times of "disorientation" involves a mother's acceptance of her lack of control in "a surrender" to what is. As Gomez explains, "a new mother who surrenders to the present moment abandons the old self that lived only for oneself and opens herself up to the new self, one who has room for truly loving both herself and others."[77] In this way, a conscious entering into her "disorientation" invites a mother into transformation.

Surrendering to the present moment also involves a conscious letting go of old false beliefs—a letting go of "shoulds" and false expectations. By surrendering to the present moment, a mother can attend to the concrete realties of her day without getting caught up in cycles of guilt and inadequacy about her role as mother. Concrete realities, including never-ending household tasks, can then be entered into with an awareness of "God in all things," enabling a mother to move with God into a new "orientation" in how she perceives and experiences her daily circumstances.

Becoming more conscious of "God in all things" gives perspective to a mother feeling isolated. It has been said that it takes a village to raise a child, and the burden of raising children should not be left solely on a mother's shoulders. A mother can be reminded of her belonging within a community of faith, surrounded by a "cloud of witnesses" (Heb 12:1). On a more concrete level, joining a mothers' prayer group is an option. Connecting with other mothers who are also conscious of their spiritual journey can be a great reminder of the reality of God and a practical source of strength.[78]

Tapping into whatever gives her strength is very important in the life of any mother. A mother can identify what energizes her—what is life-giving—and take steps to ensure these elements are present in her life. For some mothers, tapping into the support of a partner is crucial when adjusting to the process of becoming a mother. Barclay explains her finding that "the nature of the social support gained through relationships with the woman's partner, family, friends, other mothers, and health professionals was crucial as women became mothers."[79]

---

77. Gomez, "Early Motherhood and the Paschal Mystery," 145.

78. Websites such as www.mothersprayers.org demonstrate the value of such groups, with women from ninety countries involved in the "Mothers Prayers community" (Montegrande "My Journey to Mothers Prayers," 113).

79. Barclay, "Becoming a Mother," 726.

Prayer and Mothers

Prayer in the life of a mother needs to be realistic and simple. The environment a mother lives in is very different from the monastic lifestyle. The practice of attending is itself a prayer. Perhaps other ways of praying that require sitting for extended periods of time are not realistic for "on call," sleep-deprived mothers. However, there is nothing stopping a mother putting some small prayer practices in place to help remind her to engage with God. Examples of these kinds of prayers practices include lighting a candle, a form of *lectio divina*, a quick examen, centering prayer, welcoming prayer practice, journaling, and prayers in daily duties.

Lighting a Candle

Lighting a candle is a simple way to enjoy a visual reminder of the presence of a loving God in the midst of daily chores. A candle "evokes symbolic awareness,"[80] and lighting a candle in a regular "prayer spot" within one's home is one way mothers can foster engagement with the Holy One. Lighting a candle gives the space needed to pause amidst a mother's busy life. As Hebblethwaite says, "we need to find a way of moving from the vibrations of bustling activity to the still presence of God who lies at the heart of them."[81]

Modified Lectio Divina

One possibly powerful way for a mother to pray is to read only a couple of verses from the book of Psalms and choose a phrase that speaks to her heart that can then be remembered and repeated throughout the day. Mother and theologian Deirdre Cornell describes her own disorientation: "While this new life took shape inside my body, pushing for room, I felt my outward life slipping away." This led to her finding an anchor in prayer: "Savouring their poetry, I pored over the psalms, rediscovering the lines that had already saved me once . . . I marveled at the way they, in turn, baste my own small story into the seam of Christian history."[82]

---

80. Gooley, *To Share in the Life of Christ*, 112.
81. Hebblethwaite, *Motherhood and God*, 108.
82. Cornell, "Mother's Divine Office," 23.

A Quick Examen

Saint Ignatius taught his followers to reflect on their experiences twice daily for fifteen minutes in the consciousness examen. He believed this to be an exercise that "focuses and renews our specific faith identity."[83] A simplified version of the examen entails two questions, "For what moment today am I most grateful? For what moment today am I least grateful?" Practiced briefly throughout the day, this is a simple way for mothers to recognize the movement of grace in their lives. Linn writes, "Attending to our consolation and desolation can open us to sources of help and guidance that our rational minds are likely to overlook."[84]

Centering Prayer

The centering prayer has its roots in the prayers of the desert ancestors[85] and entails a set period of meditation that may be difficult for mothers of very young infants to enter into. However, for mothers who are able to create structures that allow for set meditation times, this way of prayer can be invaluable. One study specific to the centering prayer demonstrated a "change" in the way the participants related to the "divine."[86] Following participation in 11 weeks of centering prayer practice, the researcher noted an increase in a "collaborative" style of relationship where "those praying establish an experiential, interactive, and increasingly intimate relationship with God."[87] Centering prayer, then, is a tool, even a way of life, a mother could embrace to consciously engage more deeply with her God.

Welcoming Prayer Practice

Alongside centering prayer, there exists a practical component: the "welcoming prayer practice." This practice involves a simple three-step process of "feeling, welcoming, and letting go" to bring heightened awareness to what one is feeling. Welcoming prayer practice has been described as a powerful way "for turning daily life into a virtually limitless field for inner

---

83. Aschenbrenner, "Consciousness Examen," 21.
84. Linn, *Sleeping with Bread*, 65.
85. Bourgeault, *Centering Prayer and Inner Awakening*, 61.
86. Ferguson, "Centering Prayer," 324.
87. Ibid.

awakening."[88] For an overwhelmed mother struggling in disorientation, this is a practice that can help her regain vital perspective.

Journaling

Keeping a journal or "prayer-diary" can be a fruitful way of expressing feelings and engaging with God. In fact, "The very act of sitting down with the diary signifies a readiness to commune with the self; and the very act of writing may place you inside the mystery of self-healing and self-recreation."[89] In moments of painful disorientation, a mother can briefly journal as a way of working through her feelings and thoughts.

Prayers in Daily Duties

Kathleen Norris suggests we pray during repetitive tasks: "What we dread as mindless activity can free us, mind and heart, for the workings of the Holy Spirit, and repetitive motions are conducive to devotions such as the Jesus prayer or rosary."[90] Contemporary studies demonstrate "favorable psychological and physiological effects" with praying the rosary,[91] and the Jesus prayer can contribute to an "increased physiological relaxation response."[92] Thus, entering into daily prayer practices has physical and emotional benefits that may help in times of disorientation. A mother can also develop prayer habits by which hanging up the clothes can become her "prayer time" or feeding her baby can become her "meditation."

When taking steps to assist oneself in this journey, patience and gentleness are required. Byrne observes, "perfectionism, willful striving for spiritual achievement, and expectations of complete spiritual wholeness are major obstacles . . . we are always only on the way."[93]

4: Limitations and Future Directions

Mothers too are always "on the way" in their journey of becoming. Brueggemann's scheme is one way of understanding the journey of motherhood

---

88. Bourgeault, *Centering Prayer and Inner Awakening*, 135.
89. Rainer, *New Diary*, 114.
90. Norris, *Quotidian Mysteries*, 83.
91. Bernardi, "Effect of Rosary Prayer," 1446.
92. Meany, "Effectiveness of the 'Jesus Prayer,'" 63–67.
93. Byrne, "Journey," 576.

and its potential for spiritual transformation. However, Brueggemann's approach is open to criticism. Ashbrook has observed the simplicity of Brueggemann's scheme in relation to the spiritual journey.[94] He refers to Brueggemann's scheme as a "three phase paradigm" and suggests a more comprehensive interpretation of the spiritual journey to be found in Teresa of Avila's description of the spiritual journey outlined in *The Interior Castle*.[95] Here, Teresa of Avila uses the three-phase paradigm within each of the seven different mansions—or stages of spiritual growth—that Ashbrook believes to provide a more "comprehensive" or informative approach. However, it could be said that the simplicity of Brueggemann's scheme is its strength, making this way of interpreting life's experiences in a spiritual sense accessible to all.

The purpose of this chapter has been to begin a discussion of two topics that require further research: prayer and new mothers as well as spiritual preparation for new mothers. This chapter's practical suggestions on prayer for new mothers have only been a starting point. While there has been much research on prayer, contemporary research on the value of prayer specific to new mothers is lacking, as is scholarship on the suggested benefits this might have on moving through the painful disorientation of becoming a mother. There is an obvious need for further research in this area.

Another purpose of this chapter has been to begin a discussion of the need for positive ways to spiritually prepare women for motherhood. One possibility could include the development of faith-based programs to prepare women for first-time motherhood. Another challenge to the Christian community is determining how to provide ongoing spiritual and practical support to new mothers, perhaps using means such as pastoral counseling and visitations as well as faith-based mother's groups to help new mothers through their experience of painful disorientation and towards surprising reorientation.

Conclusion

This chapter has explored the potential for spiritual transformation within matrescence. New motherhood is increasingly challenging in western society due to the changing role of women, the conspiracy of silence surrounding motherhood, secularization, and the frenetic pace of life. Motherhood's journey involves a significant process of "becoming." Contemporary research has revealed a significant lack of preparation for mothers prior

---

94. Ashbrook, "Book Reviews," 103.

95. Ibid., 104.

to having babies. Mothers experiencing disorientation require words with which to voice these experiences and a framework with which to interpret motherhood's challenges. A conversation between Barclay and Rogan's contemporary midwife studies and Brueggemann's scheme of spiritual reorientation enables an interpretation of the experiences of motherhood that can lead to a transformative engagement with disorientation. This interpretation sheds light on the reality of God's presence within the losses and the new beginnings of early motherhood. It demonstrates ways that, in the midst of disorientation, mothers can remain stuck or choose hope.

"Because the glory of God, as St. Irenaeus reminds us, is the person fully alive, our vocation as human beings entails a commitment to continuous human growth. Human life is a gift from the creator, who couples the gift of life with a call—a call to us to be co-creators, freely fashioning our lives into something beautiful for God."[96] Mothers, then, are called to listen to the voice of God within their personal experience of motherhood and are called to grow and fashion their lives not within false expectations, but within the freedom of their identity based in God. By choosing hope, a mother participates in her own "re-creation" and becoming a part of "all things new." She becomes a woman of whom it can be said, "strength and dignity are her clothing, and she laughs at the time to come" (Prov 31:25).

Bibliography

Aschenbrenner, George. "Consciousness Examen." *Review for Religious* 31 (1972) 14–21.
Ashbrook, Thomas. "Book Reviews." *Journal of Spiritual Formation and Soul Care* 3 (2010) 103–105.
Atkinson, Bridgette. "Gaining Motherhood, Losing Identity?" *Midwifery Digest* 16 (2006) 172–74.
Au, Wilkie. *By Way of the Heart*. New York: Paulist, 1989.
Barclay, Lesley. "Becoming a Mother: An Analysis of Women's Experience of Early Motherhood." *Journal of Advanced Nursing* 25 (96) 719–28.
Bernardi, L. "Effect of Rosary Prayer and Yoga Mantras on Autonomic Cardiovascular Rhythms: Comparative Study." *British Medical Journal* 323 (2001) 1446–49.
Bourgeault, Cynthia. *Centering Prayer and Inner Awakening*. Plymouth, UK: Cowley, 2004.
Brueggemann, Walter. *Abiding Astonishment*. Louisville: Westminster John Knox, 1991.
———. *Deep Memory, Exuberant Hope: Contested Truth in a Post-Christian World*. Minneapolis: Fortress, 2000.
———. *Hopeful Imagination: Prophetic Voices in Exile*. Philadelphia: Fortress, 1986.
———. *Like Fire in the Bones: Listening for the Prophetic Word in Jeremiah*. Minneapolis: Fortress, 2006.

96. Au, *By Way of the Heart*, 19.

———. *Praying the Psalms*. Winona, MN: Saint Mary's, 1982.
———. *Remember You Are Dust*. Eugene, OR: Cascade, 2012.
Byrne, Richard. "Journey: Growth and Development in Spiritual Life." In *The New Dictionary of Catholic Spirituality*, edited by Michael Downey, 565–77. Collegeville, MN: Liturgical, 1993.
Chittister, Joan. *Scarred by Struggle, Transformed by Hope*. Grand Rapids: Eerdmans, 2003.
Cornell, Deirdre. "A Mother's Divine Office." *America* 187 (2002) 23.
Faricy, R. "The Heart of Christ in the Writings of Teilhard de Chardin." In *Spiritualities of the Heart: Approaches to Personal Wholeness in the Christian Tradition*, edited by Annice Callahan, 170–85. New York: Paulist, 1990.
Ferguson, Jane. "Centering Prayer as a Healing Response to Everyday Stress: A Psychological and Spiritual Process." *Pastoral Psychology* 59 (2010) 305–329.
Gandolfo, Elizabeth. "Mary Kept These Things, Pondering Them in Her Heart: Breastfeeding as Contemplative Practice and Source for Theology." *Spiritus: A Journal of Christian Spirituality* 3 (2013) 163–86.
Gomez, Cristina Lledo. "Early Motherhood and the Paschal Mystery: A Rahnerian Reflection on the Death and Rebirth Experiences of New Mothers." *Australasian Catholic Record* 88 (2011) 131–50.
Gooley, Laurence. *To Share in the Life of Christ: Experiencing God in Everyday Life*. Saint Louis: Institute of Jesuit Sources, 1997.
Hebblethwaite, Margaret. *Motherhood and God*. New York: Chapman, 1984.
Helminiak, Daniel. *Spiritual Development: An Interdisciplinary Study*. Chicago: Loyola University Press, 1987.
Linn, Dennis. *Sleeping with Bread: Holding What Gives You Life*. New York: Paulist, 1995.
McVeigh, Carol. "Motherhood Experiences from the Perspective of First-Time Mothers." *Clinical Nursing Research* 16 (1997) 335–48. http://cnr.sagepub.com/content/6/4/335.refs.html.
Meany, John. "The Effectiveness of the 'Jesus Prayer' and Relaxation on Stress Reduction as Measured by Thermal Biofeedback." *Journal of Pastoral Counseling* 19 (1984) 63–67.
Mercer, Ramona. "Becoming a Mother Versus Maternal Role Attainment." *Journal of Nursing Scholarship* 36 (2004) 226–32.
Merton, Thomas. *New Seeds of Contemplation*. New York: New Directions, 1972.
Montegrande, Rosa. "My Journey to Mothers Prayers." *Madonna Magazine* (2011) 113.
Moseley, Romney M., David Javis, and James W. Fowler. "Stages of Faith." In *Christian Perspectives on Faith Development*, edited by Jeff Astley and Leslie J. Francis, 29–58. Grand Rapids: Eerdmans, 1992.
Norris, Kathleen. *The Quotidian Mysteries: Laundry, Liturgy and 'Women's Work.'* Mahwah, NJ: Paulist, 1998.
Porter, Marie. "Focus on Mothering." *Hecate Archive* 36 (2010) 5. http://www.emsah.uq.edu.au/awsr/new_site/hecate_archive/Contents_36_1_2_2010.pdf.
Rainer, Tristine. *The New Diary*. Sydney: Angus & Robertson, 1978.
Ranson, David. *Across the Great Divide: Bridging Spirituality and Religion Today*. Strathfield, Australia: St. Paul's, 2002.
Rich, Adrienne Cecile. *Of Woman Born: Motherhood as Experience and Institution*. New York: Norton, 1995.

Rogan, Francis. "'Becoming a Mother': Developing a New Theory of Early Motherhood." *Journal of Advanced Nursing* 25 (1996) 877–85.

Rolheiser, Ronald. *Secularity and the Gospel: Being Missionaries to Our Children.* New York: Crossroad, 2006.

———. *The Shattered Lantern: Rediscovering a Felt Presence of God.* New York: Crossroad, 1995.

Sanna, Ellyn. *Motherhood: A Spiritual Journey.* New York: Paulist, 1997.

Schneiders, Sandra. "Feminist Spirituality." In *The New Dictionary of Catholic Spirituality*, edited by M. Downey, 394–405. Collegeville, MN: Liturgical, 1993.

Schor, Juliet B. *The Overspent American: Why We Want What We Don't Need.* New York: Basic, 1998.

Theological-Historical Commission for the Great Jubilee of the Year 2000. "The Meaning of Salvation in Jesus Christ Today." In *Jesus Christ, Word of the Father, the Saviour of the World*, translated by Adrian Walker, 121–42. New York: Crossroad, 2000.

Thomas, Trudelle. "Becoming a Mother: Matrescence as Spiritual Formation." *Religious Education* 96 (2001) 88–105.

———. *Spirituality in the Mother Zone: Staying Centered, Finding God.* Mahwah, NJ: Paulist, 2005.

Thompson, W. G. "Spirituality, Spiritual Development, and Holiness." *Review for Religious* 51 (1992) 646–58.

12

The Loss That Does Not Diminish

Transition Parenting as a Response to God's Covenant

Patricia A. Smith

Being with our children as they grow up is an extraordinary, life-giving, joyous adventure. We watch them grow as we ourselves grow, looking on as they transform from someone who we almost feel is part of ourselves into a quite separate, independent entity. There comes a time—for some a clear-cut point, for others a muddy borderland—when children reach adulthood. Earlier this year, two events that happened to occur in the same week brought that time home to me very clearly. My youngest son left home, and my second-eldest son welcomed his first baby daughter into the world. Both events filled me with strong emotions and poignant memories of the birth of my own children, when I was overwhelmed with feelings of joy mingled with apprehension for the weeks and years ahead.

The years have passed, and those first wobbly baby steps have firmed through tentative ventures and bold leaps—through school, college, relationships, employment, and marriage—into the confident strides of adulthood. Watching my youngest pack his belongings into his car and drive away with a cheerful wave brought home to me what I had lost and would never get back again: being the center of a child's world, the beginning and the end of every day, their comfort and inspiration, their moral reference point, and the first one they came to with their hurts and their excitements, their problems and their triumphs. Holding my baby granddaughter showed me plainly that my son and his wife are at the beginning of the very same journey—a beginning I had actually helped make possible—which, in my own way, I had shaped and prepared my son to take. It reminded me that every loss along this complex journey of motherhood has in fact been a storing-up of treasure.

The Christian Family

The domestic church—the Christian family—is a community sustained by the living exchange of love in a communion of shared beliefs challenged by new questions and sustained by honest listening and ongoing dialogue.[1] When children—as the relatively passive recipients of education and spiritual formation—begin to transition to a more active and independent participation in the domestic church, the role of parents changes and the shape of the domestic church undergoes revolutions, particularly in the balance of power and responsibility, in relationships, and in the way communication is carried out. Some parents' initial and natural reaction to their children's growing independence is a sense of loss. At times the change is experienced as bereavement: some mothers experience a period of grieving when their child is weaned; many mothers feel bereft when their child starts school full-time. When the child leaves home as an adult, the sense of losing something precious and irreplaceable can be intense and long-lasting. And yet every parental effort from birth up until this time has been towards the fulfillment of this moment.

This chapter suggests that we may gain some insights into these changes by considering them in the light of Brueggemann's framework of covenant living and response. Brueggemann's framework provides us with the opportunity to examine how we can "make sense of motherhood" (and indeed parenting) during these critical transitional stages of the parent-child relationship, which are too frequently overlooked.

In his foundational theology of the Old Testament, Brueggemann draws out three critical dimensions of the covenant relationship and what they imply for the human person: that God's sovereignty over all of creation offers us the opportunity to respond with obedience and deference; that the reliability of God's faithful providence allows us to trust that humanity

---

1. Wendy Wright identifies the Christian family as "domestic church" (Wright, "Christian Spiritual Life," 188). See also Calef, "Radicalism of Jesus the Prophet"; and Bourg, *Where Two or Three Are Gathered*. Both speak strongly about Christian life in the domestic family context.

is welcomed "to use, enjoy and govern all of creation"[2] and so to come decisively into relationship with God; and that God continues in the dialogue of the covenant relationship actively and interactively, calling us to discernment of God's intentionality and its implications. Brueggemann says that obedience, trust, and discernment—the disciplines the human person engages in when they respond in a covenant context—together "provide a foundation for a life of buoyant freedom, free of fear and cynicism, a life rooted in complete commitment to Yahweh, full adherence to Yahweh's sovereignty, and full confidence in Yahweh's reliable ordering of reality."[3]

The blueprint for the Christian family is laid out here. The Christian family is defined by acknowledgement of God's sovereignty. Conforming our will to God's will allows us to be formed as God's people: we are enabled to live righteously, make choices, and form values in accordance with building up the kingdom. "The Christian family, in its discipleship, is called to seek in its own life and in the life beyond its door the justice that the reign of God requires."[4] Living justly in this way is the foundation of the domestic church—the underlying architecture that defines it as a place of worship and love.

God's sustaining creation invites us to unconditional trust whose expression is the freedom to "have life and have it to the full" (John 10:10), so that the stories we create are vibrant and bursting with the life God promises: "The gathered church community and the domestic church . . . are both communities of storytelling. They help us know who we are."[5] Our personal stories and our family stories connect us to more than our own genetic forebears and to our offspring. By allowing us to identify with the broader experience of the Christian community, they provide us with a reminder of God's unfailing love throughout the generations.

The mutual exchange of God's involvement now in our lives—the to-and-fro of petition and comment and of help and complaint—must be honored by discernment on our part. As we question and accept learning, we grow in deeper and deeper experience of God, in true wisdom, and in holiness, which is the wholeness of the human person before God. This immediate dialogue with God keeps the domestic church from becoming a museum and provides it with the impetus to grow and respond to unremitting change. Dialogue with God and God's creation is replicated in our communion with each other in the domestic church, in the way we talk to

---

2. Brueggemann, *Theology of the Old Testament*, 456.
3. Ibid., 460.
4. Calef, "Radicalism of Jesus the Prophet," 63.
5. Wright, "Christian Spiritual Life," 185–92.

each other and relate to each other with love and respect, and in the way we expect and enable lives of justice and freedom.

Obedience

The freedom promised by the covenant between God and humanity is "not unqualified, autonomous freedom but a new summons to obedience."[6] This obedience is not slavish compliance that takes no account of God's will for the human person or of the complexity of the work to be undertaken in bringing about the kingdom of God and the creativity needed to accomplish it. Instead, this obedience seeks "to act according to the covenant intentionality" of God.[7] This is crucial to unfolding the essential nature of the human person as God has created that person to be. To be fully human is to live in accordance with God's will for human nature, to match human intentionality with God's. By cooperating with God's will for good for all creation, the human person nourishes the relationship of God to all creation. Implied in obedience is listening[8] with an attitude of attention towards God, coupled with active interiorization of what God is communicating. To truly listen is to consider, to apply, and to act in compliance with what one has heard. Thus, the act of listening is expressed in the practice of justice.

The Practice of Justice

Justice is expressed in "active engagement in doing God's will and making the world to be the creation that God intends . . . The call of God, in short, is to discipleship . . . The ground of the call is . . . that God has a powerful intentionality for the world that, when enacted, will make a decisive difference for good in the world."[9] Living a life in pursuit of justice brings the person into closer relationship with God. As Brueggemann suggests, "it is through the question of justice that communion is mediated."[10] He explains that "full communion is the measure of being a finished self in the presence of God . . . the full, hoped-for self is a self who will live in full communion with God, enjoying God's presence, being utterly safe, at home, at peace in God's

---

6. Brueggemann, *Interpretation and Obedience*, 147.
7. Ibid., 1.
8. Ibid., *Theology of the Old Testament*, 460.
9. Ibid., *Word that Redescribes*, 93.
10. Ibid., *Message of the Psalms*, 168.

presence."[11] Impediments to justice actually prevent the person becoming a "finished self."

Justice in Practice

The time of transition from dependence to independence is not a constant or a predictable progression. Caldwell states that the one consistent issue of adolescent development is change.[12] Parks describes the current climate of change as "a culture making its way through a set of rapids."[13] Many young people reach adulthood without gaining independence, and many become independent by choice or by force before they reach the legal age of majority. As Parks says, "chronological age does not serve as a consistent indicator" of adulthood.[14] Nor does leaving home indicate adulthood. As Allan and Crow explain:

> Young people can achieve a significant extension of independence by entry into the labor market while still several years away from finally leaving home. In addition, it is unusual for dependence to cease completely as soon as a young person leaves the parental household.[15]

If the Christian family is to actively pursue justice, then its members—both parents and offspring—need to carefully consider many aspects of their relationship to the community during this transitional time. Rubio describes "intentional practices of resistance"—that is, practices of "resistance to everything in our culture that diminishes persons"—that "can enable the majority of Christians who live in families to value both relationships and social change, to connect love and justice."[16] We will consider some of the implications for the domestic church in two areas of immediate relevance to the expansion of independence: economic life and hospitality.

---

11. Ibid., *Texts under Negotiation*, 42.
12. Caldwell, *Leaving Home with Faith*, 15.
13. Parks, *Big Questions*, 4.
14. Ibid., 9.
15. Allan and Crow, *Families, Households and Society*, 44.
16. Rubio, *Family Ethics*, 234, 243.

Economic Life

Employment usually brings with it a measure of the financial independence that is so critical to the perception of personhood and self-worth and is also closely allied to control over one's life and future. Since employment is such a significant sign of the young person's growing independence, it is important that the kind of work and the workplace itself are chosen carefully: work should be sought in a sustainable industry that promotes wellbeing and respect for others, and these workplaces should respect just labor laws as well as the dignity of employees, whether they are teenagers or adults.

In her defense of Christian family life, Julie Rubio speaks consistently about the importance of work for forming the human person.[17] She states, "a person's work is her vocation. In her work she realizes herself as a person."[18] Each person has more than a calling to an active vocation in the world: they have a responsibility as a disciple to exercise their calling as fully as possible. Rubio argues that vocation is an integral part of the unique being God has created. Striving for abundant life in the kingdom entails bringing that vocation to fulfillment. Rubio goes further to say that "all persons have something important to do in this world by which they will realize their very selves. The work that persons do is a fundamental part of their moral life."[19] She contends that the Christian vocation is to mission beyond the intimate locus of the family, not only to allow the full response of the individual to God's intentionality for them but also so the Christian family may more fully live out its vocation to be a sign of Christ's love for the world.

How the young earner disposes of his or her income also needs to be considered in the light of justice. Simplicity as a practice of justice implies curbing unnecessary spending as well as prudent stewardship of income.[20] Learning to manage a limited income is another important aspect of stewardship. Fair dealing between parent and offspring cuts both ways. Unpaid work in the family has economic consequences and needs to be acknowledged, particularly through equitable access to control over life-choices.

---

17. Ibid., "Dual Vocation," 178–210.
18. Ibid., 194–95.
19. Ibid., *Family Ethics*, 52.
20. Ibid., "Practice of Sex," 246.

Hospitality

"To be at home is to have a place in the scheme of life—a place where we are comfortable; know that we truly belong; can be who we are; and can honor, protect, and create what we truly love."[21] In a community of independent people living under one roof, each must take care to extend hospitality to the others. This entails welcome: maintaining an environment that is open to everyone in the community and making sure that common spaces are accessible to everyone. It includes respecting each other's need for privacy. It also means welcoming each other's friends with generosity and openness. Allowing for differences in taste and interests and making space for them is part of supporting each other's emotional health and helping each other to live a fully realized life.

Welcome should also extend beyond the narrow family circle: "As an expression of mercy, the Christian family will strive to practice a hospitality that is attentive to the marginalized, the outcast, the lonely."[22] Enabling each other to do what we see as our work in bringing about the kingdom of God is not only a matter of compassionate engagement but also a practical enactment of discipleship.

Trust

The God of the covenant is not detached and transcendent but is instead engaged, listening, and responding to all of creation, continually and endlessly in attentive dialogue with humanity. "The human person is, at origin and endlessly, dependent on the attentive giving of Yahweh in order to have life."[23] God's faithfulness is such that "human creatures live in a world that leaves them elementally free of anxiety, because of the goodness, reliability, and generosity of Yahweh."[24] God's covenantal fidelity imbues us with trust that goes beyond confidence to a firm assurance that we are held securely within the loving hands of One who has never failed to hold us close, to pour out abundance on us, to comfort us, and to hear us. The discipline of trust teaches us to risk what threatens us now, trusting in God's promises.

---

21. Parks, *Big Questions*, 34.
22. Calef, "Radicalism of Jesus," 64.
23. Brueggemann, *Theology of the Old Testament*, 453.
24. Ibid., 456.

The Practice of Freedom

"Yahweh's profound commitment to fidelity and compassion generates life-space for wondrous human freedom in the world."[25] We can be so certain of God's provident love that we are emboldened to speak freely and address our legitimate concerns to God, pleading for those things we confidently expect God to provide for us under the terms of the covenant. Brueggemann puts it strongly in his assertion that freedom implies human persons are free to take the initiative in opening dialogue with God. The human person "is invited, expected, and insistently urged to engage in a genuine interaction."[26] There is expectation on both sides of the covenant: God's expectation that humans trust in God's promises and humanity's confidence that God's compassion is unchanging from age to age.

Brueggemann tells us that the means by which we maintain the dialogue implied and nourished by freedom is in the dialogue of complaint-petition-thanksgiving. Making petition is demonstrating trust and living the relationship of sovereignty and obedience: "Both the courage to speak petition and the buoyancy of thanksgiving are linked to assertions of confidence and trust in Yahweh."[27] With trust in God's providence and eternal, unfailing, loving care, we engage in active conversation with God, seeking to exercise initiative within our own world to bring it closer to the kingdom.

Freedom in Practice

Mission

"Cultivating a capacity to respond—to act—in ways that are satisfying and just" is one of the crucial signs that mark a young adult beginning to interact independently with the world.[28] In this time of great enthusiasm and energy, a young person is very open to God's interactive presence; by engaging with this flood of inspiration, parents can be graced with new energy for enacting justice. Supporting each other's efforts is an opportunity to make a greater contribution than each can make alone. Cloutier and Mattison talk about marriage as "a life-long practice of self-giving love" that is exemplified in service to others and "a mission of mercy and service" to the wider

---

25. Ibid., 457.
26. Ibid., 458.
27. Ibid., 474.
28. Parks, *Big Questions*, 6.

community.[29] The grace of freedom is essentially outwards from the heart of the domestic church to the wider church and outside community. Calef puts this clearly:

> The individual Christian family both learns the tradition of the extended family and contributes to it in a mutual service that builds up both the individual family and the extended family . . . as it seeks to live its common life in faith, hope, and love and to witness to these gifts in relationships beyond the family.[30]

Rubio reiterates this point: the domestic church is founded on the fundamental relationship between parent and child, but this is no more than a springboard for full engagement with one's public vocation.[31]

As children become increasingly independent, they and their parents have a new freedom and responsibility to choose how best to live as servants of the kingdom and to support others in their exercise of that freedom. There is sometimes an assumption by young adults that their parents' caring role will continue unabated, or that parents will continue to provide physical care or economic support to the young adult who, at the same time, is claiming to be fully independent. For parents to abandon the opportunities that come with independence by slavish iteration of child-minding, economic dependence, or provision for physical needs repudiates the practice of freedom for both parent and child.

Control

From the moment a child is delivered, the process of separation from its mother begins. The journey from complete dependence to independence—from egocentrism to competently building relationships with others—involves change on many levels for the mother that can sometimes be perceived as deep loss. Parents and children experience changes in identity that may be threatening, isolating, liberating, challenging, often confusing, and possibly catastrophic.

Autonomous direction of behavior is one of the rights and markers of becoming an adult. Parents can cede control gracefully or obstinately, eagerly or reluctantly. They can hoard management of the young person's life until it is pried away from their dying fingers, or they can push the young adult out the front door, suitcase in hand, on their eighteenth birthday.

---

29. Cloutier and Mattison, "Bodies Poured Out in Christ," 219–22.
30. Calef, "Radicalism of Jesus," 63.
31. Rubio, "Dual Vocation," 192.

Similarly, children may dig themselves into the family home and refuse to leave. Parents need to recognize that their offspring are gifted with freedom to make new choices in an increasingly different context from their parents. Parents need to be prepared to die to self-interest and to die to the longing for the predictable safety of the status quo. The parents' sacrifice opens the way to the kingdom for the child, and their own willingness to come closer to the will of God is transformative for parent and child alike.

Discernment

Obedience relies on discernment of God's intentionality—a sifting of perceptions that is less logical calculation than a sensitivity to God's will, to the pastoral context in which it must be applied, and to the current social and emotional climate. To discern the parameters of God's intentionality, we need to be prepared to accept that the world is "other than we had taken it to be because the world is the venue for God's reign." The world is not fixed or obvious but rather a complex system where God is actively establishing God's kingdom.[32] Discernment is "a delicate recognition that reality is an intricate network of limits and possibilities, of givens and choices that must be respected, well-managed, and carefully guarded, in order to enhance the well-being willed by and granted by Yahweh for the whole earth."[33]

Discernment happens as a result of "an act of imaginative construal"[34] to explore what God may be communicating and how it connects to our current circumstances. The process of discernment involves what Brueggemann calls the "zone of imagination . . . that operation of receiving, processing and ordering that transpires when my mind wonders in listening to a text, a reading, in praying."[35] Discernment intervenes when we study and reflect, and it influences our reactions to what we have studied, especially in behavior and changes to the way we think. While discernment is a personal and largely private activity, it is nonetheless "partly shaped by the community."[36] Discernment is shaped through the history the community gives to the individual and is also shaped by the competing inputs that constantly surround the individual.

When we come to reflect on God's action or pray for discernment for a course of action, our understanding—or construal of events—is influenced

---

32. Brueggemann, *Word that Redescribes*, xiv.
33. Ibid., *Theology of the Old Testament*, 465.
34. Ibid., *Interpretation and Obedience*, 1.
35. Ibid., *Texts under Negotiation*, 62.
36. Ibid.

by our own way of listening and understanding but also by our community and our contemporary circumstances. Parks emphasizes the connection of the imagination to the action of the Holy Spirit: "The human being is most mature and true to his or her own nature when the powers of the imagination are fully awake, alive to the presence of Spirit—the deep motion of the universe."[37] Parks adds, "It is by means of the imagination that we entertain the great questions of our time and craft the dreams we live by."[38] But the imagination needs to be shaped as a tool. We need to harness the discerning imagination with "sustained, disciplined, concrete intentionality," as Brueggemann says.[39] Discerning can mean battling against accepted wisdom, resisting the conventional, and even overturning what the world holds to be unavoidable or even desirable.

The Practice of Wisdom

Brueggemann's concept of imagination reminds us that each person has gifts of self—of unique insight—to bring to the process of uncovering God's intentionality, but at the same time it tells us that the people around us—our community—can be a balancing factor in our discernment. The relationship between the human person and God, which in itself constitutes a microcosm of the Christian community, cannot exist in isolation: "Human persons are not isolated individuals but are members of a community of those authorized by the life-giving breath of the Holy Spirit."[40] The Christian community, which arises out of God's love, exists to nurture and respond to that love.

Brueggemann tells us "that true wisdom is to adhere to the commands and that the keeping of commands entails the practice of wisdom."[41] True wisdom considers God's will with a careful eye and a generous heart and clings to the commands it perceives. Enacting those commands in true obedience cannot be done without this wise consideration: justice without wisdom may be merely rash action or self-centered imposition. Listening must be modulated by wisdom—the silent voice of the Holy Spirit, which informs clear-sighted discernment. At the very least, wisdom tells us how to enact justice in accordance with God's will. The practice of wisdom is the active, intelligent, and inspired application of the fruit of discernment.

37. Parks, *Big Questions*, 107.
38. Ibid., 105.
39. Brueggemann, *Word that Redescribes*, 106.
40. Ibid., *Theology of the Old Testament*, 453.
41. Ibid., 464.

Wisdom in Practice

Listening and Communicating

Wisdom encourages genuine listening, where each listener hears the human person in their whole context: the subtext of their poverty or frustration, the overtones of their loneliness or anxiety, the background noise of their age or inexperience. In the negotiations that surround the transition from dependence to independence, communication steeped in wisdom brings patience, tolerance, and forbearance to the negotiating table. In this way, discussions are positive activators, not forums for destruction and backbiting. The young adult needs the experience of being listened to as much as they need practice at listening. Parks states that the central work of the young adult is "the birth of critical awareness and the dissolution and re-composition of the meaning of self, other, world, and 'God.'"[42] Being listened to is having a mirror held up to one's beliefs so that one may examine them all the better.

Individuals have unique "imaginations" and therefore approach communication with one another and with God from unique positions. Thus, "Discerning wisdom draws on a wide spectrum of experience including insight, intuition, imagination, understanding, analysis, dialogue, and spiritual apprehension."[43] When parents and children communicate honestly and courageously, they dare to make their private thoughts public. They do not keep silent; they voice their problems, their hurts, and their hopes.

Wisdom and Hope

Listening with hope is the very heart of wisdom. We discern with more than human understanding that we are a people who wait, trusting in God's faithfulness. Brueggemann talks about the tension between God's abiding faithfulness and God's frequent failure to appear, underlining the tension between Good Friday and Easter Sunday, which still continues in the Christian consciousness.[44] Parents are familiar with holding their children in hope: hope for their future, their happiness, and their cooperation with God's intentionality. When they give permission—however reluctantly or eagerly—for their children's adulthood, they are gifting their children with the same hope. This is especially important when it is most needed—when neither is well prepared for the transition—as in the case of disabled chil-

---

42. Parks, *Big Questions*, 5.
43. O'Murchu, *Adult Faith*, 82.
44. Brueggemann, *Theology of the Old Testament*, 402.

dren, or children at risk, or parents who are emotionally or economically dependent on their children, or when previous efforts at independence have ended in disaster.[45] Wisdom tells us that a young person is entitled to the dignity of adulthood by virtue of God's call to reach full potential in God's eyes, no matter what form that may take. Hope tells us that we must always prepare ourselves for new possibilities. As Brueggemann suggests, "endless anxiety about money, sexuality, physical fitness, beauty, work achievements . . . in the end, all of these anxieties are rooted in an ideology that resists a notion of limitless generosity and extravagant abundance."[46] Wisdom in practice acknowledges God's surprising and endless generosity.

Spirituality

Each person's experience of God is unique by its nature, as unique as each person is. Within the Christian family, spiritual development is an abiding concern. While the parent has responsibility for the spiritual development of dependent children, upon reaching adulthood the child assumes that responsibility. The adolescent's choice of faith or worship practice is a matter for his or her own conscience. Discussing how modes of worship were instrumental in forming Israel's identity, Brueggemann comments, "worship life, over time, takes on an internal logic of its own in the community of practice, an internal logic not accessible to outsiders."[47] The worship life that a family has participated in together helps to form the family in ways that are difficult to be objective about. This worship life continues to resonate in the spiritual identity of the young adult even after the worship practice itself has fallen out of use. If the family has a developed history of participating in worship, the identity of the family is partly bound up in the tradition of worship they have held in common: "In families where faith was important, it became like a tapestry, woven into their way of life at home and in their commitments to participation in the life of a faith community."[48]

If a young person makes a decision to depart from the family's faith tradition, whether to abandon worship altogether or to choose a different tradition, it will have repercussions for the whole family. Such a decision may be a source of contention for two reasons. Brueggemann concludes that because it has its own internal logic, the community's worship life is rarely

---

45. Allan and Crow discuss the special situation of dependents with a disability (Allan and Crow, *Families, Households and Society*, 45).

46. Brueggemann, *Theology of the Old Testament*, 559.

47. Ibid., 653.

48 Caldwell, *Leaving Home*, 31.

talked about or even reflected on. This suggests that members of a family may not have the tools for discussing their normal practices of worship. At the same time, Brueggemann insists there must be "intentional lines of defense and maintenance if a peculiar identity is to survive."[49] If means of defense are not available, then older members of the family may well feel that the family's identity, insofar as it is bound up in traditional worship, is under threat by the departure of the new young adult. And yet, as Parks says, "the spiritual quest is integral to the developmental process."[50] The domestic church must be the ideal place to provide opportunities for discernment through faith experiences and different approaches to prayer.

Modeling of genuine faith-seeking by adult members of the Christian family may be exactly the kind of missionary activity Bourg speaks of when she says that "the mission of domestic churches can be described as moving persons towards those ideals, goals, or ends God has designed for them so that they reach the fullness of their potential as humans."[51] Bourg's concern is the domestic church's role in educating its children in virtue through the practice of examining and understanding their ordinary lives as series of actions deliberately committed to love.

Conclusion

The parent-child relationship reflects and witnesses to God's covenant of love. This covenant of love, like the parent-child relationship, was initiated before the child even knew the parent. God's covenant of love is endlessly forgiving, boundlessly loving, sustaining, and creating. As our children take their first steps towards adult independence, our response in a covenantally human way is with obedience, trust, and discernment. We accept and permit each other to take up our own lives, especially our relationships with God and others, according to our own judgment and responsibility; we seek God's will in awareness that there is a plan for ourselves and our children that is neither of our making nor within our control. We are accepting, indeed joyfully welcoming, of God's action "in the fray" of our lives. In Brueggemann's words, "full of steadfast love and compassion, Yahweh is like a father who pities, like a mother who attends. Yahweh is indeed for human persons . . . willing and powering them to newness . . . That is the hope of humanity and in the end its joy."[52]

49. Brueggemann, *Theology of the Old Testament*, 653.
50. Parks, *Big Questions*, 198.
51. Bourg, *Where Two or Three Are Gathered*, 42.
52. Brueggemann, *Theology of the Old Testament*, 491.

Bibliography

Allan, Graham, and Crow, Graham. *Families, Households and Society*. Hampshire, UK: Palgrave, 2001.

Bourg, Florence Caffrey. *Where Two or Three are Gathered: Christian Families as Domestic Churches*. Notre Dame, IN: University of Notre Dame Press, 2004.

Brueggemann, Walter. *Interpretation and Obedience: From Faithful Reading to Faithful Living*. Minneapolis: Fortress, 1991.

———. *The Message of the Psalms: A Theological Commentary*. Minneapolis: Augsburg, 1984.

———. *Texts under Negotiation: The Bible and Post-modern Imagination*. Minneapolis: Fortress, 1993.

———. *Theology of the Old Testament: Testimony, Dispute, Advocacy*. Minneapolis: Fortress, 1997.

———. *The Word that Redescribes the World: The Bible and Discipleship*. Edited by Patrick D. Miller, Minneapolis: Fortress, 2006.

Caldwell, Elizabeth F. *Leaving Home with Faith: Nurturing the Spiritual Life of Our Youth*. Cleveland: Pilgrim, 2002.

Calef, Susan A. "The Radicalism of Jesus the Prophet." In *Marriage in the Catholic Tradition: Scripture, Tradition and Experience*, edited by Todd A. Salzman, Thomas M. Kelly, and John J. O'Keefe, 53–65. New York: Crossroads, 2004.

Cloutier, David and Mattison, William C. "Bodies Poured Out in Christ: Marriage beyond the Theology of the Body." In *Leaving and Coming Home: New Wineskins for Catholic Sexual Ethics*, edited by David Cloutier, 205–25. Eugene, Oregon: Cascade, 2010.

O'Murchu, Diarmuid. *Adult Faith: Growing in Wisdom and Understanding*. Maryknoll, NY: Orbis, 2010.

Parks, Sharon Daloz. *Big Questions, Worthy Dreams: Mentoring Young Adults in the Search for Meaning, Purpose and Faith*. San Francisco: John Wiley and Sons, 2000.

Rubio, Julie Hanlon. "The Dual Vocation of Christian Parents." In *Marriage: Readings in Moral Theology no. 15*, edited by Charles E. Curran and Julie Hanlon Rubio, 178–210. Mahwah, NJ: Paulist, 2009.

———. *Family Ethics: Practices for Christians*. Washington DC: Georgetown University Press, 2010.

———. "The Practice of Sex in Christian Marriage." In *Leaving and Coming Home: New Wineskins for Catholic Sexual Ethics*, edited by David Cloutier, 226–49. Eugene, Oregon: Cascade Books, Wipf and Stock Publishers, 2010.

Wright, Wendy M. "The Christian Spiritual Life and the Family." In *Marriage in the Catholic Tradition: Scripture, Tradition and Experience*, edited by Todd A. Salzman, Thomas M. Kelly, and John J. O'Keefe, 185–192. New York: Crossroads, 2004.

13

Conclusion

Motherhood Made Complex

BETH M. STOVELL

The central question of this book has been: How do we "make sense of motherhood" in relation to various aspects of theology? A secondary question has been: How do we make sense of motherhood in the Judeo-Christian traditions? Joining international Jewish and Christian scholars together for this project with personal commitments to these questions has allowed for deeper investigation into the complexities of motherhood from biblical and theological perspectives.

Our journey through motherhood has spanned experiences leading up to birth and birth itself to letting go of children as they move into adulthood and all the complex spaces of mothering in between. It has incorporated questions from the Hebrew Bible, the New Testament, and a variety of branches of theology, including systematic theology, spiritual theology, and practical theology. This conclusion explores some of the major themes that have surfaced in our exploration and, based on these findings, suggests some potential trajectories for future research.

Orienting Motherhood Themes

While each of the chapters in this volume has articulated a view of motherhood unique to each scholar's subject area and particular focus in motherhood, several themes have arisen that cross disciplinary boundaries. These themes include viewing motherhood as a liminal space that sits in the already-not yet tension of our experience of the world; cultivating an awareness of motherhood's ability to evoke a spirituality that echoes Christ's death and resurrection and the associated experiences of grief and hope; valuing the theology of the everyday that accompanies experiences of motherhood; appreciating the gender complexity presented in Scriptural accounts of motherhood; exploring how mothers can be models for ministry; and remembering the mothers and children who are often overlooked, forgotten, or even despised within religious communities and within society.

Already-Not Yet and Motherhood as Liminal Space

The contributions of Ruth Sheridan, Erin Heim, and my own contribution point to a view of motherhood as a liminal space that captures an aspect of the "already and not yet" experience of motherhood.[1] In these contributions, motherhood exists in liminal spaces, whether in the liminal space of waiting for birth and recovering from the birthing process (as in Sheridan), in the liminal space of adoption (as in Heim), or in the liminal space of our birthing expectations as the Spirit births us (as in my chapter). Motherhood exists in the liminal spaces between suffering and hope, death and new life, as motherhood is constantly "becoming" what motherhood will be. Both Heim and Sheridan speak of motherhood as something that happens in the gaps and in the middle spaces. My chapter suggests that the biblical metaphors of motherhood point also to our own eschatological becoming, which is always a work in progress: our spiritual rebirth is already a present truth, and yet this rebirth is still on its way to becoming in all its fullness.

Death and Resurrection, Grief and Joy: The Contours of Motherhood for Biblical and Spiritual Understanding

Because motherhood exists in these liminal spaces, it makes sense to speak of the cost of motherhood and its rewards. As these chapters have demonstrated, motherhood is neither a consistent flow of joy and happiness, nor is it only a path of grief. Ruth Sheridan and Cristina Gomez have compared motherhood to Jesus' death and resurrection in different yet related ways.

---

1. Other theologians have examined the impact of notions of liminal space on theology and spirituality, particularly on a theology of the marginalized. See Lee, *From a Liminal Place*; McNaughton, "Because I Walked It," 35–44; and Carson, "Liminal Reality and Transformational Power," 99–112.

By exploring how John 16 relates Jesus' death and resurrection with the metaphor of motherhood, Sheridan opens up a much-needed discussion on the experiences of death and resurrection in the process of birth itself. Gomez explores how new motherhood, in its experiences of struggle and joy, also mirrors Jesus' death and resurrection.

Sarah Massa and Patricia Smith approach the grief and joy of motherhood using Brueggemann's theology as a dialogue partner. Massa points to the disorientation many women feel at the start of motherhood, while Smith bookends this discussion by reflecting on the experience of grief and joy as mothers move into a new phase of motherhood with adult children. From its beginning to its end, motherhood is a journey of grief and joy. The two lie intermingled in the struggles and joys of each day, in the transition and transformation of each new stage. This intermingling draws mothers into a new orientation toward Yhwh and into new opportunities to show covenant faithfulness as they experience Yhwh's faithfulness to them.

Theology of the Everyday and a Theology of Motherhood

In unique ways, Rebecca Lindsay, Claudia Herrera, Gomez, and Massa all reverberate with an increased feminist and Latina/o awareness of the theology of the everyday.[2] These contributors provide new lenses through which to view motherhood and the everyday practices of mothering in light of theological questions. Gomez focuses on how motherhood, particularly early motherhood, mirrors the paschal mystery through the everyday experiences of mothering. Lindsay points to a new way of thinking about ministry and motherhood that renews the liturgy and sacraments in the everyday spirituality of mothering. Herrera uses the concept of *lo cotidiano* within Latina theology to describe a theology of the everyday that helps us to understand Mary as mother, emphasizing *lo cotidiano*'s value for the spiritual journey of all mothers and as metaphor for Latina theology and spirituality. Massa reflects on the everyday experiences of new mothers in relation to Brueggemann's concepts of disorientation and new orientation in the psalms, showing the ability to use spiritual practices in new motherhood as a means to a new orientation toward God.

Each of these scholars re-evaluates the place of the ordinary and the everyday in spiritual practice and point to the need for the renewal of place

---

2. Examples include Espín and Diaz, *From the Heart of Our People*; Conde-Frazier, "Participatory Action Research," 235; Aquino, "Theological Method in US Latino/a Theology," 38; Miller-McLemore, *Also a Mother*, 167; Miller-McLemore, *In the Midst of Chaos*, 5; and Soskice, *Kindness of God*, 24–25.

for mothers and children in spiritual life. Motherhood provides a place for increased spiritual awareness, and motherhood provides a new lens for spiritual experience.

Can Mothers Be Men? Gender and Motherhood

Three of our contributors pointed to the ambiguity surrounding gender within biblical depictions of motherhood. These contributors demonstrated that we cannot simply assume that all metaphors we generally associate with motherhood are thereby only associated with women. My article pointed to the use of overlapping male and female metaphors in the depiction of God as Warrior and God as Mother in Isa 42, suggesting greater complexity to the question of gender and motherhood than one might expect.[3] Anthony Rees explored the notion of Moses as mother and the debate within Numbers about who exactly "mothered" Israel and therefore who is in charge of parenting her. Alicia Myers explains the complexities in Pauline nursing metaphors and their relationship to gender, overturning our modern expectations of mothering and nursing related to gender.

This awareness that not all biblical metaphors associated with motherhood concern only females should cause us some pause. We cannot simply make gendered assumptions related to how mothering shapes women—not if Scripture itself provides space for men in our discussions of motherhood. As we develop theological reflections on what these mothering metaphors mean, we must think carefully about the complexity of gender questions and see motherhood as a metaphor with meaning not only for women but also for all people.

Mothers as Ministry Models

Herrera and Lindsay have demonstrated that motherhood is not a barrier to ministry (as unfortunately others have suggested, whether directly or indirectly) and instead both explore in different ways how mothers can become powerful metaphors for ministry. Lindsay explores this in terms of being a deliverer of God's body and God's word. Herrera explores this through the action of birthing God in the model of Mary, the mother of Jesus. For Herrera, *abuelas* ("grandmothers") and mothers are the bearers of the good news among Latinas. Thus, motherhood should not be seen as something

---

3. I have explored elsewhere the complexity of gender and metaphors in Isaiah in Stovell, "Divine Warrior and Shepherd."

that keeps women from active ministry. Instead, motherhood can provide a means to deeper understanding of the nature of ministry, the sacraments, and the nature of the church.

The Forgotten Mothers and the Misunderstood Children

Shayna Sheinfeld begins our volume with a series of frequently overlooked, forgotten, or even hidden stories of motherhood in the Hebrew Bible. These stories cause a struggle for interpreters because these mothers become mothers by less than ideal means: incest and subversion. Yet these mothers' stories are redeemed in rabbinic literature by their outcome. What began in violence, negligence, or desperation ends in creating the birth line for the messiah. Thus, the biblical narratives do not provide us with a tidy story even in the birth lines of the great heroes of the faith. These stories themselves are wrapped up in the messiness of motherhood, which, in its complexity, has the potential both for great sadness and great promise.

Heim provides a picture of motherhood often overlooked both in scholarship and within different religious contexts: adoption and motherhood. By focusing on these stories of mothering, Heim highlights a need to remember these forgotten mothers. Heim illumines the value of the experience of each member of the adoption triad: biological mother, adoptive mother, and adoptee. Each holds a unique place in our understanding that helps us to better appreciate the Apostle Paul's depiction of adoption and its applications for the church today.

Louise Gosbell's discussion of infanticide and exposure in the ancient world provides a window into ancient views of motherhood in relation to children deemed less desirable and also into modern questions about the lives of disabled children and their mothers. Gosbell reminds us that we are not as distant from these debates as we might at times believe. Thus, we need to think carefully about not only the theological implications of motherhood but also the ethics of motherhood in society today.

These contributions remind us that we should not limit our discussion of motherhood to only mothers who became mothers in ideal circumstances, mothers who were able to keep their children, mothers who became mothers via biological means, and mothers who gave birth to healthy children deemed "normal" by society's standards. To do this is to forget many mothers (and children) among us and to diminish their stories. If we forget them, we also lose the richness of their contributions to our theological understanding.

Potential Ways Forward for Further Research

Based on the themes of this volume, this section discusses how the findings of this volume could be used in future research.

Motherhood and Biblical Studies

In the areas of Hebrew Bible and New Testament, several potential directions for future research arise. Sheinfeld's contribution points to the complexity of how motherhood is reinterpreted within rabbinic literature and the value this provides for reflection on notions of motherhood in the Hebrew Scriptures. There is more space for examination of other stories of mothers, metaphors of mothers, etc., and consideration of how they are reflected upon in rabbinic literature. My article suggests the value of conceptual frameworks for motherhood in the Scriptures. Further research could explore the complexity of various conceptual frameworks related to motherhood throughout the Scriptures. The question of gender and motherhood present in Rees and Myers' work suggests the need for more careful analysis of texts related to gender and motherhood. Unconventional forms of motherhood also need further exploration. For example, Heim's work on adoption and motherhood has demonstrated that the current work on this aspect of motherhood has not gone far enough to explore the complexities of this experience of mothering. Gosbell's contribution opens the door for further discussions on the theological significance of mothering children with disabilities.

Motherhood and Systematic and Spiritual Theology

Motherhood provides rich resources for systematic and spiritual theology that this volume has only begun to touch upon. Gomez, Lindsay, Massa, and Smith have provided first steps into examining motherhood's impact on understanding Christ's death and resurrection, the impact of mothering on ministry, new ways of orienting a mothering spirituality, and new ways of growing spiritually from the transitional places of mothering. Each of these trajectories could lead to further research on the significance of motherhood for theology. How might the images of motherhood—such as notions of God as mother and Christ as mother (in the vein of Julian of Norwich)—provide further examination of these themes in systematics? How does the history of mothering images in spiritual theology, both Jewish and Christian, help us think deeply about mothering today? We have only begun the journey toward the wealth of riches motherhood has to offer systematic and spiritual theology and vice versa.

Motherhood and Practical Theology

Herrera's contribution reminds us of the value of socially and culturally contextualized understandings of the spirituality of motherhood. In this way, practical theology is a friend to explorations of theology and motherhood. While motherhood is a shared experience that crosses socio-cultural divides and can thereby be seen as a common experience, Herrera's chapter on Mary's motherhood as a metaphor for Latina spirituality has demonstrated how a reading of motherhood that is contextually located within the experience of a particular culture can reveal layers within the spirituality of motherhood unique to that culture. There are more socially contextualized metaphors of motherhood yet to be plumbed for their theological depths. Perhaps a new generation of practical theologians will heed this call and dive in.

Conclusion

Motherhood provides a space for reflection on the already-not yet experience of spirituality, providing a liminal space for spiritual reflection. Motherhood moves us into the spaces of death and resurrection, of grief and transformation, where we can be joined to the sufferings of Christ and also to his glory. Motherhood reminds us that spirituality is not only for those who can journey into solitude and silence, it also occurs in the struggles of everyday experience. Motherhood reminds us of the complexity of God's image within both male and female and the implications of this image for our conceptions of gender. Motherhood provides us with new frameworks for understanding our roles as disciples and as ministers in the world. Motherhood extends past our simplistic pictures of the *ideal* mother or the *ideal* child and into the realms of forgotten mothers and children society has deemed less than ideal. Yet these forms of motherhood share with us new theological insights that have often been overlooked along with these marginalized mothers and children. Motherhood is the journey that begins when new life is formed and ends only in death. This journey provides deep reservoirs for theological meaning.

Ultimately, no book can ever fully "make sense of motherhood," but the hope is that this volume has initiated some first steps toward exploring the meaning of motherhood in biblical and theological terms. The complexity of motherhood will make every instantiation of mothering unique and yet, as this book has shown, motherhood can have a shared shape, a common ethos, and ultimately a shared, yet complex theology.

Bibliography

Aquino, María Pilar. "Theological Method in U.S. Latino/a Theology: Toward an Intercultural Theology for the Third Millennium." In *From the Heart of Our People: Latino/a Explorations in Catholic Systematic Theology*, edited by Orlando O. Espín and Miguel H. Díaz, 6–48. Maryknoll, NY: Orbis, 1993.

Carson, Timothy L. "Liminal Reality and Transformational Power: Pastoral Interpretation and Method." *Journal of Pastoral Theology* 7 (1997) 99–112.

Conde-Frazier, Elizabeth. "Participatory Action Research." In *The Wiley-Blackwell Companion to Practical Theology*, edited by Bonnie J. Miller-McLemore, 234–43. Malden, MA: Wiley-Blackwell, 2011.

Espín, Orlando O., and Miguel Diaz. *From the Heart of Our People: Latino/a Explorations in Catholic Systematic Theology*. Maryknoll, NY: Orbis, 1999.

Lee, Sang Hyun. *From a Liminal Place: An Asian American Theology*. Minneapolis: Fortress, 2010.

McNaughton, Lynne. "Because I Walked It: Pilgrimage as Spiritual Practice During Life's Transitions." *Transitions* 26 (2008) 35–44.

Miller-McLemore, Bonnie. *Also a Mother: Work and Family as Theological Dilemma*. Nashville: Abingdon, 1994.

———. *In the Midst of Chaos: Caring for Children as Spiritual Practice*. San Francisco: Jossey Bass, 2007.

Soskice, Janet Martin. *The Kindness of God: Metaphor, Gender and Religious Language*. Oxford: Oxford University Press, 2007.

Stovell, Beth M. "Divine Warrior and Shepherd as an Echo of Exodus in Isaiah 40:10–11: Contributing Voice." In *Isaiah*, edited by and primarily authored by Carol J. Dempsey. Wisdom Bible Commentary. Collegeville, MN: Liturgical, forthcoming.

Modern Authors and Subjects Index

Abortion, 112, 113, 116
Adoption, vii, 23, 65–80
Adulthood, 130, 135, 200, 203
Aichele, George, 48, 63
Allan, Graham, 193, 201, 203
Allély, A., 104, 115
Amundsen, D. W., 103, 106, 110, 115
Aquino, María Pilar, 154, 160
Arbel, Vita Daphne, 83, 98
Aschenbrenner, George, 183, 186
Ashbrook, Thomas, 159, 160
Askren, Holli A., 74, 79
Atkinson, Bridgette, 172, 177, 178, 186
Attention, 148
Attridge, Harold, 81, 92, 98
Au, Wilkie, 186

Baby, Babies, xx, 116, 137, 151
Bachelard, Sarah, 148, 151
Baker, Denise Nowakowski, ix, xvi, xix, xxiv, 15, 64, 99
Ballard, C. G, 63, 76,
Ballard, Richard L., 79
Baraitser, Lisa, 47, 48, 63
Barclay, Lesley, 165, 171, 173, 181, 186
Barrett, C. K., 52, 55, 59, 63
Batailles, Georges, 49, 63
Beauty, 138
Becoming, 126, 128, 135, 165–66, 171–81, 186–88
Beginning(s), 60, 157, 179
Beker, J. Christiaan, 79
Belleville, Linda L., 36
Belonging, 67, 69, 71, 72

Benjamin, D. C., 19–22, 25–26
Bergmann, Claudia D., 32–37
Berlin, Adele, xxv, 11, 15, 40, 41
Bernardi, I., 184, 186
Besser, Avi, 68, 71, 76, 80
Betchel, C., 116
Bird, Phyllis, 11, 12, 15
Birth, iv, vii, xix, 23, 27, 29–37, 39, 41, 63, 83, 85, 98, 99, 103, 106, 110, 115, 126, 132; born, 36, 40, 41, 74, 80, 123, 135, 174
  born again, 35, 38, 39
Blachman, Esther, 9, 15
Blenkinsopp, Joseph, 36, 40
Bloom, Kathaleen C., 74, 79
Bonfante, Larissa, 86, 98
Boswell, J., 102, 115
Boundaries, 67, 69, 71, 72, 79
Bourg, Florence Caffrey, 190, 202–3
Bourgeault, Cynthia, 183, 184, 186
Braaten, Carl, xxi, xxiv
Bradley, Keith, 88–90, 97–98, 102
Breastfeeding, 82, 85, 86, 89, 91, 98, 187
Brennan, K., 104, 115
Brisson, L, 105, 115
Brockington, I. F., 49, 63
Bronner, Leila L., xx, xxiv, 4, 9, 12, 15
Brown Hughes, Amy, xiv, xvi,
Brown, Raymond E., 59, 63
Browning, Don, xxi, xxiv
Brueggemann, Walter, xxiv, 165–69, 171, 175–80, 185–86, 190–92, 195–96, 198, 199–203, 206
Bunge, Maria, 138, 151

213

Byrne, Richard, 177, 184

Caldwell, Elizabeth F., 193, 201, 203
Calef, Susan A., 190, 191, 195, 197, 203
Campbell, M., x, 117
Cannold, Leslie, 137, 151
Carey, Gemma, 137, 151
Carr, Ann, xxi, xxiv
Care, 56, 63, 64, 80, 150, 152, 186
Carson, Timothy L., 205, 211
Caruth, Cathy, 49, 63
Chaos, 139, 140, 146, 152, 206, 211
Child, Children, xxiv, xxv, 56, 79, 80, 98, 102, 106, 110, 111, 115–17, 138, 140, 151, 152, 188, 208, 211
    Biological, 69, 74
    Daughters, vii, xx, xxv, 3, 4, 5, 7, 9, 11, 13, 15, 80
    Healthy, viii, 100–117
    Infants, iv, viii, 101, 102, 104, 106, 107, 116, 121
    Newborns, 106, 108–10, 115–16
    Sons, 38, 82, 92–95, 97, 203
Childbearing, iv, vii, 27, 29, 30, 31, 33, 35, 37, 39, 41, 99
Childbirth (see also birth, born), 32–38, 40, 45, 49, 57, 62–64
Chittister, Joan, 179, 187
Christ, iv, xiv, xvi, xix, xx, xxi, xxiii, xxv, 27, 30, 39, 67, 68, 73, 74, 78, 80, 94, 95, 96, 97, 123, 126–38, 141–45, 149–51, 156, 157, 163, 178–79, 182, 187–88, 194, 197, 203, 205, 209–10
Christ's death, xxiii, 129, 205, 209
Church, iv, ix, x, xxi, xxiv, 29, 41, 80, 102, 111, 116, 122, 134, 135, 136, 138, 142, 143, 145, 151, 152, 157, 163, 164, 203
Cloutier, David, 196, 197, 203
Coakley, Sarah, 137, 139, 141–42, 144, 146–52
Coats, George W., 17, 26
Cohick, Lynn, iii, vii, ix, xiv, xv, xvi
Community, ix, 39, 41, 116, 158, 164
Conde-Frazier, Elizabeth, 154, 156, 164, 211
Context, ix, xi, 16, 41, 79, 99, 103, 166

Conway, Colleen, 96
Coogan, Michael D., 22, 26
Cooper-White, Pamela, 145, 152
Corbeill, Anthony, 86, 98
Corbier, M. 110, 116
Corley, Kathleen, 66, 79
Cornell, Deirdre, 182, 187
Covenants, viii, ix, 189
Cowan, Margaret Parks, 10, 11, 15
Creation, 83
Creedy, Debra K., 49, 63
crisis, xxi, 18, 25, 28, 33, 36, 37, 38, 39, 121, 125, 132
Cross, 122–24, 127–28, 135
Crow, Graham, 193, 201, 203
Cruver, Dan, 70, 75, 79–80,
Culture, 64, 99, 103, 116, 152
Cuneen, Sally, xxi, xxiv

Daly, Mary, 29, 40, 128, 134
Darr, Kathryn Pfisterer, 30–33, 40,
Dasen, V., 105, 116
Daughters, vii, xx, xxv, 3–15, 80
De Vaux, R. 21, 26
Dean Jones, Lesley, 98
Death, iv, viii, 40, 54, 64, 85, 98, 121, 124, 126, 128–29, 135, 187, 205
Defective, Deformed, 108–10, 115–16
Delbridge, Arthur, 16, 26
Delcourt, M., 105, 116
Demand, Nancy, 85, 98
Development, ix, 41, 49, 63, 99, 106, 117, 187–88
Diaz, Miguel, 154, 164, 206, 211,
Discernment, 151, 198
Discipleship, iv, vii, 27, 39, 41, 54, 56, 203
Disorientation, viii, 165–66, 170–71, 175, 177, 180
Dille, Sarah, xx, xxiv, 27, 31–33, 37, 40
Disability, 116
Dixon, Suzanne, 87, 90, 98, 103, 116
Divine, ix, x, xii, xvii, xxv, 26–28, 33–34, 40–41, 109, 182, 187, 207, 211
Dodd, C. H., 59
Dunbar, Nora, 72, 79
Dunn, James, 79

Egan, Harvey D., 129, 134
Esau, Amy M. Lash, 3, 72, 79
Espín, Orlando O., 164, 206, 211,
Evans Grubbs, J., 98, 107, 116
Experience, iv, viii, xxiv, 121, 123–25, 135, 151, 164, 167–78, 186–87, 203
Exposure, viii, 100–108, 110, 115–16

Family, xi, xxi, xxiv, xxv, 56, 64, 69–79, 80, 88–89, 97, 98, 103, 106, 115–17, 152, 190, 193–94, 203, 211
Fant, Maureen B., 88, 98
Faricy, R., 177, 178, 187
Fass, Dan, 30, 40
Father, Fatherhood, xxiv, 24, 27, 29, 40, 53, 66–69, 78–81, 88, 91–98, 128, 134, 151, 188
Fears, 92–93, 98
Ferguson, Jane, 183, 187
Ferngren, G. B., 108–10, 116
Fessler, Ann, 74, 79
Fiorenza, Elisabeth Schüssler, xxi, xxiv, 128, 135
Fisher, Allen P., 71, 79
Flemming, Rebecca, 82, 84, 98
Flusser, David, xxi, xxiv
Forgiveness, vii, xx, 37, 45, 47, 49, 51, 53, 55, 57, 59, 61, 63, 208
Fowler, James W., 161
Francis, Pope, 40, 59, 64, 112, 155–58, 163–65, 187–88
Fravel, Deborah Lewis, 68–71, 74, 79
Freedom, 170
French, Valerie, 56, 64
Fuggle, Sophie, 49, 64

Gallop, Jane, 46–48
Gandolfo, Elizabeth, 180
Garcia-Johnson, Oscar, 158, 164
Garcia-Rivera, Alejandro, 158, 164
Garland, R., 103, 106, 116
Gaventa, Beverly Roberts, xxi, xxiv, 156, 157, 164
Gebara, Ivone, 155, 164
God, iv-xxv, 4, 9–16, 19, 27–41, 53, 59, 67–69, 73–74, 77–78, 92–94, 97–98, 109–15, 121–23, 128–71, 175, 177–202, 206–11
Grief, 205
Groaning, vii, 65, 67, 69, 71, 73, 75, 77–80
Grow, Growth, 69, 78, 80, 137, 187, 203
Giubilini, A., 112–13, 116
Gleason, Maud W., 89, 98
Glover, Stephen, 113, 116
Goizueta, Roberto S., 159, 160
Gomez, Cristina Lledo, iv, viii, ix, xvii, xxiii, 124, 135, 181, 187, 205–6, 209
Gooley, Laurence, 182, 187
Gonzalez, Michelle A., 153, 164
Greenspahn, F.E., 10, 15
Grenholm, Cristina, xxi, xxiv
Grenz, Stanley J., 29, 30, 39, 40
Gries, Stefan Thomas, 4, 15
Grmek, M. D., 107, 116
Grotevant, Harold, 68, 69, 72, 74, 79
Gruber, Mayer I., 32, 40

Harrington, Daniel J., 37, 40
Harris, Stephanie, 69, 80,
Harris, W.V., 116
Health, Healthy, viii, 100–117
Hebblethwaite, Margaret, 182, 187
Helminiak, Daniel, 161
Hemelrijk, Emily A., 89, 98
Herrera, Claudia H., viii, x, xxiii, 154, 164, 206–7
Hispanics, x, 153, 156, 159, 160, 164
Hogan, Linda, xx, xxiv
Holy, xx, 13, 28, 34, 38, 39, 128, 154–57, 163, 166–71, 182, 184, 199
Home, 56, 64, 193, 201, 203
Hooker, Morna, 73, 80
Hopes, x, 73–77, 177–80, 186–87, 200–201
Horsfall, Jan, 49, 63
Hoskyns, Edwyn,
Humanity, 40, 113, 116, 123, 186, 199
Husbands, 27
Huys, M., 106, 116

Identity, 15, 72, 79, 98, 116, 135, 161, 172, 177–78, 186
Imagery, xxiv, 41, 60, 151
Imago Dei, xix, 116
Infanticide, viii, 100, 101, 102, 104, 107, 108, 115, 116
Infants, iv, viii, 101–7, 116, 121
Isasi-Diaz, Ada Maria, 155–56, 159–60, 164

Javis, David, 161
Jenson, Robert W. xxi, xxiv
Jesus, x-xix, xxiii-xxiv, 10, 27, 34–39, 45–46, 52–64, 82, 92–98, 121–23, 128–35, 143, 154, 157–63, 179, 184, 187–91, 195, 197, 203–7
Jobes, Karen, 93, 98
Johnson, Elizabeth A., 29, 40
Johnson, Mark, 33, 37–38, 40
Joüon, Paul, 31, 40
Journey, xxv, 177, 181, 184, 187, 188
Joy, vii, xx, 37, 45, 47, 49, 51, 53, 55, 57, 59, 61, 63, 164, 205
Justice, 164, 192–93

Kantor, Bela, 68, 71, 76, 80
Keener, Craig S., 59, 60, 64
Kellas, Jody Koenig, 69, 80
Kelley, N.,109, 110, 116
Kimel, Alvin F., 27–29, 40
King, Helen, xii, 7, 9, 10, 13, 14, 41, 83, 85, 98
Kingdom, 34, 41, 139
Kirk-Duggan, Cheryl A., xx, xxv

Kittay, Eva Feder, 30, 40
Kitzinger, Sheila, 124, 135
Knowlton, Linda Goldstein, 65, 80
Koester, Craig R., 92, 98
Kohler, Julie K., 72, 79
Kovacs, Jason, 67, 80
Kranstuber, Haley, 69, 80

Labor, vii, 31, 37, 45, 49
Lakoff, George, 33, 37, 38, 40
Lang, Justin, xxi, xxiv
Laskaris, Julie, 86, 98

Latinas, viii, x, xxi, xxiii, 135, 153–64, 206–7, 210
Lee, Sang Hyun, 205, 211
Leftkowitz, Mary R., 88
Levine, B. A., 18, 26, 79
Leys, Ruth, 49, 64
Life, ix, xvi, 26, 41, 64, 67, 70, 80, 83, 88, 98, 104, 113, 115–16, 125, 134–35, 182, 187, 190–91, 194, 203, 211
Lifton, Betty Jean, 74, 80
Lindars, Barnabas, 58, 64
Linn, Dennis, 183, 187
Listening, 162, 186, 199–200
Live, Living (see also Life), 38, 40, 67, 78, 80, 104, 115–16, 123, 132, 135, 168, 180, 191–92, 203
Loades, Ann, 32, 40
Løland, Hanne, 150
Longman, Tremper III, 33, 40
Loss, viii, 173, 189, 191, 193, 195, 197, 199, 201, 203
Love, xxi, xxiv

Mackellar, C., 112
Maier, Christl M., xx, xxv
Malm, Karen, 75, 80
Mankowski, Paul, 29, 40
Marriage, xxi, xxv, 84–85, 203
Martell-Otero, Loida I., 161
Mary, Maria (Mother of Jesus), v, viii, ix, xvii, xxi, xxiii, xxiv, 29, 40, 64, 98, 122, 134, 153–64, 180, 187, 206–7, 210
Maternal, xxiv, 47, 56, 62–64, 80, 187
Matrescence, iv, viii, 121, 123, 125, 127, 129, 131, 133, 135, 165, 167, 169, 171, 173, 175, 177, 179, 181, 183, 185, 187, 188
Matthews, V. H., 19, 20, 21, 22, 25, 26
Mattison, William C., 196
McFague, Sally, xx, xxv
McMahon, Martha, 126, 135
McNaughton, Lynne, 205, 211
McVeigh, Carol, 173–74
McWilliam, Janette, 115, 124
Meany, John, 184, 187
Melamed-Hass, Sigal, 68, 71, 76, 80

Memory, 63, 116, 180, 186
Menn, Esther Marie, 9–11, 14–15
Mercer, Ramona, 177, 179, 187
Merton, Thomas, 180, 187
Metaphor, vii, viii, xii, 30–37, 40–41, 64–65, 79, 82, 89, 95, 99, 152–63, 211
Mihalios, Stefanos, 60, 64
Milgrom, J., 19, 26
Milk (see also nursing), viii, 81, 82, 85, 89, 91, 93, 98–99
Miller, Patrick, 33, 40, 203
Miller-McLemore, Bonnie, xxi, xxv, 137, 139–48, 150–52, 164, 206, 211
Minerva, F., 116
Ministry, viii, ix, x, 136, 149, 150, 152, 207
Miscall, Peter, 48, 63
Moloney, Francis J., 37, 40, 59, 61, 64
Monro, Anita, 137, 139, 144–52
Montegrande, Rosa, 181, 187
Moore, Bruce, 16, 26,
Moore, Russell, 66, 67, 70, 80,
Moore, Stephen D., 48, 64, 96
Morris, Leon, 37, 41
Moseley, Romney M., 161
Myers, Alicia D., viii, x, xv, xxiii, 81, 88, 91, 98, 99, 207, 209
Mystery, iv, viii, 40, 121, 123, 124, 125, 127, 129, 131, 133, 135, 181, 184, 187

Narrative, 15, 41, 76, 79–80
Neusner, Jacob, 8, 15
Newborn, 106, 108, 109, 110, 115, 116
Neyrey, Jerome H., 37, 41
Norris, Kathleen, 184, 187
Nursing (see also milk), 79, 86, 98, 102, 186–88
Nutrix, viii, 81–99
Nuth, Joan M., xix, xxv

Obedience, 192, 198, 203
O'Murchu, Diarmuid, 200, 203
Ordain, 138
Orientation, 170
Oswalt, John, 31, 41

Pace, S., 25–26
Pain, 74, 171, 178
Palliser, Margaret Ann, xx, xxi, xxv
Parent, viii, 19, 25, 79, 189, 197, 198, 200, 203
Parks, Sharon Daloz, 15, 193–96, 199–203
Paschal, iv, viii, 121–35, 181, 187
Pastor, 135, 150, 187, 211
Patterson, C., 105, 107, 116
Paul VI, Pope, 122, 135
Pelican, Jaroslav, xxi, xxiv
Pelphey, Brant, xx, xxv
Perez, Zaida Maldonado, 7, 10, 13
Perry, Peter S., 92–93, 98
Person, personal, 82, 92–93, 98, 187
Perspectives, iii, iv, xxiv, 41, 64, 82, 164, 187
Pilgrimages, viii, 153–54, 162, 211
Pippen, Tina, xx, xxv
Pitsios, T. K., 104, 116
Porter, Marie, 167, 174, 187,
Porter, Stanley E., xii, 34, 41
Post-Partum, 49, 173
Powery, Emerson, 73, 80
Practices, 41, 106, 115–16, 152, 187, 192–96, 199–200, 203, 211
Prayer, 165–69, 176–87
Pregnancy, viii, 153
Presence, Present, 79, 180, 188
Priel, Beatriz, 68, 71, 76, 80

Rahner, Karl, ix, 122, 127–35
Rainer, Tristine, 184, 187
Ranson, David, 180, 187
Reality, 211
Rees, Janice, xi, xxii, 207, 209
Reid, Barbara E., 128, 135
Reid, Daniel, 33, 40
Reinhartz, Adele,
Relationship, 80, 140
Remember (see also Memory), 161
Reorientation, 175–77, 180
Resurrection, xxiii, 27, 36, 37, 39, 45, 46, 54, 56, 59, 63, 122–27, 131–34, 141, 144, 160, 163, 205–6, 209, 210

Rich, Adrienne Cecile, 123, 124, 135, 174, 187
Richlin, Amy, 86, 99
Richo, David, 130, 135
Rogan, Francis, 165–66, 171–73, 177, 186, 188
Rolheiser, Ronald, 168, 188
Rose, M. L., 103–6, 116
Rubio, Julie Hanlon, xxi, xxv, 193–94, 197, 203
Ruether, Rosemary Radner, xx, xxv, 29, 41
Rushton, Kathleen P., 45, 57, 64

Safrai, S., 56, 64
Sakenfeld, K. D., 19, 26,
Salvation, 83–84, 99, 164, 188
Sandnes, Karl Olav, 38
Sanna, Ellyn, xxi, xxv, 174–75, 188
Schmitt, John J., 33, 41
Schnackenburg, Rudolf, 57–58, 64
Schneider, T. J., 5, 6, 11, 12, 15
Schneiders, Sandra, 188
Schor, Juliet B., 188
Scott, E., 55, 103, 106, 108, 112, 116
Segovia, Fernando F., 52, 64
Sherwood, Yvonne, 48, 64
Shochet, Ian M., 49, 63
Shortt, Rupert, 152
Singer, P., 103, 112
Slee, P. T., 106, 117, 152
Smith, George Adam, xi, xxiv, 31, 206, 209
Smolin, David, 70, 74, 80
Social, 15, 19–22, 25–26, 64, 115, 151, society, xix, xxiv, 26, 40, 80, 99, 116, 152, 193, 201, 203
Soeur, Anne-Etienne, 41
Solevåg, Anna Rebecca, 83, 99
Sons, 38, 82, 92, 93, 95, 97, 203
Soskice, Janet Martin, 32, 137, 139, 142–52, 206, 211
Spears, B., 117
Speiser, E. A., 6, 11, 15
Spirit, iv, vii, xv, xx, xxii, 27–41, 68, 77–78, 128, 142, 147, 150, 154–58, 163–64, 184, 199, 205

Spirituality, viii, xvi, xxv, 119, 122–35, 138–211
Stanley, A. K., xii, 29, 34, 40, 41, 49, 63
Starhawk, 29, 41
Stefanowitsch, Anatol, 4, 15
Stemberger, G., 4, 15,
Story, ix, xii, xx, xxiv, 15, 74–76
Stovell, Beth, xi, xiii, xv, 32, 33, 37, 41, 207, 211
Strack, H. L., 4, 15
Struggle, 123, 164, 179, 187
Suffer, suffering, vii, xx, 37, 45- 63, 73–76, 79, 95
Systematic, 147, 152, 164, 209, 211

Tarango, Yolanda, 156, 159, 160, 164
Temkin, Owsei, 86, 88, 90, 91, 99, 106
Theology, iii-xxv, 40, 41, 79, 98, 119, 122–35, 138–211
Thomas, Trudelle, x, xi, 41, 164–67, 171, 180, 186–88, 203
Thompson, Geoff, 152
Thompson, James W., 81, 83, 92, 99
Thompson, W. G., 188
Tite, Philip, 81, 88, 96, 99
Traditions, 26, 59, 63, 116, 187, 203
Transformation, viii, 9, 11, 15, 135, 165–87
Trauma, 49, 63, 64
Trible, Phyllis, 29, 41
Trinity, 29, 40, 80
Trust, truthful, 169, 195, 186
Tull, P. K., 18, 26
Tyebjee, Tyzoon, 75, 80

Vocation, 194, 197, 203

Walker Bynum, Caroline, xiv, xvi
Walsh, Richard, 48, 63
Walters, James C., 66, 80
Walters, Jonathan, 82, 99
Washbourne, Penelope, 126, 135
Warriors, 22, 26–34, 40–41, 207, 211
Wearing, Betsy, 125, 135
Welti, Kate, 75, 80
Williams, Dolores S., 152

Wisdom, xix, xxv, 41, 64, 199–203, 211
Woman, women, vii, ix, xi, xiv, xvi, xxiv, 15, 23, 29, 31–32, 37, 40, 41, 45, 54, 57, 64, 66, 79, 82–85, 88, 98–99, 114, 123, 126, 135, 138, 142–45, 148–52, 156, 159–60, 164, 174, 186–87
Wood, Janet, 138, 152
Woolf, Virginia, 67, 68, 80

Words, xi, xxiii, 52, 64, 79, 80, 136, 144, 148, 150–52, 186, 188, 192, 198–99, 203
Work, xxv, 64, 83, 152, 187, 211
Worthy, 105, 106, 116, 203
Wright, Wendy M., 190, 191, 203

YHWH, xxii, 17–25, 32–33, 37, 39, 191, 195–96, 198, 202, 206

Zeitlin, Froma I., 83, 99

Ancient Documents Index

Hebrew Bible

Genesis

1:27	13
12:10–20	3
18:16–33	4
19	3, 14
19:26	5
19:30–37	3, 4
19:31	6, 7
19:33	6, 8
19:34	vii
24:65	11, 12
27	3
28	3
31	3
35:22	6
38	3, 9, 11, 14, 15
38:11	9
38:13–14	12
38:14	xi
38:16	13
39	13
46:20	13

Exodus

15	vii
16	20
16:20	20
32:33	20
34:33 35	xi

Numbers

1–20	18
1	26
11	20, 26
11:12	18, 19, 94
11:13	20
11:15	25
14	22
14:14	22
14:22	22
15:38	14
20	22
25	xi, 24

Deuteronomy

25:5–10	9
30:19	21
34:10	23

Ruth

4:17	7
4:18–22	7

Nehemiah

9:32	33

Psalms

24:5	33
24:8	33
33	98
31:25	160
37:3	169
48:6	60
78:65	33
87:1–4	170
103:1	176
103:4–5	176
110:2	14

Proverbs

18:1	8

Isaiah

1–39	36
10:21	vii
16:16–22	41
21:3	60
26:11	vii
26:16–19	60
26:16–21	60
26:17	60
37:32	vii
40	vii
40:10–11	8, 41, 211
42	xv, xix, xxii, 28–40, 207
42:10–17	vii, 14
42:13–14	30
42:13	32, 33
42:14	19, 37, 60
46	14
66:7–14	60

Jeremiah

4:31	60
6:24	60
13:21	60
14:17	24
18:12	24
20:11	vii
22:23	60
22:24	14
48:41	60
49:22	60
49:24	60
50:43	60

Hosea

13:13	60

Micah

4:9–10	60

Zechariah

14:3	33

New Testament

Matthew

13:33	45
16:21	27
16:24	127
24:8	27
24:9	60
24:21	55, 60
24:29	60
28:10	160

Mark

8:34	127
13:8	27
13:19	55, 60

Luke

1:26–46	160
1:34	157
1:38	157
1:39	157

1:47	157
2:10–11	159
2:16	157
2:17	161
2:18	161
2:19	157, 160, 163
2:22–52	160
2:34–35	160
2:51	160
7:32	55
9:23	127
13:21	45
14	x
16:22	68
16:29	21

John

1:19–12	xi
2:10–45	59
2:20	27
2:34–35	160
2:51	160
3	xv, xix, xxii, 28, 34, 36–39, 41
3:15	12
4:21	55
4:23	55
5:28	55
8:20	55
9	12
10:10	191
10:11	8
11:31	55
11:33	55
12:23	55
12:27	55
16	xv, xxiii, 37, 60, 206
16:15	13
16:20–22	vii, 8, 37, 45–49, 52, 55, 58, 63
16:21	27, 36, 37, 45, 64
16:33	175
19:25–27	160
20:11	55
20:13	55
20:15	55

Acts

1:14–10	160
14:22	60
15	82
15:20	82

Romans

8	xxiii, 66, 67–71, 73–74, 77–80
8:12–25	vii, 67–79
8:15–23	66, 68, 71, 73, 77
8:15	68
8:18	74
8:20–21	68
8:20	46
8:20–23	73, 78
8:22	46, 60, 69
8:22–23	69, 73, 78
8:23	67, 68, 71, 78
8:24–25	73
8:25	75
8:26	78
8:28	177
8:29	68
8:29–30	73
8:37–39	78
9:2	55

1 Corinthians

3:1–3	81
7:26	60
10:11	60

Galatians

4:19	46
4:29	27

Colossians

1:24	55

1 Thessalonians

2:7	27

Hebrews

2	92, 93	1:17	68
2:10–13	92	2	99
2:21–25	95	2:20	27
5	92	2:20–25	95
5–10	92	2:21–25	95
5–6	95, 98		
5:12–14	55, 92		
5:12	82		

1 John

2:20	27

James

1:18	27

Revelation

7:14	55
12:2	60
12:5	60

1 Peter

1–2	68, 95

Old Testament Pseudepigrapha

1 En 64:4	60

Dead Sea Scrolls and Related Texts

1 QHa 3:3–18	60	1 QHa 15:20–21	94
1 QHa 3:9	60	1 QHa 17:35–36	94

Pseudo-Phocylides

Sentences, 184–85	108

Mishnah, Talmud, and Related Literature

Babylonian Talmud

b. B Qam. 38b	9	*b. Yebam.* 77a	9
b. Yebam. 63a	9	*b. Sanh.* 98b	60
		Shabb. 118a	60

Other Rabbinic Works

Genesis Rabbah

38:9	9	85:4	10
38:11	10	85:5	9
51:8	7, 8	85:7	12
51:9	8	85:8	12
		85:9	13
		89:1	13

Apostolic Fathers

Didache 2.2   108–9

Nag Hammadi Codices

Apocalypse of Peter, 8:10   109

Greek and Latin Works

Aeschylus

Chor. 523–50	86
897–930	86

Aristotle

Eth. nic. 1.3	89
1.7.15	83
1.10.11	83
2.6.11	83
4.9.1–8	83
7.5.4	83
7.7.6	83
Gen. an. 2.2.735b33–35	85
2.4.740a35–6.745b21	84
2.7.746a2–4	85
4.8.769b	104
4.8.776a31–776b4	86
4.8.777a6–8	85
4.8.777a22–26	85
Hist. an. 9.1.608b8–15	83
Part. An. 2.1.646b21–2.3.650b13	84
Pol. 1335b19–21	106

Athenagoras

Leg.	
35.1	108
35.6	113

Augustine

City of God, 16.8	109
Epistles, 98.6	110

Aulus Gellius

Noct.att. 12.12–15	86–87
12.20	87
12.21–23	87

Cicero

Amic. 74	90
Brut. 210–12	87
Laws, 3.8.19	104
Tusc. 3.1.2	90

Clement of Alexandria

Ecl. 41	109
48–9	109
Paed. 3.3–4	109

Epictetus

Diatr. 2.16	90
2.16.39	81
3.24	90

Euripides

El. 969, 1206–1207	86
Med. 573–75	94
Or. 527–30	86

Hippocrates

Carn. 6.594	85
Genit. 9.483	84
Glands, 16.572	85
16.573	84
Joints, 55	107
Lev. R. 14.3	85
Mul. 1.33–34	85
Nat. Puer. 19.532	85
30.2–9	85

Homer

Il. 22.77–90	86
Od. XI. 583.141	129
593.141	124

Justin Martyr

First Apology, 27	109

Juvenal

Sat. 6.592–94	87
6.592–601	84

Lactantius

Divine Inst. 6.20	109
7.187	109

Livy

History of Rome, 1.4	104
41.21.12	105
27.37.5 105	
39.22.5	105

Obsequens

De Prodigiis, 14	105

Ovid

Am. 2.14	84

Oxyrhynchus Papyri

P. Oxy. 939:13	55

Philo

Creation,	83
QG, 1.33 83	
Spec. Leg. 3.110–119	108
3.115	108

Plato

Resp. 4.443d-e	83
460c	105
Symp. 201d-12c	95
212.a	95
Theaet. 148e-51d	95
Timaeus, 19a	105

Pliny the Elder

Nat. 28.123	86

Pliny the Younger

Ep. 6.3	90

Plutarch

Am.prol. 3.495d-496a	85
3.496a-496c	87
3.496b-496c	87
[Lib. Ed] 5 (3c-d)(3e)(3f)	87–89

Pseudo-Hermogenes

Prog. 16	91

Quintilian

Inst. 1.1.1–9	89
2.4.5–6	81
11–12	83

Seneca

On Anger, 1.15.2	103
Helv. 16.3–4	84
Ep. 45.13–33	91

Soranus

Gyn. 1.4.19–23	84
2.10	106
2.13.12	86
2.19.88	88
2.20.89–40.109	88
2.21.46	91

Suetonius

Aug. 65.4	103
Nero 50	90

Tacitus

Agr. 4	87
Dial. 28.6	91
28–29	91
29	87–88
Ger. 20	87
Hist. 5.5.3	108

Tertullian

Apol. 1.15	109

Valentinian I

Cod. Theod. 9.14.1	111

www.ingramcontent.com/pod-product-compliance
Lightning Source LLC
Chambersburg PA
CBHW072023240426
43667CB00044B/2260